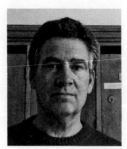

ROBERT CLARK

$\mathcal{D}$ark $\mathcal{W}$ater

Robert Clark is the author of the novels *In the Deep Midwinter*, *Mr. White's Confession*, and *Love Among the Ruins* as well as the nonfiction books *My Grandfather's House*, *River of the West*, and *The Solace of Food: A Life of James Beard*. He lives in Seattle.

Dark Water

ART, DISASTER,

and REDEMPTION *in* FLORENCE

Anchor Books
A DIVISION OF RANDOM HOUSE, INC.
NEW YORK

Dark Water

Robert Clark

FIRST ANCHOR BOOKS EDITION, OCTOBER 2009

Copyright © 2008 by Robert Clark

All rights reserved. Published in the United States by Anchor Books,
a division of Random House, Inc., New York, and in Canada by Random House
of Canada Limited, Toronto. Originally published in hardcover in the United States
by Doubleday, a division of Random House, Inc., New York, in 2008.

By kind permission of Ripley Hugo, lines from "The Towns We Know and Leave Behind,
the Rivers We Carry with Us" by Richard Hugo. © The Estate of Richard Hugo.

The Library of Congress has cataloged the Doubleday edition as follows:
Clark, Robert, 1952 Apr. 9–
Dark water : flood and redemption in the city of
masterpieces / Robert Clark—1st ed.
p.   cm.
Includes bibliographical references.
1. Floods—Italy—Florence.   2. Florence (Italy)—History—1945–   I. Title.
DG738.792.C58 2008
945'.5110926—dc22 2008001695

Anchor ISBN: 978-0-7679-2649-2

Author photograph © Caroline Johnson
Book design by Jennifer Ann Daddio
Map designed by David Cain
Title page photo by Heather Perry, National Geographic Collection/Getty Images
Photographs by David Lees courtesy of Time & Life Pictures/Getty Images © Time Life Pictures

www.anchorbooks.com

Printed in the United States of America
10   9   8   7   6   5   4   3   2   1

FOR ANDREW,
vero fiorentino

così, giù d'una ripa discoscesa,

travammo risonar quell'acqua tinta,

si che 'n poc'ora avria l'orecchia offesa

So down that steep bank the flood
of that dark painted water descending
thundered in our ears and almost stunned us . . .

—DANTE, *INFERNO* XVI, 103–105

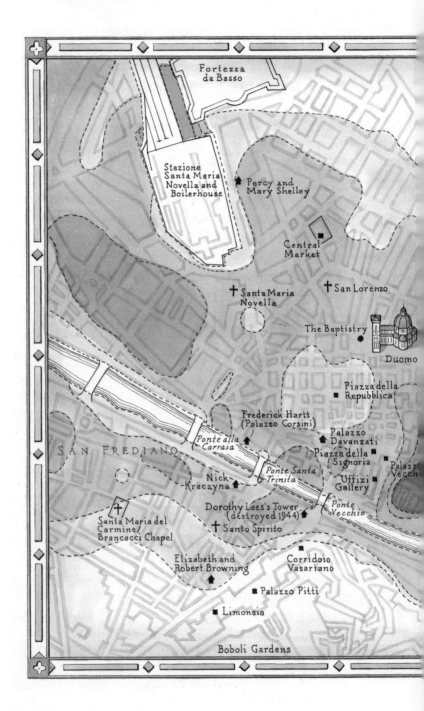

Fortezza
da Basso

Stazione
Santa Maria
Novella and
Boilerhouse

Percy and
Mary Shelley

Central
Market

† Santa Maria
Novella

† San Lorenzo

The Baptistry

Duomo

Piazza della
Repubblica

Frederick Hartt
(Palazzo Corsini)

Palazzo
Davanzati

SAN FREDIANO

Ponte alla
Carraia

Piazza della
Signoria

Palazzo
Vecchio

Nick
Kraczyna

Ponte Santa
Trinita

Uffizi
Gallery

Dorothy Lees's Tower
(destroyed 1944)

Ponte
Vecchio

Santa Maria del
Carmine/
Brancacci Chapel

† Santo Spirito

Elizabeth and
Robert Browning

Corridoio
Vasariano

■ Palazzo Pitti

■ Limonaia

Boboli Gardens

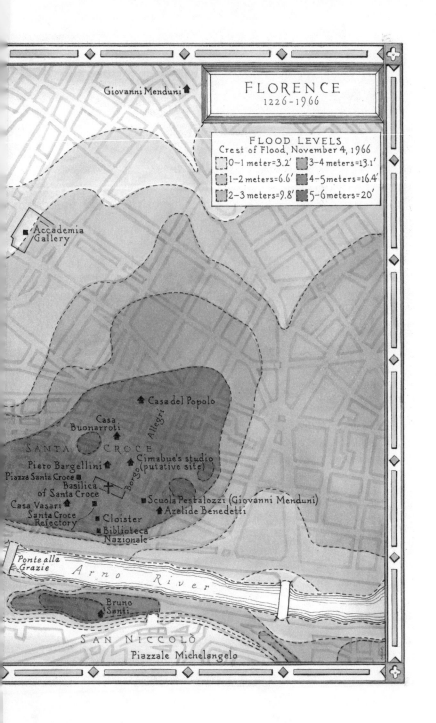

FLORENCE
1226-1966

FLOOD LEVELS
Crest of Flood, November 4, 1966
0–1 meter=3.2'   3–4 meters=13.1'
1–2 meters=6.6'   4–5 meters=16.4'
2–3 meters=9.8'   5–6 meters=20'

Giovanni Menduni

Accademia
Gallery

Casa del Popolo

Casa
Buonarroti

SANTA   CROCE

Piero Bargellini   Cimabue's studio
Piazza Santa Croce   (putative site)
       Basilica
    of Santa Croce

Casa Vasari   Scuola Pestalozzi (Giovanni Menduni)
Santa Croce   Azelide Benedetti
Refectory
        Cloister
        Biblioteca
        Nazionale

Ponte alla
Grazie
           Arno   River

           Bruno
           Santi

SAN   NICCOLÒ
Piazzale Michelangelo

One

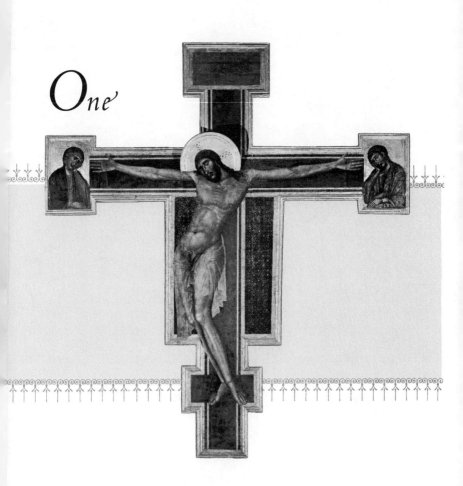

I grandi fiumi sono l'immagine del tempo,
Crudele e impersonale. Osservati da un ponte
Dichiarano la loro nullità inesorabile . . .

The great rivers are the image of time,
Cruel and impersonal. Observed from a bridge
They declare their implacable nullity . . .

—EUGENIO MONTALE,
   "L'ARNO A ROVEZZANO"

Cimabue *Crocifisso*, c. 1288 (photographed before November 4, 1966) *(ArtResource Inc.)*

*T*here is Florence and there is Firenze. Firenze is the place where the citizens of the capital of Tuscany live and work. Florence is the place where the rest of us come to look. Firenze goes back around two thousand years to the Romans and, at least in legend, the Etruscans. But Florence was founded in perhaps the early 1800s when expatriate French, English, Germans, and not a few Americans settled here to meditate on art and the locale—the genius of the place—that produced it. Over the next two centuries a considerable part of the rest of the world followed them for shorter visits—"visit" being derived from the Latin *vistare*, "to go to see," and, further back, from *videre*, simply "to see"—in the form of what came to be called tourism. The Florentines are here, as they have always been, to live and work; to primp, boast, cajole, and make sardonic, acerbic asides; to count their money and hoard their real estate, the stuff—*la roba*—in their attics and cellars, and their secrets. We are here for the view.

But it's so easy to miss so very much. The more you look, the less you see. If something is not after a fashion framed, hung on a wall, stood on a pedestal, monumentalized, encased by columns and architraves, boxed in marble, or dressed in architectural stone, it fizzles into background. If the conjunction of earth, water, and sky doesn't form a land-scape—nature on exhibition—rather than mere land, they disappear, recede into the black hole, the *gorga nera*, the underworld of the unseen.

For example, in late October 2005 I'd already been in Florence two months, gazing at art, gazing at the opaque screen of my laptop, before I noticed the plaque. I suppose we—Carrie, Andrew, and I—had settled into a routine. We were living on the Piazza del Carmine. At one end is the church of Santa Maria del Carmine, to which our elderly neighbor—known to us only as la Signora—shuffles off to mass each day. Within the church is the Brancacci Chapel and its frescoes by Masaccio. History's first art historian, a Florentine named Giorgio Vasari, called them *la scuola del mondo*, "the art school of the world," the essential work that every other Renaissance artist came to study, the spark that set off the fire. The image that most of us know best is the *Expulsion from the Garden of Eden*, the harrowed and weeping figures of Adam and Eve stoop-shouldered, clutching their genitals, the shame and the pity that launched the fallen world. You look at them and for a moment it seems that all that too began just here.

At the other end of the piazza is an enormous palazzo I'd heard belonged to the Ferragamo family, the shoe and fashion dynasty from Naples to whom it's said many things in Florence belong. Sometimes you can see into the central garden and its lemon grove through the gate. Once I saw a Labrador retriever gamboling among the trees. I've never seen anyone coming or going, but then Florence seemed to me very much about boundaries and privacy—secret and hidden things. That sense was abetted by the annoyingly narrow sidewalks upon which two people can scarcely pass each other without one of them having to step off the curb. The walls of the palazzi press right up against the street, fiercely rusticated, studded with massive ring hitches and iron sconces for riders and torches that disappeared long ago. The walls ascend beyond your sight and inside the palazzi, I've heard, descend nearly as far in layers of cellars, tunnels, and strong rooms. You're not, of course, meant to see any of this. You're not even meant—so the unnavigable sidewalk seems to intend—to stop here, to consider it.

Between the church and the palazzo with the lemon grove—between the naked shame of Adam and Eve and the veiled upstart pride of the Ferragamos—is a café and bar called Dolce Vita. I'm told it was the chicest nightclub in Florence during the nineties and that, after a brief decline at the turn of the millennium, it's come back as *il più trendy* place in the city. Unlike its unforthcoming neighbors, it spills outward into the piazza, past the jetty of the outdoor seating area, and, as the night ripens, onto the street, where the police are writing tickets for the double- and triple-parked Alfas, Mercedeses, Lamborghinis, and Ferraris. I've never stopped here—never mind gone inside—but I've pressed through the beautiful throng in the evenings and perhaps squeezed past an Italian celebrity, a soccer star, a Medici or Frescobaldi or, unbeknownst to me, a Ferragamo.

My life, rather more circumscribed, was across the street. Our apartment was on the second floor of what is called a palazzo—as is any large edifice built around a central cortile—but the building is scarcely grand. I suppose it's four or five hundred years old, and the stonework is pitted and frayed. A family of emigrants from somewhere in the Philippine archipelago lives across the cortile, and adjacent to them the multifloored apartment of the aristocratic owners ranges upward to a series of terraces. There's a crest over the door and I've caught a glimpse of the gold-framed paintings inside and the fusty, once elegant furniture that signals the presence of minor nobility or old money in ebb. Then there's la Signora and us. I've never seen anyone else who lives here. In the cortile there is a heap of rubble and broken stucco. Every three or four weeks someone turns up and, unseen, hauls away a fraction of it. I suppose it will all be gone in a year or so.

I worked in the mornings in our living room and I could see la Signora trudge by, a scarf pulled over her head, through the window that looks out onto the common corridor between our apartments. Inevitably she was looking for her cat, who had wandered into the hall. *Amore, tesoro. Vieni quà a Mama*, she'd call, pushing her lips out from the stumps of her teeth as though in a kiss. I went down to the vestibule for the mail each day around eleven, and sorted through the bills—gas, electricity, water, school lunches—each of which would have to be paid in cash at the post office, signed and countersigned, stamped and stamped again. It was on one of those trips that I noticed, above the rank of ten mailboxes, an inscription:

IL IV NOVEMBRE 1966

L'ACQUA DELL'ARNO

ARRIVÒ A QUEST'ALTEZZA

and beneath it a long red line. The Arno, it said, had reached this height on November 4, 1966.

It was carved in the same squarish, Roman script you see in other inscriptions on walls around the city. They usually seem to be quotations from Dante marking places where he perhaps saw Beatrice; where an eminent family or personage that he later met in Purgatory or, more likely, Hell once lived; or a simple stanza of his heroic melancholy, connected to nothing more than Florence, the glory and pity of it.

The line was well above my head, a good seven or so feet from the floor. I didn't make much of it. I knew about the flood. In Minnesota, where I grew up, we'd heard about it at the time, for weeks, in issue after issue of *Life* magazine. But there were other such markers around the city, recording not just the crest of the great 1966 flood but those of 1177, 1333, 1557, 1740, 1844, and 1864. I supposed there would, of course, be more floods. Florence proved—in its squabbling and treacheries, its beauties arising miraculously from its corruptions; in all that Dante recorded and that drove him into exile as Adam and Eve went into exile; and in his descent to Hell, circuit of Purgatory, and return—that what goes around comes around.

Most afternoons I worked a little more and then Carrie or I picked up Andrew from school. I generally took him to a park, a large walled expanse that was once the cloistered garden of the church of Santa Maria del Carmine. Andrew played soccer with the Italian kids, and had learned to negotiate his place in the game with relative ease despite his still very basic Italian. What took time was setting up the *partita* in the first place, even though there were only a half dozen players. Everything had to be discussed, argued, and arbitrated, and it often seemed to me that these arrangements took longer than the game that eventually got played; nearly as long as it takes the kids' fractious elders in Rome to form a government.

So I passed much of the autumn sitting on a park bench while Andrew played, and in that time I managed to work my way through *Il Piacere*, the masterwork of the self-styled decadent and protofascist Gabriele d'Annunzio. The novel's argument seemed to be that a surfeit of beauty, of the aesthetic, must end in moral and spiritual bankruptcy. But who could believe that, in this city of masterpieces where I had Masaccio's Adam and Eve at one end of my block and the secret lemon grove of the Ferragamos at the other; where the light and trees even then, close on the November anniversary of that terrible flood, had scarcely begun to color?

In the evening we often ate at the Trattoria del Carmine, which is perhaps a hundred feet up the street from our door. Under an awning there is a little *terrazza* that extends into the piazza and there or sometimes inside we were accustomed to eat our *crostini*, *ribollita*, *pollo arrosto*, and *tagliata di manzo*, passing an hour or so with a bottle of Morellino di Scanso. It was always pretty much the same—in the mode of la Signora and her cat, of the daily mail, of the debris in the court-yard—and I liked this. So perhaps it was habit that blinded me. In any case, for more than two months I didn't notice the photograph hanging at rafter height in the trattoria's side dining room.

Maybe it didn't bear noticing: at most eleven by fourteen inches, it was faded, off kilter, and muddy in tone. The first thing that caught my attention was a car in the upper left-hand corner. The car was leaning crazily on top of something, and that something was, I made out, an awning, and the awning upon which this car was poised was the awning of this restaurant, the awning I'd been eating under for some weeks.

Of course, you couldn't see the restaurant. What you saw were the upper stories of the surrounding palazzi, cars floating, and, everywhere, water. It was only because I was inside this restaurant and had realized that the photograph must be connected to it in some way that I was able to place its locale, to frame the image it contained within a context. It was a photograph of the Piazza del Carmine, probably taken from the top of the church. You couldn't see most of the piazza. In the lower left-hand corner the frame ended at what must be the tall double doors to our palazzo, only the lintel visible above the water. It was up to the second-floor windows in some of the more modest buildings at the very head of the piazza. In the middle, where the cobbled pavement should have been—where police were just now beginning to issue the evening's parking tickets to the patrons of Dolce Vita—a car floated, apparently in a circle, lazily spinning as though hovering over a clogged drain.

The next morning when I collected the mail I looked at the plaque again, now with much more curiosity, even with a sort of anxious urgency. I tried to imagine myself standing before these mailboxes with a foot of water over my head, paddling back to the landing just below our door while cars drifted by outside, water lapped the feet of Masaccio's Adam and Eve, and carp from the river swam among the lemon trees.

Rereading the inscription, it struck me as odd that this seemingly public monument should be placed in the unfrequented privacy of our unprepossessing vestibule, apparently for the sole benefit of the two dozen or so tenants and their guests. Was the water especially high here? It was easy to establish from a guidebook that the flood crest in this part of Florence had indeed been high, but not as high as in, say, Santa Croce, where Cimabue's crucifix was inundated along with scores of other artistic, architectural, and bibliographic masterworks. It was the fate of those objects that had brought the flood of 1966 to the world's attention. It took place *in* Firenze, in streets and quotidian spaces as ordinary as the vestibule where I got my mail, and left thirty-three *fiorentini* dead and five thousand families homeless. But in the eyes of the world it happened to this other city, to Florence, this visible efflorescence of transcendent beauty, of humanity's rarely seen better self, and nowhere more than here. More was at stake than a city, human habitations and enterprises, or even thirty-three human bodies.

Where, exactly, did this place called Florence exist? Surely not just in the imagination. Yet you could say many more people had visited Florence than had ever set foot in Firenze, even if only in their mind's eye. What was its history? Who were its founders? Could a river wash it away?

I remembered a little more. Everything I'd known about the flood came from *Life* magazine in 1966, when I was fourteen years old. And now it almost seems that everything I knew about the larger world then had been contained in pictures on those pages. Color television and live news reports by satellite scarcely existed, so insofar as you saw things that existed or happened far way, you saw them through photographs, and preeminently so in *Life*.

Perhaps that is why those years between, say, 1962 and 1968 seem to me not so much a story as a gallery, a series of two-dimensional images set in a line. If they have a theme it seems to be human goodness—or at least the desire to be good—stymied by tragedy, a world a little more optimistic about its prospects than today seems wise.

So there are space launches and supersaturated colors and youth; Selma, Carnaby Street, World's Fairs (Seattle, New York, Montreal), and the Ho Chi Minh Trail; and then the great funerals—Kennedy, King, and Kennedy. There's also a great deal of Italy, Italy being important for its historic art; for its contemporary design, fashion, film directors, and stars; and as home to a Catholic church that just then seemed in the vanguard of the era's idealism. Among the superfluity of photographs I remember from *Life* are shots of the papacy of John XXIII, the Second Vatican Council, Fellini, Gucci, and Loren; the funeral of Pope John and the accession of Pope Paul; the new pope's travels to America and the Near East; and then this flood. After that for me there was more television and moving images, less print, and—as my childhood ended, my youth became larger than anything in *Life*— much, much more me. So I stopped seeing things in that particular way, and perhaps that is why those images seem to form a unique strand—especially those from Italy—almost as if they were all by the same hand. Which, in large part, it turned out they were.

Perhaps it was also then that I began to get out of the habit of *seeing*. And it seemed just now that it was looking rather than seeing that had blinded me to the flood, this brief but deadly collision between Florence and Firenze at the sly hands of the Arno. But it was the desire to look at art and beauty, at *images*—and what else is there to call it but imaginary?—that had brought me here, perhaps impelled by those photographs from *Life*. It was Florence that had taken me to the threshold of Firenze. So first I would look some more. I would try to make out what or who had created this imaginary place, Florence. I would look for the source of the Arno.

$\mathcal{T}$wo

Lo Corpo mio gelato in su la foce
trovo l'Archian rubesto;e quel sospinse
nell'Arno, e sciolse al mio petto la croce
Ch'i'fe' di me quando 'l dolor mi vinse:
Voltommi per le ripe e per lo fondo,
poi di sua preda m coperse e cinse.

At its mouth the swollen Archiano
found my frozen body and swept it down
the Arno, and loosened the cross on my chest
that I'd made of myself when overcome
by the pain. It spun me past the banks and to the bottom
Then covered and buried me among its prey.

—DANTE, *PURGATORIO* V, 124–129

Death Mask of Dante Alighieri, 1965 *(Photograph by David Lees)*

*H*ere is where it begins.

      A man cuts down a tree, a poplar. A second saws it into boards. The last man paints another man—or perhaps he thinks it is God he is painting—on the planks, bound together to form a cross, another kind of tree. And then comes the river, the deluge, and the end of the world.

How can this be explained? Who, except God himself, could know how everything touches every other thing, or even how just one thing touches another? Perhaps only by vision, which is itself a kind of art. So look for the river and perhaps you will find the art.

*H*ere is where it begins.

      Deep in the Casentine Forests, about twenty-five miles east of Florence, you walk steadily up the mountain from a place called Fonte dei Borbotto, "grumbling spring." There's a cross—there is always a cross—at the head of the trail and halfway along the ascent you reach a small lake called Gorga Nera, "black throat." The story has it that the lake is bottomless and connects underground all the way to the Tyrrhenian Sea, beyond Pisa where the Arno ends. Thunderous sounds are supposed to issue from the Gorga Nera—explosive thundercracks, shudders, and rumbles audible one hundred miles distant—that signal or, it is said, cause earthquakes, landslides, and, not least, floods.

After a mile there's a crossroads. The trail to the left goes up to the summit of Monte Falterona. In the winter there would be snow here, a glaze on the beech trees and escarpments of sandstone. And once, ten million years ago, all this was underwater. If you go straight there's a slight descent of perhaps one hundred feet and, after three-quarters of a mile, a fall of rocks against a slope. Amid them a stream of water seeps out. This is the Capo d'Arno, the head of the Arno. A plaque set in the rocks tells you so.

Or rather, Dante tells you. The plaque doesn't so much name this place as refer you to the poet. Like most everything regarding Florence and Tuscany, Dante is your guide, just as Virgil was his guide downward into Hell and upward toward Purgatory and Paradise. The plaque incorporates lines from the fourteenth canto of *Purgatorio*. Two spirits ask Dante where he's from, but Dante is evasive: his home, he allows, is somewhere along a river that rises on Monte Falterona. One of the shades deduces it's the Arno, and the other wonders why Dante should be hiding its name. No wonder, the first ghost responds: everyone who lives along that river is mired in vice and sin, "flee[ing] virtue like a snake." It's only right that the name of this "miserable valley" should perish. Upriver, he adds, dirty pigs and slinking dogs feed, and as it swells into Florence "the damned and accursed ditch" supports wolves and foxes, or rather, we're given to understand, their human equivalents. Dante might indeed be reluctant to disclose this place as home. The river, like the city it sustains, is an object not of local pride but of shame. Dante has met these two ghosts on the level in Purgatory inhabited by those guilty of the sin of envy. As Florentines, they know whereof they speak.

In Dante's poem the source of the Arno is scarcely less unsavory than the sewer it widens to downstream: the owners of the land it springs from, the Guidi family, are burning in Hell as Dante has already reported in his first volume, *Inferno*. Their particular crime—one that both virtuous and less virtuous Florentines could join together in decrying—was minting short-weighted gold florins, the international currency Florence gave the whole of Europe, the very essence of her glory, avarice, and greed.

Less disreputably, the monks of Camaldoli have owned much of the watershed to the east of here for almost a thousand years. Outside their hermitage they groomed the trees and cleared away the debris from the forest floor until the woods were less a wilderness than a cloister, light shafting down among the columns of beech. And in the fourteenth century the building and works department of the cathedral of Florence, the Opera del Duomo, would take over the Conti Guidi woods. They would harvest—some say strip—timber from the mountain and the Casentine Forests to build and maintain the architects Arnolfo di Cambio and Filippo Brunelleschi's Duomo, the majestic and pitiful heart at the core of Florence.

All that aside, this place is dark and spectral, like the *selva oscura*, the dark wood, where Dante finds himself at the beginning of his poem. It's cloudy and ash gray. Just beyond the Capo d'Arno is another *gorga* called Lago degli Idoli, where an enormous cache of Etruscan votive statues was found in 1830. Uncanny and weird in themselves, it was stranger still that they should be found so far from any known human habitation. Then, as now, mad pigs, wild boars with their tusks, prowled the ground. Vipers slithered up the oaks and beeches and fell on unsuspecting charcoal makers, hunters, and loggers. People have seen this happen, just as they've heard the Gorga Nera bellow and groan. It rains serpents here.

*H*ere is where it begins.

A little southeast of Monte Falterona and the Capo d'Arno there is another mountain in the Casentine Forests called Monte Penna. On its flank, upslope from the Arno, is a forest pierced by rock outcroppings, fissures, and chasms called La Verna. Around 1220 its owner, Count Orlando of Chiusi, donated it as a retreat to the itinerant preacher and mystic Francis of Assisi. Head of a monastic order now numbering thousands and of a charismatic movement that was sweeping Europe, Francis needed to be alone merely to pray, to feel himself in the company of Lady Poverty, to become once more a holy fool, God's juggler, his clown.

At the end of the summer of 1224, Francis ascended to La Verna for the last time. On the way up he and the handful of brothers accompanying him met a peasant with a donkey. The peasant thought he recognized him—the whole world had heard about Francis—and asked him if he was indeed Francis of Assisi. Francis admitted that he was, and the peasant told him, "Be as good as folk say you are that they may not be deceived—that's my advice."

The others were appalled at the peasant's presumption, but Francis prostrated himself on the ground before him. Francis had seen—as he was always seeing—Christ in human faces, in the least of them. Then he began to pray, and because the peasant was thirsty, a spring welled up out of a rock. They all drank, the donkey included, and the water ran down to the Arno.

Francis spent a month at La Verna. He meditated in the forest and prayed in a cave. No one could find him here except God. At dawn on September 14, after spending the night at the bottom of a gorge, he had a vision, or rather, something befell Francis: an angel hovered overhead and rained down ecstasies upon him. Then Francis saw that the angel was crucified, was pinioned on the sky like a butterfly. He felt pain interleaved with joy, the sear of one shading into the other, and he looked down and saw wounds on his hands, his feet, and his side, the stigmata of the crucified Christ. Autumn came. The mists formed, the leaves fell, and the sky went gray. The beeches, spindly and bare, looked like lepers and cripples walking.

Two years later Francis was dead. From the day of his vision onward, he had declined. He weakened. The wounds throbbed and seeped. He'd swallowed suffering whole, drunk the Arno and all its cursed misery down. He'd given Christ a face people hadn't seen before, a human face, the peasant's face. Until then Christ had been the Redeemer as the judge and king of the universe: he was painted enthroned, stern and impassive. Now he was the Redeemer as the man of sorrows, the god who became human to the quick and the marrow in order to lay claim to human wretchedness.

All this and what happened over the next hundred years might have been called the Franciscan revolution, larger than anything since the Christianizing of the Roman Empire eight centuries before. Until now it had seemed that God had been up and man had been down. But now God, in the person of Christ, of Francis, of the poor, the hungry, and the afflicted, was down here. The foreground and the background, God and man, history and prophecy, were one horizontal flowing thing. Christ was most fully human in his suffering body; man was most fully Christ in Francis's suffering body. You could not quite pry them apart. People would need to learn to see this, to see God in the wounds Francis had received above the river.

෧←

*J*ere's where we begin, the painter said. The apprentice boy
stood nearby, across the expanse of the panel, about nine Florentine ells—fourteen feet—long and a little less broad, a chalk-white
lowercase *t*. It had taken weeks to get this far: planing the planks
smooth, laying down coat upon coat of size to attach the canvas to the
wood, and then eight layers of gesso—gypsum from Volterra ground
up and boiled—polished and rubbed to glassiness.

They were going to make a man, a Christ on a cross. It was a sculpture in the sense it was a *crocifisso*, a crucifix made of wood, but it was
also a painting, the body rendered on the front-facing panels of the
cross in two dimensions. The boy might eventually be made a painter:
he could sketch rather well. In fact, the painter had found him sketching—so the story goes—while shepherding sheep and had been so impressed he'd persuaded the parents to let him take the boy to Florence
as an apprentice. But they weren't going to sketch, not yet. First they
were going to mark the panel with chalk lines and compasses, inscrib-
ing circles, triangles, and arcs. The painter, Bencivieni di Pepo, had
made a painted panel crucifix before for the church of San Domenico
in Arezzo. He knew the rules. The square of the cross contained an
equilateral triangle that could in turn be bound by a circle in which you
could then interpose a perfectly proportioned spread-eagled human
body, *homo quadratus.*

But of course this body wouldn't be perfectly proportioned: it
would be bent, distended, suffering in every limb, expression, and gesture, dead or near dead. So Bencivieni made three points in relation to
the arms and foot of the cross and, as the boy watched, began to mark
out other circles and then from these, segments of arcs. Those lines
would determine the curve and leftward slump of the body, the sag of

the arms, the collapse and tilt of the head and neck: the exact magnitude and measure of the suffering, the pity, and the horror.

When all that was in place, Bencivieni would draw a figure in willow charcoal and then go over it with a squirrel-hair brush dipped in a wash of ink. Afterward they would lay down gold leaf and burnish it. You are supposed to burnish gold on a damp winter day, so let us say it is February 1288, in a studio in Florence on the street called Borgo Allegri. This painted cross will hang over the high altar of the new Franciscan church on the east side of the city, which will itself be named after the cross, Santa Croce. So it will need to be especially beautiful and therefore gilded for the honor and glory of God. But it also needs gold because when you mix the ground colors—white lead, cinnabar, lapis—with egg (use yolks from town hens: they're paler) to make tempera and brush them stroke by tiny stroke over the gold, something happens to them: the rivulets of blood catch fire; the pallid flesh seems always to be not quite cold, to be dying just now; the wounds refuse to close. The whole painting becomes luminous and palpable. It is not so much seen as seeing, pursuing and then laying hold of the viewer.

Bencivieni di Pepo knew all these things: his art consisted of his knowing them. It was not a matter of inspiration, never mind genius: a Christ was a Christ, a Madonna was a Madonna. The thing was to make them well. He'd made many. When he began this crucifix he was forty-seven years old. He'd worked in Rome, Bologna, and Pisa. He'd designed mosaics for the Florence Baptistry eight years earlier, and it was there—working in that most Byzantine of media—that his images became less eastern, his faces less hawklike and severe, the deep lines (almost carved like bas-relief) replaced by a softer stroke, more rounded and modeled; bodies not set down on panels or tile but incarnated, pulled nascent and breathing from their ground.

The painted crucifix Bencivieni had painted for Arezzo fifteen years earlier was identical in almost every respect—size, composition, color—to the one he painted for Santa Croce, and yet the first was an icon and the second a presence: the Arezzo cross had a beautiful and grave power—we are moved to see a God brought so pitifully low—but the Santa Croce cross will, if you let it, make you weep; not just for Christ, but for anyone who has to suffer and die; for yourself; for everyone and anyone in particular.

Bencivieni had been laboring hard, even in middle age, and was now the most active and important painter in Florence. He'd also been given a nickname: "Cimabue," or "bull head," doubtless in recognition of his stubborn perfectionism. His colleague the sculptor and architect Arnolfo di Cambio was just then building the very church Cimabue's cross would occupy. He would follow that project with the massive Palazzo Vecchio and then in 1300 he'd be made *capomaestro*—head architect and builder—of the new Duomo. But it was Arnolfo's sculpture that excited the most interest among his fellow artists, not just other sculptors but painters too. His statues had the curves and chasms of real flesh, and even when he carved relief figures on a slab you felt you might walk around and see the people from the back. Cimabue and Arnolfo would have talked at length about their work and about the Santa Croce and Duomo projects. Some years later, Cimabue's apprentice boy, now himself known as Giotto, would get the commission for the Duomo's bell tower.

What Cimabue and Arnolfo were after was not something new or different but that same perennial image—human flesh and God's embrace of it—made deeper, more vividly, more completely themselves. It was Francis of Assisi's doing: grasping the God who had entered us, the one who—crazily, heedlessly in love with humankind—took the form of a decrepit, heartsick man. How did you render that in tempera or stone, extending the notion outward into the whole creation like the Dominican Thomas Aquinas had, saying "God is in all things deeply"? How could you put that into words? How could you put skin on the bones of the world?

There was another young man around Florence then, Durante degli' Alighieri, or Dante for short. He knew everyone or at least knew *about* everyone in town. He was in that sense a natural-born politician, if not a deft one. He had good friends and even better enemies: their treachery and the exile it sent him into were his making as a poet. In an exquisite act of creative revenge he put them and practically every other Florentine in their place—in Hell, Purgatory, or Heaven—and wrote the greatest poem in history. Its subject was not gods or heroes but mere persons and Dante's own befuddled, jerky passage among them. He's lost his way in the world, or rather his longing had lost track of what it was it loved. He thought it was a person: Beatrice had died young and now he, middle-aged, had to seek her among the dead.

They'd met at the head of the Ponte Santa Trinità—or, rather, her presence, her living image, simply struck him, poured out and seized him, though she said not a word. The Arno and the city, the river and the world, rolled by, but it was only she that he saw. To find her, he has to visit every circle of the next world, to meet most everyone that he's known in Florence or their kin, to learn every evil they've ever done. And of course everyone here too had lost what they love: life, which is love breathing, speaking, walking. *I' non averei creduto che morte tanta n'avesse disfatta*, he wrote: "I could not believe death had undone so many." It was this that Cimabue's crucifix contained: the unnumbered dead in one human yet divine person who, in his affliction, was love. It is that love, more even than Beatrice, that Dante has lost and now learns to long for again.

The Ponte Santa Trinità had been built by the Frescobaldi, the ancient aristocratic family of the Oltrarno, the other bank of the Arno.

Their son Dino was Dante's collaborator in the group of young poets creating the *dolce stil novo*, "the sweet new style" of verse. The bridge had been erected in 1252, destroyed in the flood of 1269 when Dante was four years old, but reconstructed in 1290, just in time for him to meet Beatrice there. But on the northern end of the bridge in 1300, a street fight between rival Florentine political factions, the "White" and "Black" Guelphs, precipitated a power struggle in the city that ended two years later with the exile of Dante, among others. It was said that afterward Dino Frescobaldi recovered Dante's notebooks for the *Divine Comedy* and had them sent to the poet in his hiding place, thus making possible its composition.

In that same year, 1302, Cimabue died. Giotto had continued as an apprentice and member of his studio for some years after the Santa Croce *Crucifix* was finished. In the early 1290s they'd gone to Assisi to paint frescoes in the new church dedicated to Saint Francis. It's sometimes unclear exactly who painted which ones: some are attributed to both master and apprentice, some to Giotto alone (perhaps executed later in the decade when Giotto began to work independently), and some entirely to Cimabue.

Their names and careers were always entwined, albeit less and less to Cimabue's advantage. The story of Cimabue's discovery of the genius shepherd boy tending his flock became legendary in the telling of Lorenzo Ghiberti (creator of the Duomo's baptistry doors) in his *Commentaries* and, later, in Vasari's *Lives of the Artists.* In one of Vasari's anecdotes Giotto tricks his master by painting a tiny fly on a panel so realistically that Cimabue tries to brush it away; elsewhere, the master is portrayed as a vain and prickly perfectionist who would rather burn a painting than let anyone criticize it. Giotto, by contrast, wears his talent lightly, has many friends, and is as devout as he is shrewd.

Dante knew how good Cimabue and Giotto were at their art, and—it goes without saying—how good he himself was: his great poem grapples with the problem of genius even as it manifests it. The ambitious new thing Dante created in the *Commedia* is classical—colossal, Roman, panoramic—in scope but Christian in scale: no more than tales, the intimate rendering of frail and embarrassed human persons from an overweening provincial town built on the insubstantial ruins of an outpost of a great empire. It was an epic of weak little men—"an ingrate, malign people . . . avaricious types, envious and proud"—who were nonetheless capable, like Cimabue, Giotto, and Dante, of making great things, human works of timeless consequence and beauty.

In the seventeenth canto of the *Inferno*, in the midst of describing himself in an extravagantly imagined flight over Hell, Dante reminds himself of Icarus, the headstrong son of the patient artificer Daedalus:

> . . . *quando Icaro misero le reni*
> *sentì spennar per la scaldata cera,*
> *gridando il padre a lui "Mala via tieni!"*
> . . . *when poor Icarus felt his shoulders being*
> *plucked through the warming wax,*
> *his father crying to him, "You're going down a bad road!"*

One of the themes of the canto is the misuse of art and here the young artist Icarus (as opposed to his father, the artisan Daedalus), drunk on inspiration and egoism, flies too high and destroys himself. Dante and his fellows already sense the pitfalls of being a self-acknowledged artist, the vain, mad, and self-destructive character that will emerge in their city in the Renaissance and peak in the Romantic era.

Dante was acquainted with Cimabue and knew Giotto well enough to model for him, or so the story goes. In the poem he uses their respective careers as an example of the already apparent slipperiness of celebrity and reputation: "where once Cimabue held the field, now the talk's of Giotto, such that the former's fame is obscured."

It doesn't seem that Cimabue resented his pupil, or perhaps he simply died too soon to realize he'd been eclipsed. In any case he either left Giotto his house in Via Ricasoli or Giotto took it over. The following year Giotto began painting the Scrovegni Chapel in Padua and with those frescoes made his own reputation. In the 1320s he would return to the place his life as an artist had begun, Santa Croce, to paint the great cycle of frescoes of the life of St. Francis in the Bardi and Peruzzi chapels. Then Giotto would design the lofty escarpment of the Campanile. The base was faced by a frieze of twenty-one relief sculptures by Andrea Pisano, the creator of the south doors of the Baptistry. Among these exemplars of crafts and professions—plowman, farmer, shepherd, carpenter, blacksmith, and architect—the architect and his sculptor placed an incongruous image on the southeast corner: Icarus, a sly footnote that seems to say be careful of art, of towers, and of great heights.

Cimabue's reputation, meanwhile, would increasingly be based on his having been his pupil's master rather than on his own art, a lesser talent who recognized and nurtured a greater one. Thus began a process that one art historian later referred to as "the curse of Cimabue": the decline in his historical and critical status, the damage to or deterioration of his existing works, and the removal of his name from important works once attributed to him. Except for a handful of "lesser" works, there would not be much left of Cimabue except his cross. But that, perhaps, was all there was anyway. Dante tried to tell Florence this: reputation turns to ruin, wealth to poverty, pride to disgrace, inspiration to despair. The cross, earthbound as Icarus's plucked back, is a monument to those facts, the picture of Dante's poem, the pierced flesh of Francis's wounds, the river cleaving Falterona and scouring Florence away.

*B*y 1302 what Vasari would call "the rebirth of painting in Florence"—the abandonment of the eastern, iconic tradition by Cimabue and the creation of a native style by Giotto—was under way and might well have continued without interruption. But over the next hundred years it seemed that the progress of art in Florence stalled as the city underwent one catastrophe after another.

In 1304 the Ponte alla Carraia (then built of wood) collapsed from the weight of the crowd during a dramatic pageant depicting Hell on the river. The Florentines had tempted fate, it was said—there was surely a kind of vain mockery of divine justice in attempting to re-create the Inferno on the Arno—or perhaps they were being punished for one of their myriad vices. The most likely candidate in the opinion of many was sodomy, for which Florence enjoyed an international reputation, anal intercourse being known as "the Florentine vice" in French and simply *Florenzen* in German.

In subsequent years, fire followed famine and the standoff between the White and Black parties continued, punctuated by eruptions of violence. Alliances were formed and broken that brought the rest of Tuscany into play, control of Pisa, Lucca, and Siena changing hands with seasonal regularity. All these machinations, insurgencies, and intrigues would be studied and recorded in detail by Niccolò Machiavelli two centuries later. His interest in Florentine history was entirely political, but he halted his account long enough to note that "in 1333 the waters of the Arno had risen throughout Florence more than twelve braccia, and by its overflow had destroyed some of the bridges and many buildings."

In fact the flood of November 4, 1333, was the greatest yet seen on the Arno, cresting, by Machiavelli's estimation, twenty-four feet above normal. More detailed accounts report the four-day-long downpour; the thunder, lightning, and gales; then the scramble from rooftop to rooftop by means of planks and ladders as the torrent ran through the streets below; and the cries for divine mercy so loud and frequent that they drowned the thunder cracks and the seethe of water.

The death toll was said to exceed three thousand persons, and ten times as many animals. Certainly there was nothing to eat or even to drink. Every source of grain and therefore bread was spoiled or destroyed along with the mills in which it might have been ground. So too the *pescaie*—the rock dams on the Arno above and below the city where fish were caught—washed away together with the Trinità and Carraia bridges. Water reached the top of the high altar in the Duomo and up to the second story of Arnolfo's recently completed Palazzo Vecchio. In the Oltrarno the palazzo of the Frescobaldi at the end of the Ponte Santa Trinità was devastated as were the humbler dwellings where Florence's artisans and shopkeepers lived. Coursing westward into the San Frediano quarter, the flood breached and undermined recently constructed defensive walls designed to withstand entire armies.

As in other floods, the previously undeveloped area on the northeastern edge of the city was inundated most deeply. Now it was home to the new church of Santa Croce and its vast Franciscan establishment of cloisters, dormitories, and teaching facilities. The water struck here first, breaking through a three-hundred-foot section of city wall adjacent to the monastery and flooding in fifteen feet deep. The floor of the church had been built high above the surrounding street and piazza, and the altar still higher: the water crested just shy of the top. Cimabue's cross hung overhead, untouched and unmoved.

A little upstream the ruined Ponte Vecchio had been reduced to a sluice, the sewer grate against which thousands of tons of debris from Falterona downward piled up. The ancient totemic statue of Mars had fallen into the Arno. Dante had spoken of the Mars legend in the *Inferno*, putting it into the mouth of one of the Florentine suicides that inhabit the seventh circle of Hell: "I was of the city that traded patrons / Mars for John the Baptist. On that account / Mars with his craft will make her grieve forever." Unless his statue remained intact, those who built the city "would have done their work in vain." And then the shade, seemingly in reference to his own suicide, but still seized by the Mars legend, adds *Io fei giubetto a me de le mie case*, "I made my house into my gallows." And that, with its tangle of angular, cadaverous trees and jutting planks, was how the Ponte Vecchio must just then have appeared; that was what Florence—flouting Mars, flouting John the Baptist—had made of itself.

*I*t would take 150,000 gold florins—an amount then equal to the entire economy of some of Florence's neighbor states—to rebuild the city after the 1333 flood, but work began the following year, as did the construction of Giotto's design for the Campanile of the Duomo. But alongside the restoration was the labor of understanding the reasons for the flood. The preachers and priests, of course, focused on human sin and divine retribution, but the lay intellectuals and writers of Florence took a broader approach, employing both pagan and Christian methodologies. Giovanni Villani noted the matrix of inauspicious astrological signs at the time of the flood before turning to the Old Testament to explore precedents ranging from the deluge to the destruction of Sodom. By providing examples of God's previous behavior, these parallel cases might explain how and why he had visited calamity on Florence and, read subtly and assiduously, even have forecast it.

There were also individual witnesses and reports to be taken into account: some said there had been advance rumblings from the Gorga Nera or that villages upstream had been remiss in their usual petitions to San Cristoforo, the protector of river dwellers. And on the night of the flood a holy mystic living in his hermitage at Vallombrossa had seen a troop of demons mounted on horseback whom he overheard saying, "We're going to submerge the city of Florence on account of its sins, if God permits us." The hermit prayed and made the sign of the cross, but it was not enough to stop them.

So no matter how one approached the problem—by way of theological casuistry, biblical exegesis, signs and visions, or the revival of Greco-Roman knowledge and culture that would soon be known as the Renaissance—it came down to sin. It was evident to anyone with eyes to see that Florence was up to its neck in sin, and so the city being drowned was an apt Dantean punishment: in the poet's Hell, the penalty not only fit the crime but imitated it. Florentines were known for their excessive interest in the exquisiteness of their clothes and cooking, their outsized civic and personal pride, and of course their fondness for anal intercourse, be it homosexual or heterosexual—unhappy wives had been known to denounce their husbands to the authorities for insisting upon it—but Florence stood out most of all for avarice and envy: lust for the florin, particularly someone else's florins, together with their house, their furnishings, their good fortune, their beauty (and that of their spouses, children, and lovers), and their talent.

All this went without saying, but perhaps to underline the point, in December 1334 the Arno rose and flooded again, not to the level of 1333, but sufficiently to wash away the temporary spans erected prior to the rebuilding of the Carraia, Santa Trinità, and Vecchio bridges. Five months later an earthquake on Monte Falterona caused a landslide that descended down the mountain and into the Arno, bearing with it an enormous quantity of liquid the color of ashes from which masses of vipers emerged together with, locals said, a four-footed serpent the size of a dog. The debris, dark and noxious, rendered the water from the Arno undrinkable all the way to Pisa.

However, as Niccolò Machiavelli was able to note, politics returned to its normal modes within the next five years. Chafing under the rule imposed by the noble families from the other side of the Arno, the Frescobaldi joined the Bardi (the other chief aristocratic family of the Oltrarno and Giotto's patrons in the Santa Croce chapel) in a conspiracy to overthrow the government on All Saints' Day 1340. The plot was discovered and the head of the Frescobaldi family put to death. Florence would remain in political turmoil for the rest of the century even as a middle-class, upstart family named Medici emerged from obscurity.

Meanwhile, flood reconstruction continued. Taddeo Gaddi, who had been Giotto's apprentice just as Giotto had been Cimabue's, supervised the rebuilding of the Ponte Vecchio while simultaneously painting his masterwork frescoes *The Last Supper* and *The Tree of Life* in Santa Croce's refectory. His teacher, dead eight years, was already becoming a mythic figure, not least in the work of the young poet Giovanni Boccaccio, whose father was an employee of the Bardi family. Boccaccio would make his own name with the *Decameron*, tales set amid a calamity that befell Florence in 1348. It destroyed no bridges, breached no walls, and left no trace of mud, only the collective reek, both in the present moment and in the memory, of sixty thousand bodies, two-thirds of the people of Florence, dead of plague in the course of six months.

There had never been so much prayer—pleas, supplications, and penance—in Florence, nor so much silence, save for the bells, tolling for upward of five hundred souls per day. The river flowed by, the dry-docked hulk of the unfinished Duomo and the half-built stump of Giotto's Campanile loomed, and the pyres burned. In October the worst was over, and the praying could stop. It seemed, in any case, to have accomplished very little. Perhaps it had saved those who survived, left behind enough of the living to bury the dead.

There was a decline of religious faith thereafter in Florence, or at least a concomitant rise in fatalism, in the shrug of ceasing to seek consolations. Perhaps it fostered a skepticism that cleared the path for the Renaissance, but more largely a pall of self-loathing seemed to lie over the city. Filippo Villani, nephew of the chronicler of 1333, contrasted "the excellence of our forefathers amidst the ignominy of this present age." But even their masterpieces and monuments were crumbling, infected by the plague of despair that beset the city: the Palazzo Vecchio "through its own weight is collapsing on itself and is falling apart with gaping cracks within and without, foretelling its own ruin"; the still unfinished Duomo "has developed a fissure and seems about to end in a hideous ruin."

Mars, deposed from his place on the Ponte Vecchio, was free to go about the business of vendetta. And Christ, suspended above the altar in Santa Croce, hadn't even been able to protect Francis's monks from flood and plague in Francis's own church. Their bones were heaped up like driftwood in the crypt beneath the refectory. In time the corrosive minerals and salts from their decay would leach upward into Gaddi's frescoes and eat away the colors. No one should have been surprised that prayer availed nothing: on Cimabue's cross, Christ's eyes were not only averted but closed. He saw nothing, spoke nothing, and was deaf as well. Cimabue, like Francis, had meant to show Christ's suffering and how he followed it deep into death in order to save us. But now it seemed he never came back, nor would we.

*O*ne hundred and twenty years after Cimabue made his *Croci-fisso* another poplar was felled, this one big enough to hew a whole body. It would be neither a Mars nor a Christ—no triumph here, or even pity or resignation—but a Magdalene, more dead than alive, as though pulled from the river half drowned. The sculptor was Donato di Niccolò di Betto Bardi, called Donatello. In his twenties he'd been in Rome with Filippo Brunelleschi, and they'd measured and recorded the forms and dimensions of ancient buildings, which Brunelleschi would subsequently translate into a new architecture in Florence. They also dug up statues, or pieces of statues—feet, shards of legs and arms—and in them Donatello discovered something that the sculpture of Arnolfo di Cambio had begun to hint at: a palpable musculature, flesh laid on muscle over sinew and bone, limbs that might flex, tense, or go slack. And with that Donatello began to make Davids, Old Testament prophets, and Christian saints carved as Greeks and Romans might have carved them, sculpture that belonged to what would later be known as the Renaissance.

Donatello made his *Maddalena* in the last decade of his life, in 1454, and in many ways it was a throwback, a sculpture half medieval and half Renaissance, a pitiful soul inhabiting a heroic body, a St. Francis or Cimabue Christ in the form of a classical ruin. Mary Magdalene stood with her hands folded in supplication at the end of her decades of penance, her beauty turned cadaverous, clothed in the matted hanks of her once glorious red hair. Toothless and gaunt, her expression was the wrung-out rag of a gasp. She might have been a female Christ or Francis, for all intents dead except for the fact that she hasn't quite yielded herself entirely to suffering, to universal pity. She's still the particular Mary Magdalene to whom this particular trial has happened: there was still some vigor in the muscles of her arms, in the grip of her feet on their pedestal. She'd submitted herself to penance without quite surrendering her capacity for defiance. She was still *this* Mary, the individual with a unique history, character, and passion, the kind of person everyone was beginning to become in the Renaissance.

The *Maddalena* was installed against the southwest wall inside the Bapistry, under Cimabue's mosaic, angled to the font at which Dante was christened. She remained there—wretched, immobile, slashing the room at eye-level with her gaze—for 512 years.

*A*cross the piazza, the Duomo was completed a decade later, in 1463, topped by the dome of Donatello's friend Filippo Brunelleschi. Brunelleschi, by now a man of many unfinished projects, had himself died almost two decades earlier. But time in Florence flowed at the pace of fossilization or erosion, punctuated by cataclysm, attendant on nothing, least of all men—not even Brunelleschi; he of the Duomo, the churches of Santo Spirito and San Lorenzo, the Ospedale degli Innocenti, and Palazzo Pitti; he whom people called Icarus on account of his audacity.

For example, Brunelleschi built and patented a massive barge called *Badalone* ("sea monster") to haul marble up the Arno for the Duomo. It sank spectacularly on its first voyage in 1428. Two years later, when Florence was at war with the city of Lucca, he advanced a scheme to defeat the Lucchese by means of an artificially induced flood on a tributary of the Arno. In the event, Lucca's army succeeded in breaking through the channel dug by Florence such that the water ran in the opposite of the direction intended and drove back the Florentines.

A boy like Leonardo di ser Piero da Vinci, born in a village just above the Arno in 1452, would have seen the wreck of the *Badalone* a little upstream, the beams and ribs pinned to the river bottom by tons of white marble, and he might even have heard of the abortive drowning of Lucca. But Leonardo was already possessed by the Arno, the river and its valley; the braid and curve of the watercourse; the whorls, eddies, bars, tangles, and snags; the bridges and ferries; the mills and weirs; the fish, the men, and the birds.

Leonardo would have Giotto's intensity and acuity of vision but also Dante's: *Così, giù d'una ripa discoscesa, / travammo risonar quell'acqua tinta, / sì che 'n poc'ora avria l'orecchia offesa*—"so down that steep bank the flood / of that dark painted water descending / thundered in our ears and almost stunned us." He would paint dry riverbeds, chasms, valleys, and canyons without rivers, rivers without channels, flooded landscapes from which the water had withdrawn, but, still more, limitless deluges and inundations, water without shores.

Someone would have to write all this down, or rather to explain it—the city and the river; their mutual savagery—someone who was Leonardo's equal in the medium of words and analysis, the parsing of Florence's passions and wiles. Niccolò Machiavelli was born seventeen years after Leonardo, but they became contemporaries in history by way of the Medici ascendency that began with Cosimo de' Medici's return from exile in 1434. Leonardo would become Leonardo in the Medicis' Florence—he would paint its women against savage Arnoscapes—and Machiavelli would become Machiavelli— diplomat, pundit, chronicler, flack, and oracle—in their employ. He possessed a capacious and highly attuned mind through which to sieve both the finer and grosser tendencies of his fellows: on the one hand, *popolo universale di Firenze, sottile inteprete di tutte le cose* ("a people universally known as subtle interpreters of every situation"); on the other, prodigies of cruelty who dealt with an anti-Medici conspirator by hanging him on a gibbet, interring the body in his family's tomb, then exhuming it to drag it through the streets by the noose with which he was executed, at last heaving his corpse into the Arno, Dante's ditch, so that he would know peace in neither soul nor body.

It was the time that would later be called the High Renaissance. In 1476 Leonardo painted his first masterpiece, his portrait of Ginevra de' Benci. Soon after, he was denounced for sodomy, once in April and again in June. This was not an uncommon charge: among the family names that figured in the records of the Florence vice squad (the Ufficiali di Notte, or "Night Officers") were Bardi, Frescobaldi, Machiavelli, and, indeed, Medici. Leonardo's colleague Sandro Botticelli would be accused of the same charge once or twice in each successive decade. The notoriety of another painter, Giovanni Antonio Bazzi, was such that he was given and worked under the sobriquet "Sodoma."

Leonardo escaped the charges and, although guilty many times over, evaded punishment then and in the future. The belief that God's distaste for sodomy might be expressed in floods and other disasters was still current, though presumably not in the minds of Leonardo and his fellows. But Leonardo, a man of many preoccupations—his next masterpieces, *The Virgin of the Rocks*, *Lady with an Ermine*, and *The Last Supper*, were painted in fits and starts, asides to his other interests—was nonetheless especially preoccupied with cataclysms. Acknowledged today as an engineer and anatomist, he was also a hydrologist, albeit one less interested in stream flows and drainage than in cataclysms, water as scourge and tragedy, on the rampage in torrents, vortexes, and floods. Transpiration was too placid for his tastes: he favored the idea that water moved through underground chasms from the sea to the tops of mountains in a manner similar to the legendary Gorga Nera of Monte Falterona.

When the Medicis were deposed in 1494, Leonardo decamped for Milan and remained there while Florence fell under the spell of the Dominican demagogue Savonarola. He returned six years later, after the monk had been burned alive and, as was the custom, his ashes were dumped into the Arno, which would, Florentines hoped, convey them onward to Hell. In the interim Leonardo had painted *The Last Supper*, planned the abortive casting of a seventy-five-ton, two-story-tall bronze horse, and begun to put his thoughts on hydrology to paper, ultimately in a manuscript he called *The Book of Water*.

The contents were to include channels, pipes, dams, pumps, and even a metaphysics of water, the river as time-space continuum: "The water you touch in a river is the last of that which has passed and the first of that which is coming. Thus it is continuously in the present." But it was the violence of unbound water that most fascinated Leonardo:

> *Amid all the causes of the destruction of human property, it seems to me that rivers hold the foremost place . . . Against the irreparable inundation caused by swollen proud rivers no resource of human foresight can prevail, for in a succession of raging and seething waves gnawing and tearing away high banks, growing turbid with*

the earth from plowed fields, destroying the houses therein and
uprooting the tall trees, it carries these as its prey down to the sea
which is its lair . . .

In *The Book of Water* these images are reduced to a thesaurus of chaos: "revolution, turning, submerging, rising, declination, elevation, caving, consuming, percussion, descent, impetuousness, retreating, crashing, rubbing, inundation, furrows, boiling, relapsing, springing, pouring, overturning, serpentine bends, murmurs, roars . . . , abysses, whirlpools, precipices, tumult, confusions, tempests . . ."

The mind of Leonardo, the engineer and lucid polymath, seemed almost to break down beneath this torrent of words, transfixed by his obsession as the flood bore down on him; undone in his attempt to grasp the eternal present of water in flow, water not just as disorder but annihilation. Nonetheless, Leonardo did not share his contemporaries' near unanimous belief in the Mosaic deluge: surely, he asked, a deluge of such proportions must have swept fossil remains far downstream to the sea rather than deposit them in river valleys: and if there was indeed a worldwide flood in the first place, where did all that water go when it receded?

Leonardo returned to Florence in time for the moderate but, to him, impressive floods of November 1500, noting darkly that *li monti sono disfacti dalle piogge e dalli fiumi*, "the mountains have been unmade by the rain and rivers." In a more dispassionate mood, he also posited that the cutting of the Casentine Forests was a major factor in flooding on the Arno, presaging the concepts of both deforestation and ecosystem that would be current four hundred years later.

The next four years marked the summit of Leonardo's career as a hydrologist, his obsessions and paranoia harnessed to practical and scientific ends. He mapped not only the Arno but the other rivers of central Italy and drew up a study for a reclamation project incorporating both the Arno and the Tiber. In the midst of these projects, he painted the *Mona Lisa*, placing his subject against a background of the upper Arno in the vicinity of the Casentine. And, in late 1502, he met Niccolò Machiavelli.

Florence was just then engaged in one of its recurrent sieges of Pisa with the aim of taking control of its assets by starving it out of existence. In response Machiavelli and Leonardo together conceived a grand project with both strategic and hydrological benefits: the diversion of the Arno around Pisa and the straightening of its course by means of a channel. Florence would attain faster and surer access to the sea, floodwaters could be controlled and contained, and Pisa would die of several varieties of thirst. Leonardo drew up the plans in 1503, including what would today be called time-motion studies calculating how much earth a given number of men might dig per day. He also made preliminary sketches for an enormous excavating machine, which like so many of his inventions went unbuilt.

Work began the following year on the most pressing phase, that of diverting the river away from Pisa. Neither Leonardo nor Machiavelli was given a role in the actual work, which the government had put in what it regarded as surer hands. Two thousand laborers were put to work and more than seven thousand gold ducats spent but the result was no more than a few ditches that, in the mode of Brunelleschi's Lucca project, were breached or ran backward. Florence would fight with Pisa for another five years and Leonardo's larger scheme, the taming of the Arno, was summarily and permanently abandoned.

Failure succeeded failure. Machiavelli had used his influence to secure a commission for Leonardo to paint a magisterial fresco for the great council chamber of the Palazzo Vecchio. But only the center section was ever completed and the same experimentation with oil colors that led to the deterioration of *The Last Supper* apparently spoiled this one too. By 1504 Leonardo's masterpieces were now behind him, and his reputation was being eclipsed by the young Michelangelo Buonarroti, whose *David* was erected just outside the Palazzo Vecchio as Leonardo toiled fitfully on his fresco within.

Michelangelo's habits of mind and soul—his obsessions—were a little like Leonardo's: the tumid, agonized muscles and ligaments of his figures, barely contained by flesh, had a torrential force, a bursting forth akin to the unbounded chaos of a da Vinci inundation fantasy. Five years after the *David*, Michelangelo would create his own, the *Universal Deluge* of the Sistine Chapel.

That same year, 1510, Niccolò Machiavelli was denounced for sodomy with the blunt indictment that *Nicolo di messer Bernardo Macchiavelli fotte la Lucretia vochata la Riccia nel culo*, "Niccolò, son of Bernardo Machiavelli, fucked Lucretia, called Riccia, in the ass." Still in possession of his diplomat's skills, he avoided prosecution but was unable to re-ingratiate himself with the Medicis when they returned to power a year and a half later. He had performed extensive services for the republican government during their exile, an indiscretion they were disinclined to ignore. It was in the hopes of restoring himself to their favor that he wrote his masterpiece, *The Prince*, but to no avail.

Machiavelli lived on in his country house, still writing, still hoping he would be summoned back to the Palazzo Vecchio. That did not happen and, never a strapping figure to begin with, he grew scrawny, crabbed, and bitter. He wrote a play in which demons too malign for Satan decide to settle "in this city of yours [Florence]" where "we have taken over the government because here is shown confusion and pain greater than hell." He wrote a friend, Francesco Guicciardini, that "for some time now I have never said what I believe nor ever believed what I said; and if I do sometimes tell the truth, I hide it behind so many lies that it is hard to find."

He was not one for God or Francis or the cross. But he seemed to believe devoutly in Hell, or, in moments of equanimity, mere Fortune: "I liken her to one of those ruinous rivers that when they are enraged, wreck trees and buildings; they remove earth from this side, they put it on the other; everyone flees before them, everyone gives into their impetus, without in any way being able to block them."

Leonardo fared better with the Medicis. One brother, Giuliano, ruled Florence and the other, Giovanni, had just been elected Pope Leo X. Leonardo became part of Giuliano's entourage and was given Vatican commissions by Giovanni. But da Vinci, now sixty-three years old, was more dilatory and distractible than ever. His artistic output consisted in large part of exquisite, meticulous drawings of maelstroms, deluges, and floods, less figurative images than abstractions on endlessly curving lines and whorls, the fabric of creation fraying, unwinding into the merest of threads—vortexes, mandalas, and fractals—before vanishing entirely into the liquid black.

At this point, Leonardo was of no use to the Pope, the Medicis, or Florence. But François I, the king of France, wanted a genius at his court for the sheer sake of having one, and he happily took on Leonardo in 1516 for what would be the last three years of da Vinci's life. François installed him in a house on a considerable river, the Loire, and left him to his own devices: more renderings of deluges on paper, more words recounting their motions and effects in his notebooks. The latter were in the mode of his *Book of Water*—strata deposited upon strata of descriptive nouns and adjectives—but were now joined by excruciatingly imagined scenes of the pain and suffering inflicted by floods: mothers weeping for the sodden, mud-matted corpses of their children; a lone bird flying desperately over the limitless water, finding nothing solid to alight upon but an island of entangled, floating corpses. And then, altogether nothing:

Divisions.
Darkness, wind, fortune of sea,
water's deluge, fiery forests, rain,
lightnings of the sky, earthquakes and ruins of mountains,
leveling of cities.

*T*he story of the man who would tell all their stories was re-markably similar to Giotto's. In 1519, the year of Leonardo da Vinci's death, Luca Signorelli, the Florentine master painter, was passing through Arezzo, just below the great bend in the Arno. There he came upon a boy so prodigally gifted with a pencil that he recommended to the child's parents that he be sent downriver to Florence to be apprenticed.

But here the biography, the life of the artist, diverges from the legend of Giotto. Giorgio Vasari was not a shepherd or even a country boy. His family were once potters and leatherworkers, but had come from Cortona to Arezzo two generations before and acquired property and status. So instead of being sent off to an apprenticeship, Giorgio continued to grammar school, memorizing long stretches of the *Aeneid* and developing a fluid writing style in both Latin and Italian. His teacher had Medici connections, and when Giorgio did leave Arezzo for Florence in 1524 at the age of thirteen it was to join the Medici heirs, Alessandro and Ippolito, and to continue studying for two hours a day under their tutor.

He did, however, find his way into the *botteghe* of the painter Andrea del Sarto and the sculptor Baccio Bandinelli. These were not inconsequential masters, but later in life Vasari would wish it a little otherwise and so rewrote his story to include being apprenticed to Michelangelo. Even if it had been true it would have been unlikely: Michelangelo, a hermit to his obsessions—Dante, bodies wrenched and anguished, tireless labor, and stone—did not have much use or time for apprentices. Vasari also claimed that in April 1527, during an anti-Medici riot in the Piazza della Signoria, he recovered and saved the broken arm of the *David*, which had been fractured in the melee. Perhaps it even happened, or something like it: what a life Giorgio might make for himself.

Four years later, his schoolmates Ippolito and Alessandro were respectively archbishop and duke of Florence, and Vasari formally entered the service of the Medici court, producing paintings, frescoes, and interior decorations. He was now extraordinarily well connected, assiduous in acquiring friends, and flush with commissions, although in the manner of the small-town burghers who begat him, he never ceased to strive as though he were one painting away from ruin.

Perhaps he was wise not to be complacent. In 1537 Alessandro de' Medici was assassinated and replaced by a cousin, Cosimo. Vasari did not have much to fear in this development—it was an internal matter in the Medici family business—but he decided to withdraw from the courts of Florence and Rome for a time, not simply to Arezzo but into the Casentine, the country of Francis's wounds and the Arno headwaters.

He went on retreat, not with the friars in the tangle of the La Verna woods, but among the monks at Camaldoli who managed their forest as a kind of deeply shaded park, less wilderness than architecture. It was a congenial place, created by God, refined by man, and Vasari would in future years make a retreat here each summer. He had visitors—his friend Bindo Altoviti came up from Rome to requisition large timbers for the construction of St. Peter's—but of Camaldoli he would mainly say *Quivi il silentio sta con quella muta loquella sua*, "Here lives silence with its mute eloquence." But art and the great artists were inescapable: in one of the cells, he was shown a small painted crucifix on a gold background "with Giotto's name written upon it in his own hand."

Vasari underwent no great personal or spiritual transformation but simply withdrew into himself, and thereby withdrew from himself a little, retreating for a while from the life he was forever building up before anything—disaster, time, other people—could tear it down, the exhausting, incessant fashioning and fabrication of his own biography.

Except for the month each year he spent with the Camaldolese monks, he was in continuous motion, shuttling between commissions in Florence, Rome, Venice, and Bologna as well as villas and religious establishments in between. It struck him around 1542 that he was a man of at least some means and ought to appear to be so. He bought himself a house in his hometown in Arezzo, remaking it in his own image, or the image he was busy becoming. He began by decorating its grandest room with murals on the theme of fame and the artist. Whether this represented vanity or aspiration cannot be said. He was transfixed by the classical virtues—labor, fortitude, justice, plenty, and liberality—and surely, after all, one ought to be ambitious in pursuing them.

In Rome, he tracked down Michelangelo, his idol, and dogged if not quite befriended him: Giorgio felt their intimacy even if Michelangelo did not, saw that this genius was no less than the reincarnation of Dante, and wondered how he might pay him his due beyond mere imitation. Then, dining at the court of Cardinal Alessandro Farnese in Rome, someone tossed out the idea that Vasari might write a book about the great artists, showing how the masters of the Greek and Roman world had been reborn in the masters of the present age and recent past; how after a thousand years of barbarism and stagnation, art had been resurrected on the banks of the Arno.

Vasari seized on the idea. He saw he might work not just in the tradition of the Florentine chroniclers such as Villani, but of the ancient masters like Plutarch and in particular Pliny and his *Natural History*. It would be an epic about beauty and fame but also a genesis of the world that Vasari inhabited and devoted himself to. The book would begin with Cimabue and end, of course, with Michelangelo.

The Lives of the Most Excellent Italian Architects, Painters, and Sculptors from Cimabue to Our Times took five years to write. Vasari, as always, had numerous other projects under way, and some could scarcely be refused. In October 1546 the Farnese Pope, Paul III, asked him to make a large panel painting for the convent Paul's niece, Faustina di Vitello Vitelli, Contessa di Pitigliano, was about to enter as a novice. The subject was to be the Last Supper. The finished painting measured a substantial length of just under twenty feet by eight and a half feet tall. It was completed in two months, a speed doubtless made possible by the employment of apprentices and subcontractors in the preparation of its five connecting panels. As opposed to the meticulous preparation of *tavola*, canvas, and ground practiced by Cimabue and his generation, the paint was applied straight onto the gessoed wood. Vasari was done with it in time for it to be installed for Faustina's— now Sister Porzia—first Christmas in her new home, the Convento delle Murate in Florence.

The panels were mounted in the refectory, where the painting surely caused a stir among the nuns. Its scale might have seemed even larger than its considerable actual dimensions because of Vasari's composition. He placed Christ and the disciples around an oval table, behind which we see not a wall or a window but an elevated balustrade, also oval in form, from which several figures overlook the diners like spectators in an amphitheater. It's the instant of Jesus' revelation that one of the disciples will betray him. Peter recoils, stunned, and John has seemingly fainted into his master's arms. The other disciples eye one another or confer in disbelief. Judas, seated a little distance from the others and at an oblique angle to Jesus, has averted his eyes from his victim and turns toward us, his arms akimbo, his right leg contorted in the manner of Michelangelo.

It's an electrifying moment rendered without much electricity, delivered without the pity of Giotto two hundred years earlier or the shock of Caravaggio a half century later. The colors were muted and the expansive, stately setting was more akin to Raphael's *School of Athens* than to the modest, claustrophobic upper room suggested by the New Testament. The mood was almost languorous: for the inscription above Christ's head, Vasari chose the placid "Do this in memory of me" rather than the more urgent "This is my body." Vasari was nothing if not a Renaissance man, both classical and Christian, as drawn to virtue as to charity. He portrayed the moment in an almost stoic mode, Christ more noble than suffering, his passion rendered dispassionately.

It was a long way from the Casentine La Verna of Francis to this place, Vasari's arena in which the onlookers at the balustrade mirror us, an audience rather than witnesses. It's a stage, this arena, and we are less sharers in Jesus' desolation—God taking on betrayal and suffering with us and for us—than spectators of a great man at a great moment in history. Vasari has created—has seen and made us see—not the Last Supper but a painting of it, a monument called *The Last Supper.*

It was not a failure. It was not substantially better or worse than Vasari's other paintings, and it had something to say about the distance Florentines had come from the thirteenth century—from Cimabue to Michelangelo—and perhaps that Giorgio himself had come from Arezzo. He too wanted to be a great man, the kind of man who might be memorialized in oils or stone.

෫←

*I*n the new year of 1547 Vasari stayed in Florence and worked on *The Lives of the Artists* into the spring and summer. Then, on August 13, the city was struck by its worst flood since 1333, remarkable for both the speed in which the water crested and for occurring in high summer rather than autumn. It surged into the Piazza Santa Croce and dumped what one chronicler called "infinite" timber, carcasses, and debris right up the steps of the church to the great doors and higher. The Ponte Vecchio was slammed and plugged by a thicket of olive and fig trees. In Vasari's own neighborhood the water was almost sixteen feet deep. He may have been away in Arezzo or on his annual retreat with the Camaldoli monks, surrounded by the notes and manuscripts for his book.

When the waters retreated—the mire, fermenting in the August sun, was remarkably noxious—the speculations, suspicions, and recriminations poured in. In contrast to the theological explanations put forward two centuries earlier, contemporary Florentines turned to reason and natural science, economics, and politics. To many, deforestation in the Casentine now seemed an obvious culprit, but this did not much satisfy Florence's appetite for conspiracy and backbiting. More compelling was the rumor that the Ricasoli family, who had extensive landholdings upstream, had secretly built a gargantuan dam and breached it at the height of the rains, thereby wiping out their neighbors whose property they would now be able to buy up on the cheap.

Vasari meanwhile flourished. He finished and published his *Lives* in 1550 to great acclaim. That same year, another old patron, Giovanni Maria del Monte, was elected Pope Julius III, and steered a series of Vatican commissions his way. And, finally, Vasari married, less out of desire than on the advice of higher-ups in papal and Medici circles: it befitted a man of stature to have a wife. Roman women were imputed to tend to adultery and ought to be avoided; those of Arezzo were too rustic and poor; but one from Florence, say, the daughter of a good merchant family, would be compliant and rich. Giorgio nevertheless chose a girl from Arezzo, Niccolosa Bacci, but bargained hard on the dowry, settling for a healthy eight hundred florins. The marriage would be childless.

Three years later, Pope Julius III died, but shortly afterward Vasari formally entered the service of Duke Cosimo de' Medici at an annual salary of three hundred ducats. The Medicis, who had taken over the Pitti Palace in the Oltrarno as their residence, were completely refurnishing the Palazzo Vecchio as their seat of government. They put Giorgio in overall charge as architect, interior designer, and painter of murals and frescoes depicting the Medici in a range of heroic postures.

Vasari was in the midst of these labors when, in 1557, another late summer flood struck, at least as large or larger than that of ten years before. As then, it descended with tremendous velocity, carrying away the Ponte Santa Trinità and two of the five arches of the Ponte alla Carraia. This time the water not only submerged the piazza and steps of Santa Croce, but swept inside. A block to the west on Borgo Santa Croce was the house Giorgio and his wife had rented only three months before. The ground floor, used as a stable, was inundated, but the living quarters upstairs were unaffected. Vasari might have taken counsel from Michelangelo—more talented and here also shrewder than him—who advised his family to avoid Santa Croce real estate: "the cellars flood every winter, so think it over and be well advised."

But it could be said that Vasari profited from the disaster: what had been an extensive building program by the Medici became, after the flood, a full-scale urban renewal project. The tax records office had been severely damaged and Vasari was given the task of constructing a new depository. Then, a year later, the Medici decided that the area between the Arno and the Ponte Vecchio should be razed and the grounds occupied by a massive government complex called the Uffizi, "the offices." Vasari was made both architect and builder, and to complete the project the Medici had him then construct an above-ground enclosed arcade (known today as the Corridoio Vasariano), connecting the new buildings all the way to the Pitti Palace by way of the Ponte Vecchio.

But Vasari would always think of himself as a painter. In 1561 he was given the chance to do something great, an enormous fresco in the Palazzo Vecchio commemorating the Battle of Marciano at which Florence had decisively defeated Pisa in 1509. However, the wall Giorgio was to paint was already occupied by another fresco, Leonardo's *Battle of Anghiari* of 1505, perhaps the most magnificent of da Vinci's many unfinished works. It would have to be either torn from the wall and removed or overpainted. Vasari went ahead, with which method and with what reluctance we cannot say. He rendered his own battle scene as a bloodless massacre, throats being cut, pikes thrusting, horses rearing, but with little of the energy he envied in Michelangelo or even much conviction, and certainly none of the stunningly unified chaos Leonardo's original was said to possess. Unlike Leonardo, Giorgio finished his painting and in the far distance of the background, among the copycat ranks of infantrymen, this most conventional of painters strangely and inexplicably wrote *cerca trova*—"seek and find"—in tiny letters.

By way of thanks for this and other services, Duke Cosimo bought Vasari the house he had been renting in Santa Croce. He filled the walls with murals: allegories of the foundation of the various arts, portraits of the great artists he had praised in the *Lives*, and a vast work called *The Painter's Studio* or *Zeusi and the Beautiful Maidens*. These frescoes were the last works he would paint with his own hand. It was as though he was not simply reflecting his own interests and vocation, but mirroring them back upon himself in his home, encasing himself inside his own monument. Over the fireplace he frescoed a bust of himself—a painting of a memorial sculpture, a replica of a replica—surmounted by the face of Michelangelo. To either side of the two of them, the master and his most avid disciple, he placed portraits of Cimabue and Leonardo.

All this while he had been at work on a second, revised edition of the *Lives*. Vasari's painting often had a certain secondhand quality—motifs and content appropriated from an imagined classical past, style from the artists he worshipped—but in the *Lives* he was not content merely to pass on previously recorded legends and anecdotes. He delved into and employed primary sources—letters, journals, and public records—in a way that anticipated the methods of modern history writers. His aim remained the adulation of the artists he loved and the glorification of Florence as the cradle of the revival of art, but he grounded most of his enthusiasms and prejudices in the particulars of facts and evidence. He had invented the field we call art history, but still more he was a tremendous storyteller, the lives of his great men always in forward motion, pressing onward to their destinies.

For his second edition Vasari added new material (particularly about Michelangelo), but he also deepened his exploration of his original subjects, visiting, for example, Assisi to examine Cimabue's frescoes. He also inserted himself into the second edition, citing his own work for the Vatican and the Medicis. What he had to say about himself is neither especially humble nor grandiose, but his treatment of his Medici patrons was a little fulsome. He credits the family with bringing Masaccio back to Florence to paint the frescoes that would launch the second phase of the Renaissance in the 1420s. They were also supposed to have persuaded Luca Della Robbia to start making ceramics. Neither of these stories were true.

Vasari's tendency was to praise rather than to blame or gossip, although he opined that Botticelli died miserably on account of his "bestiality." But he attracted enemies and rivals. Benvenuto Cellini began his own autobiography while under house arrest for sodomy and portrayed Vasari as "Giorgetto Vassellario"—"little Georgie the Vassal"—a flunky for the Medicis and a scabby liar compulsively scratching himself with grubby, jagged fingernails. For his part Vasari praised Cellini's work in the *Lives* and described him, not inaccurately, as "courageous, proud, lively, very prompt, and very terrible." A friend of Vasari's could only wonder at his restraint: "To put that pig of a Benvenuto into your book shows how gentle and tolerant you are."

O n February 11, 1564, Michelangelo died in Rome. His corpse was sent to Florence, addressed to Giorgio Vasari. It remained for some days in the courtyard of Vasari's house in Borgo Santa Croce. Before burial on March 12, the coffin was opened and it was said the body showed no sign of decay or corruption, as was thought to be true of saints.

Giorgio supervised and designed the memorial service (into whose planning Cellini had tried to insinuate himself, but he was rebuffed). The preparations took him until July to complete and resulted less in a requiem than a civic spectacular. Then he set to work erecting Michelangelo's tomb in Santa Croce. In fact, Cosimo de' Medici put him in charge of renovating the entire church, which had been in poor condition since the flood of 1557. But Vasari's plans extended far beyond mere repair or restoration. Rather, Santa Croce, the long-standing burial place of choice for Florentines of note, would be transformed into a gallery of great men, like Giorgio's *Lives* in three dimensions. The church of Francis and Cimabue would become a memorial temple worthy of Michelangelo.

It would also be, insofar as Vasari could manage it, stripped down and bulked up in the manner and spirit of Michelangelo, manifesting nobility in place of tenderness and frailty, muscular exaltation and endurance in place of suffering. It would, of course, remain a church: Vasari still held the world of the Camaldoli in high regard and in the *Lives* he had said "that true religion ought to be placed by men above all other things and that the praise of any person must be kept within bounds." But there was a Medici on the ducal throne in Florence and another on the throne of St. Peter in Rome, refashioning the city of Florence in the first case and the whole Roman Catholic church—in response to the Protestant reformation north of the Alps—in the second. These were persons whose appetite for praise and making their mark upon the world was formidable.

Over the next four years Vasari's energies would be consumed in the remodeling of churches from Santa Croce to the little church of Pieve in his hometown of Arezzo, of which he proudly remarked, "It may now be said to have been called back to life from the dead." Sometimes old art had to make way for new, even art by masters Vasari had valorized in the *Lives*. Thus Masaccio's *Trinità* in the church of Santa Maria Novella—much praised in the book—was covered over by a *Madonna of the Rosary* painted by none other than Giorgio himself. Times change and things change with them: revising the *Lives*, Vasari went to Milan to see da Vinci's *Last Supper* and found it already *macchia abbagliata*—"obscured by decay"—scarcely sixty years after it was painted.

Masaccio's *Trinità*, however, seemed to have been in perfectly good condition, so it was probably replaced for other reasons, perhaps because the rosary had become the preeminent devotion of the Counterreformation; and perhaps also because Vasari could not quite bring himself to refuse the commission. He was apparently not a vain or arrogant man but he was, by his own admission, a weak-willed one. What happened at Santa Croce is just as difficult to explain. In the early stages of his remodeling project Vasari decided—or acquiesced in the decision—to replace Cimabue's cross over the altar with a *ciborio* (an outsized tabernacle in which to house the consecrated Eucharistic bread) designed by himself. The installation of a *ciborio* reflected, like the rosary, another Counterreformation development: devotion to the real presence of Christ in the Eucharist. Vasari's was a gilded cylindrical cupola, a Renaissance temple at the head of Santa Croce's forum of tombs of great men. Cimabue's *Crucifix*—the sign of Francis's love for his wretched, plangent savior; of the tender and humane vision Cimabue bequeathed to Giotto and successors—was removed to the refectory, where it would remain for the next four centuries.

Three years after the installation of the *ciborio* in 1569, Vasari received the greatest commission of his career, the frescoing of the inside of Brunelleschi's dome above the high altar of Florence's Duomo. But perhaps his heart—what he loved and wanted to see most—remained more with the still-unfinished tomb of Michelangelo in Santa Croce. He saw neither project completed, but Michelangelo himself might have told Giorgio that in the grand scheme of things it was beside the point: in his old age Michelangelo had called sculpture "a grave danger to the soul," regretting that he had made "an idol of art."

Vasari understood this, at least at times: "I know that our art is wholly imitation, firstly of nature, and then, because of itself it cannot rise so high, of the works of the best masters." So Giorgio had devoted his life to making copies of copies, to an idol. Perhaps what was truly real lived at the head of the river, with Francis and Camaldoli. But Vasari was weak, too eager to please great men to become a great man himself, never mind a saint like Michelangelo: "I am as I can, not as I ought to be, and that comes from my being too much at the will of others."

In *The Lives of the Artists* he had explained how the Renaissance had come about so convincingly that the explanation would stand through four centuries. But why did it happen in Florence? He had thought about that too:

In Florence, more than anywhere else, men came to be perfect in all the arts, and especially in the art of painting, because the people of this city are spurred on by three things. For one thing, they were motivated by the constant criticism expressed by many people . . . who always judge them more on the basis of the good and the beautiful than with regard to their creator. Secondly, anyone wishing to live there must be industrious, which means nothing less than continually exerting one's mind and judgment, being sharp and ready in one's affairs, and, finally, knowing how to make money . . . The third and perhaps no less powerful motivation is a thirst for glory and honor . . . Indeed, this thirst often compels them to desire their own greatness to such an extent that, if they are not kind or wise by nature, they turn out to be malicious, ungrateful, and unappreciative of the benefits they received. It is certainly true that when a man has learned all he needs to learn in Florence . . . he must leave and sell the excellence of his works and the reputation of the city in other places . . . For Florence does to her artists what time does to its own creations: after creating them, it destroys them and consumes them little by little.

That was true enough for Leonardo, Masaccio, then Cimabue at Giorgio's half-unwitting hands, and eventually for Vasari himself, who would be remembered for the writer he became rather than the painter he wanted to be. Fame, like brushstrokes and pigment, gets obscured, overpainted, or carelessly or uncomprehendingly restored. Vasari's *Last Supper* would be restored twice over, once in 1593 and again in 1718, varnished with *beverone*—the hocus-pocus concoctions formulated by misguided restorers—that did more harm than good. It would wait in the Murate convent for its own appointment with destiny, with Napoleon, the greatest of great men, when it would be consigned to the same backwater at Santa Croce to which Vasari had consigned Cimabue's *Crucifix*. This is why men need the cross, Cimabue could have told him: because even the best of them, those of the most eminent lives, little by little consume other men, other lives. They need something—someone wounded and forgiving—to whom to confess "I am as I can, not as I ought to be."

*H*ere is it where it ends, in the delta of the grave.

The corpse of Vasari, dead in 1574, returned upriver on the Arno to Arezzo where he would be considered a great man, if not a genius.

Vasari's tomb of Michelangelo was finished a year later. More great men would find their way to Santa Croce, not all of them artists. Galileo Galilei, dead in 1642, was interred directly opposite Michelangelo. For all the pope's attempts to muzzle him, Galileo had been a man of considerable influence in Florence, and in addition to his astronomy took an interest in the Arno and its penchant for overrunning its banks. There'd been a serious flood in 1621 and a truly spectacular inundation in 1589, and once again various plans to channel, dam, or divert the river had been put forward. One of these—proposed by the engineer Alessandro Bartolotti in 1630—was quashed by Galileo, but the following year another project received his support and was approved by the Grand Duke Ferdinando II de' Medici. But that plan, too, was never carried out, at least in part on account of Galileo's condemnation by the Church.

One hundred years passed, their course fragmented by serious floods in 1646, 1676 and 1677, 1687 and 1688, 1705, and 1715, and a major deluge in 1740. Three years earlier the last of Vasari's great patrons, the Medicis, also died, and the dukedom of Tuscany was transferred to the dukes of Lorraine. The Lorraines were modernizers and promoters of Enlightenment and the cult of reason. The Medici art collections were donated to the state and the Uffizi converted to a public museum in 1769. Medici-era laws were rescinded, among them bans on forest-cutting in the Casentine. And eight years later Niccolò Machiavelli at last got his due.

Machiavelli had died in 1527 and had been buried in the family chapel in Santa Croce. But two decades later the chapel was taken over by a confraternity, and Niccolò's name, or at least his bones, was obscured. But in 1787, at the duke's behest, Innocenzo Spinazzi carved a grand tomb for Machiavelli crowned not by any religious figure, not even a cross, but an allegorical goddess of politics.

They were all here together now, the great men in their tombs, even Dante, who (although he was, like Leonardo, buried elsewhere in exile) in 1818 had a monument of his own on the south wall, halfway between Michelangelo and Machiavelli, as well as a statue in the piazza in front of the church.

Firenze was ready to be reborn as Florence; the city of art was ready to be born. In 1854, like so much else, Vasari's *ciborio* was dismantled and would be interred in the largest tomb of all, oblivion, "the great sea"—as Florentines liked to call it—into which all things are finally emptied.

Three

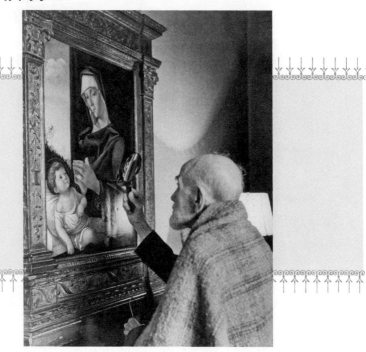

Gradually
The purple and transparent shadows slow
Had filled up the whole valley to the brim,
And flooded all the city, which you saw
As some drowned city in some enchanted sea . . .
The duomo bell
Strikes ten, as if it struck ten fathoms down,
So deep . . .

—ELIZABETH BARRETT BROWNING,
"AURORA LEIGH," VIII

Bernard Berenson inspecting a Madonna by Giovanni Bellini, 1957 *(Photograph by David Lees)*

*I*n 1799 Napoleon Bonaparte conquered Florence and began to strip the Uffizi of its artworks. Then, in 1808, in line with the Enlightenment principles in force in the rest of the French Empire, the city's monasteries and convents were closed and their members and property dispersed. Among the objects to be disposed of at the Convento delle Murate was a painting of no great distinction, a *cenacolo*, *The Last Supper* by the sixteenth-century artist Giorgio Vasari.

Vasari was famous, but not, art historians would say, a great painter: he lacked imagination and his work was a little too studied and stiff. He was a better architect, as the Uffizi had proved. But the French couldn't be bothered to loot his *Last Supper* from the Murate. It was hauled over to the church of Santa Croce and put in a chapel. The Murate became a jail and Vasari was remembered less as a painter or an architect than as a writer, as the author of *The Lives of the Artists*, the book that chronicled and codified the Renaissance, that established the reputations of the painters who, unlike Giorgio Vasari, were geniuses.

✺←

*I*n October 1819, the novelist Mary Shelley, her husband, Percy, and her stepsister, Claire Clairmont, settled in Florence in the Palazzo Marini near the Church of Santa Maria Novella. Mary was eight months pregnant and while she awaited her lying-in, day after day Percy walked the banks of the Arno and prowled the Uffizi. Claire meanwhile left for Venice in an attempt to gain visitation rights to her daughter by Lord Byron, Allegra. On October 25 "Percy took yet another river walk in a wood that skirts the Arno . . . when that tempestuous wind, whose temperature is at once mild and animating, was collecting the vapours which pour down the autumnal rains. They began, as I foresaw, at sunset with a violent tempest of hail and rain attended by that magnificent thunder and lightning peculiar to the Cisalpine regions." The flood season was in crescendo. Percy returned to the Palazzo Marini and wrote down the poem that had just then come to him and that he called "Ode to the West Wind."

Claire returned from Venice. Byron had refused to allow her to see Allegra except under supervision. On November 12 Mary gave birth to a son named Percy Florence Shelley, named for his father and for the city of his birth, and perhaps too in homage to the epiphany that had befallen Percy on the bank of the Arno. After Mary's confinement she and Claire went on almost daily excursions to the Uffizi, Percy leading them up and down the corridors, past work after work that had seized him, taken him over, like the rain and the flood wind.

That January was the coldest in seventy years. Claire took the Shelleys' other children outside into the garden to throw snowballs, while Percy and Mary stayed inside reading *The Tempest* aloud to each other. Mary began a new novel, her first since *Frankenstein*. In it, she imagines Hell on the Arno, or rather the depiction of Hell mounted in 1304 on boats and scaffolds by the Ponte alla Carraia, a macabre pageant based on Dante. Her hero, Castruccio, watches in fascination, "the terrible effect of such a scene enhanced, by the circumstance of its being no more than an actual representation of what then existed in the imagination of the spectators." But then

> *the Arno seemed a yawning gulph, where the earth had opened to display the mysteries of the infernal world; when suddenly a tremendous crash stamped with tenfold horror the terrific mockery. The bridge of Carraia, on which a countless multitude stood, one above the other, looking on the river, fell . . . with a report that was reverberated from the houses that lined the Arno; and even, to the hills which close the valley, it rebellowed along the sky, accompanied by fearful screams, and voices that called on the names of those whom they were never more to behold.*

It seemed, Mary wrote, that the Arno had "rebuked them for having mimicked the dreadful mysteries of their religion." It was the story of Icarus told on the scale of a whole, overweening city, the same story she had written in *Frankenstein* and would write again in *The Last Man*, a tale of "a fond, foolish Icarus." It was, of course, Percy's story, told again and again, until it claimed him entirely in the summer of 1822, when he drowned in the Tyrrhenian Sea.

Allegra too died, of typhus, in 1822, in the convent to which Byron had sent her. Mary returned to England, but Claire, perhaps possessed by the "Wild Spirit, which art moving everywhere," by the "Angels of rain and lightning" that her brother-in-law had found along the river, wandered through Austria, France, Germany, and Russia and, when she was an old woman, returned to Florence.

*B*etween 1830 and 1835, a Scottish geologist named George Fairholme explored the valley of the Arno upstream from Florence. In the course of his excavations he came across "a sandy matrix" in which "bones were found at every depth from that of a few feet to a hundred feet or more," bones of every sort of creature, from rabbits, bears, and wolves still native to the Arno valley to rhinoceroses, elephants, and buffalo that no one had ever imagined dwelled here. The remains of all these creatures were jumbled together, not layered in separate strata, as though swept away all at once, all at the same moment. What had swept them away was not in doubt: elephant bones were encrusted with oyster shells. There had been water, a great deal of it, and it had lingered long enough, submerged everything long enough, that the whole world was sea.

In 1837 Fairholme published a book that revealed these findings, his thesis tidily summed up on the title page: *New and Conclusive Physical Demonstrations both of the Fact and Period of the Mosaic Deluge, and of its having been the only event of the Kind that has ever occurred upon the Earth.* How many might have died in the flood, Fairholme might wonder; how many could die in such a flood today; how many in all of history? *I' non averei creduto che morte tanta n'avesse disfatta*, Dante had said: "I could not believe death had undone so many." Twentieth-century demographers estimated that six billion people have died since the pyramids were built, the age that followed Fairholme's flood. But going back forty thousand or so years since human beings first emerged they posit a total sum of perhaps sixty billion persons who have at one time or another lived on this planet. So if both Fairholme and the demographers are right, the deluge whose traces Fairholme found on the Arno washed away a world that had contained 54 billion people. That was what a flood could do.

Dark Water

O f course there were floods on the Arno: there was one in 1839, just two years after the publication of Fairholme's book, and then a much larger one in 1844. That November 3, there had been no warning except that of frantically ringing church bells upstream, but it was a Sunday morning and what was more ordinary on a Sunday morning than the ringing of bells? The Arno runs southeast from its source on Monte Falterona in the Casentine Forests east of Florence, makes a hairpin turn above Arezzo, and bears straight northwest toward the city. Under normal conditions it would take eighteen hours for a drop of water to transit the river's 150-mile course from Falterona to Ponte Vecchio, but on that day, the time would have been halved. At the bridges of Florence the Arno is capable of carrying about two thousand cubic yards of water per second: that morning the quantity would be nearly twice that. With both the amount and speed of the water almost doubled, the bridges and in particular the Ponte Vecchio acted as siphons, jetting the water with tremendous force and speed while—as debris began to plug the arches—simultaneously creating a backup behind the bridges that breached the riverbanks and poured into the low-lying eastern part of the city around Santa Croce. Underwater, in the channel of the river, the flow of sewers emptying into the Arno reversed direction. Geysers of floodwater spumed from drains and manholes.

The following year Giuseppe Aiazzi of Florence felt moved to write a chronicle of every recorded flood in the history of the city, some fifty-four since 1177. He'd watched as parishioners stood haplessly on top of the pews as the tide of water entered the churches where they sat at mass. He'd seen the slopes and escarpments of timber—tree trunks, stumps, whole hedges ripped and sucked from the ground—damming up streets and the heaped carcasses of livestock piled against walls and intersections. He was oddly struck by the color and smell of the effluents rising from the cellars and stores of merchants and provisioners, blends of wine, dye, olive oil, paint, spices, flour, and grease bound into a deep brown gesso by mud and, of course, excrement. Mattresses, picture frames, writing desks, and the corpses of household pets floated past. Rats paddled and stroked through the mire.

With a friend, a little before noon, Aiazzi climbed Giotto's belltower, the Campanile, next to the Duomo. They looked out from the top and he saw the broadening strip of water widening between the hills to the east. From this height it looked silver: the sun had come out, as though to mock the city. To the west the river had become a lake, no, a sea, a *procelloso*, a word that Giacomo Leopardi had used once in a poem: *i pesci si posar degli olmi in cima / e le damme sull'onde procellose*, "the fish resting in the tops of elms / the does upon the tumultuous waves."

In his book Aiazzi published calculations by the engineer Ferdinando Morozzi showing that, on average, there was a small to moderate flood every twenty-four years and, every one hundred, an extraordinary one; to use Fairholme's word, a deluge. The Arno flooded, it seemed, with a kind of determination, willfully, because it could and therefore would. Florence wanted something done. Three hundred years earlier, Leonardo da Vinci had noted with alarm the consequences of deforesting the mountains and hills above the river, and those warnings had been repeated. But Florence couldn't forgo wood for building, for burning, for painting upon: people wanted another solution. Leonardo himself had proposed diverting the river by canal for purposes of commerce, defense, and flood control, although nothing had come of it. In 1840 fresh projects were proposed and approved. The hydrologist and city engineer Alessandro Manetti began a program of deepening the river channel and building locks in 1840, but its completion coincided with the inundation of 1844. In the custom of Florence someone had to be blamed, on this occasion the blameless Manetti. He was laid low by nervous exhaustion, by a torrent of backbiting, and took to his bed.

John Ruskin, a young Englishman and heir to a sherry fortune, arrived in Florence the following year. Manic, melancholic, and obsessive, he would transform looking at pictures into a new discipline called art history and, with his gorgeous prose, turn aesthetics into social criticism, even into an art of its own. The flood and the accusations and calumnies in its wake were lost on him: everything, it might have been said, was lost on him except art.

You would have found Ruskin sprawled on the floor of the Bardi Chapel in Santa Croce at around ten o'clock in the morning—the only hour at which the light was right, when one could truly *see*—sketching segments of Giotto's frescoes of St. Francis in his journal. A few months earlier water had been lapping within feet of Giotto's friars arrayed in prayer around the saint's deathbed, and even now there was the dull, sour stink of damp and sewage, the bands of mud and ordure that inscribed the high water mark on the walls.

That—the damage and persisting misery apparent anywhere around the city you might look—was real, but not as real as the art Ruskin had come to see. Or rather (so it seemed to him) it was the art that allowed you to see everything else. There was a carved sepulchral slab set into Santa Croce's floor, overlooked by most people, no more than the image of an old man wearing a deeply folded cap. But Ruskin insisted that by this rather than by the city's more famous masterpieces was the best way to understand Florence and its art. The slab's unknown sculptor, if only in the carving of the folds of that cap, had genius, had the gift, and so "what is Florentine, and forever great—unless you can see also the beauty of this old man in his citizen's cap,—you will see never."

Giotto, the shepherd boy who was transfigured into the avatar of the new Florentine painting, also had the gift, immeasurably so. Ruskin imagined that you might read of what the gift consists—of what Giotto was given by his maker—on the wall of the Bardi Chapel:

You shall see things—as they Are.
And the least with the greatest, because God made them.
And the greatest with least, because God made you and gave you
eyes and a heart.

*I*n 1847 Elizabeth and Robert Browning took an apartment in the Casa Guidi in Florence, south of the river, in the Oltrarno. They'd eloped, recklessly fled England by way of France and then Pisa. Robert made a studio for Elizabeth—"like a room in a novel," she said—furnished with pieces he found in the San Lorenzo market, among them paintings sold off from suppressed monasteries such as the Murate.

Florence transfixed Elizabeth, enchanted and took possession of her, beginning with the "golden Arno as it shoots away / Straight through the heart of Florence, 'neath the four / Bent bridges, seeming to strain off like bows, / And tremble . . ."

The city's stories became tales she had to tell. There was, for example, the legend of Cimabue's Rucellai *Madonna*. Outside Santa Croce there was a lane called Borgo Allegri—"the village of joy"— running north from the side of the church up to Cimabue's studio, and the story had it that the street was given this name on account of this painting, a stunning virgin and child for the church of Santa Maria Novella. On its completion, so it was said, the painting was carried to its home in a procession headed by King Charles of Anjou from

Cimabue's studio through the city. Thus, Elizabeth wrote, did the street acquire its name:

> *The picture, not the king, and even the place*
> *Containing such a miracle grew bold,*
> *Named the Glad Borgo from that beauteous face*

The city infused Elizabeth herself with joy. She had the freedom to live with the man she loved and, with it, a sense of utter liberty to write what and as she pleased. Outside, on the streets there was, briefly, freedom in the air. Italy seemed on the verge of casting off foreign and papal domination and of attaining nationhood. It was on her doorstep, in the Via Romana, where

> *I heard last night a little child go singing*
> *'Neath Casa Guidi windows, by the church,*
> *"O bella libertà, O bella!"*

Seeking their own liberty, the Brownings, preceded by the Shelleys, formed the advance party for a new stream of Anglo-American artists and writers who in their turn fostered a wave of tourism centered on Florence's art. Among their early visitors were Nathaniel Hawthorne, Harriet Beecher Stowe, George Eliot, Dante Gabriel Rossetti, and, not least, John Ruskin. The Brownings introduced him to the young artist Frederick Leighton. Taken by the same fervor that had seized Elizabeth, in 1855 Leighton painted a work he called *Carrying Cimabue's Madonna through the Borgo Allegri*. It was purchased by Queen Victoria.

Italy's liberty was not to be realized until 1865 and Florence would become its first capital. Elizabeth had died four years earlier, in 1861. Robert buried her in the Protestant cemetery in a tomb designed by

Frederick Leighton, who would soon paint a portrait of Icarus, a portrait, it sometimes seemed, of every one of them.

*T*here was another flood on November 5, 1864, an inundation that, according to the hydrometer at the Ponte Santa Trinità, briefly reached the level of 1844. A magazine illustration showed chest-high water behind the Uffizi and women with parasols floating down the street in skiffs. The caption celebrated "the self-denial and sacrifice" of the National Guard, the firefighters, and the police "in the supreme moments of peril" and claimed, perhaps for purposes of drama, that the river crested a foot higher than in 1844. In truth the flood lasted all of a night and a day, and damage was minimal.

There had been luck involved—the rain had stopped at a propitious moment—but also human ingenuity of a kind that the nineteenth century and the new Italy and its capital city gloried in. In the aftermath of 1844, Giuseppe Poggi and his engineers oversaw a vast array of civic improvements and expansions in the mode of Paris's Baron Haussmann. Poggi built the Lungarni—the promenades formed by walling-in the river channel—on both banks of the Arno as well as a central storm drain and sluice gate system designed to prevent the sewers from being overwhelmed as they had been in 1844. The genius of Florence extended to engineering. The Arno might flood, but 1864 proved there need be no more devastation. By the time the seat of government moved permanently to Rome in 1870, Florence might claim to be capital of something almost as significant: art, history, beauty, or at the very least tourism.

When the twenty-six-year-old Henry James arrived from Venice in October 1869, it seemed to him that Florence was already a full-fledged international destination, filled with Americans of the wrong sort: "There is but one word to use in regard to them—vulgar, vulgar, vulgar." But for all their ignorance—"their stingy, defiant, grudging attitude towards everything European"—they frequented the same sites and places Henry had come to see: the Uffizi, the Pitti Palace, the Duomo and Santa Croce, the piazzas of the Santissima Annuziata and Signoria, and the Caffé Doney. They were all there for the same reason: the art, the beauty, the ineffable "transparent shadows." So during the month he stayed to study and sightsee he met them—the middle-class tourists, the rich expatriates, and the would-be sculptors and painters fleeing the stultification of America and Victorian Britain—and they became the material of his own art. He redefined their apparent stupidity and shallowness into a kind of willful innocence and stood it in opposition to European fatalism; to the tarnish and faded color of art too often sold, stolen, or left to gather dust.

The following year, home in Massachusetts, Henry wrote a story called "The Madonna of the Future." The main character was an American painter living in Florence. For him, the apex of art is Raphael's *Madonna of the Chair* in the Pitti Palace, and it is his deepest ambition to paint a work equal to it. He has a model, a canvas prepared, and a title: "The Madonna of the Future." But he's not sure an American can pull it off: "We are the disinherited of Art! . . . We lack the deeper sense." So he never begins. His virginal model loses her youthful looks and the canvas remains blank but for a dusty layer of ground color. The artist catches a fever and as he dies, he explains, "I suppose we are a genus by ourselves in the providential scheme—we talents that can't act, that can't do nor dare!" He has believed in beauty—in what he imagines Florence to be—too devoutly, and it has paralyzed and then undone him.

As Vasari had created the artist/genius 250 years earlier, so the nineteenth century created the masterpiece: artworks whose own status exceeded anything they might represent, signify, or point to; the altarpiece that overwhelms the altar it was meant to adorn and itself becomes the altar. A painting or sculpture like Leonardo's *Mona Lisa*, Raphael's *Sistine Madonna*, or Michelangelo's *David* that had begun its life as an aid to worship or prayer or to civic or familial memory was—enshrined in the Louvre or the Uffizi—now an object of worship, possessed of a mystery and power akin to the divine. Florence, full of masterpieces, was a masterpiece too.

*I*n 1873–74 both Henry James and John Ruskin returned to Florence. Henry rendezvoused with his brother William. William—the psychologist and founder of the Pragmatist movement in philosophy—did not care for Florence as Henry did, failed perhaps to admire what his brother called "the deep stain of experience" that lay upon the city. After William left for America in February, Henry settled in an apartment on the Piazza Santa Maria Novella and stayed until the heat became unbearable in June.

He had launched himself into a novel, *Roderick Hudson*, set in Rome but full of the Florentine preoccupations of "The Madonna of the Future." Roderick Hudson is a young New England–born sculptor of exceptional promise who goes to Rome to find himself as an artist. Instead, he squanders his talent and destroys himself, a contemporary Icarus who pursues the allures of art and Europe at too great a height. His lover, of half-American, half-Continental parentage, declares, "I am fond of luxury, I am fond of a great society, I am fond of being looked at. I am corrupt, corrupting, corruption."

It might have been a cautionary tale: beware of art that is merely artificial, of beauty that is really vanity. But James's point is not to avoid art and beauty, but, because they are essential—because life is itself pointless and untenable without them—to find a way to live with them; and, for James himself, *in* them. That, rather than a moral tale, is what James was working on above the Piazza Santa Maria Novella. That same spring he'd written, "The world as it stands is no illusion, no phantasm, no evil dream of a night: we wake up to it again for ever and ever; we can neither forget nor deny it nor dispense with it." The world insisted on being visible and palpable, on being seen and felt. The question was how to see without being blinded. It seemed to James that art was the only means, and that a city like Florence was the optimal lens.

As Henry James was finishing *Roderick Hudson* in Florence, John Ruskin was in Assisi studying Giotto's frescoes. To immerse himself in the work, he'd arranged to lodge in a monk's cell just across the cloister from the lower church. But as the days passed he found himself less struck by Giotto than by his master and teacher Cimabue, about whom Ruskin concluded, "He was a man of personal genius equal to Tintoretto, but with his mind entirely formed by the Gospels and the book of Genesis; his art [was] what he could receive from the Byzantine masters—and his main disposition, *compassion*."

From Assisi Ruskin moved to Lucca and then to Florence, where he settled in the Hotel dell'Arno on the river. On a Sunday in September, Ruskin would return to Santa Croce. He would sit again—soon he'd be on the verge of lunacy, a lifelong virgin given to pedophile fantasies, a visionary frothing with manic schemes and utopias—in the Bardi Chapel at the hour in which the light would present itself. He saw two young Englishmen pass by, oblivious to Giotto, fixed on the nave's preposterous and flaccid ranks of funeral monuments, and he decided—it came upon him like the sliver of daylight he'd been awaiting in order to draw—that Giotto's gift had come to him not directly, but by way of Cimabue, his master.

"Before Cimabue, no beautiful rendering of human form was possible," Ruskin began, but admitted, "nor could I in any of my former thinking understand how it was, till I saw Cimabue's own work at Assisi . . . even more intense, capable of higher things than Giotto, though of none, perhaps, so keen or sweet." But Cimabue, it seemed to Ruskin, had sacrificed himself—emptied out his own gifts—for Giotto: "Showed him all he knew; talked with him of many things he felt himself unable to paint; made him a workman and a gentleman—above all a Christian—yet left him a shepherd."

As to the Rucellai *Madonna* and the Borgo Allegri, "recent critical writers, unable to comprehend how any street populace could take pleasure in painting, have ended by denying [Cimabue's] triumph altogether." But the truth of the story, like the truth of the Rucellai *Madonna*'s status as a masterpiece, was self-evident. Even illiterate medieval Florentines could see it and delight in the epiphany it contained. "That delight was not merely in the revelation of an art that they had not known how to practise," Ruskin continued, "it was delight in the revelation of a Madonna whom they had not known how to love."

So this was Cimabue's—or anyone's—genius; the ability to transform looking into loving. And that was what was lost on those who would not give Cimabue his due, who would not wait for the light to fall just so in his apprentice's chapel, who refused to learn to see how one thing touches every other thing: "You will never love art well till you love what she mirrors better."

Back at the Hotel dell'Arno, Ruskin had been trying to sketch from memory the dove Cimabue had used in Assisi to portray a verse from Genesis: "And the Spirit of God moved on the face of the Waters." But the effort frustrated Ruskin. "Goodness!—that I can't draw it," he recorded, and then, "That dove's wrong after all. Cimabue's wings go up. I confuse things now in a day, if I don't put them down instantly."

On March 19, 1879, Claire Clairmont, age eighty, died in Florence, the last member of the Shelley and Byron circle who had discovered Italy and Florence for a generation of expatriate artists and writers and the tourists who followed them. For the previous nine years she had been living near the Porta Romana in Oltrarno with her niece. It was said that Claire had grown progressively more eccentric with each passing year; that she prattled on about Byron, kept the windows curtained and shuttered, and, despite a lifelong and very vocal antipathy toward the faith, converted to Catholicism.

There had been, except Napoleon, no greater celebrity in nineteenth-century Europe than Byron and there were supposed to be a bundle of Byron's love letters to Claire among her effects, papers of extraordinary interest, not to mention value.

Henry James heard about them in 1887, eight years after Claire's decease, when he returned to Florence and took a villa above the city in Bellosguardo. He had become by now "someone on whom nothing is lost," who saw everything, and by means of his art aimed to render it yet more visible.

James realized that he had walked by Claire Clairmont's door, might have passed her in the street. The story he'd heard was an incident of what he called "the visitable past," "the poetry of the thing outlived and lost and gone." He put his thoughts on what he'd heard into his notebook:

> *Certainly there is a little subject there: the picture of the two faded,*
> *queer, poor and discredited old English women—living on into a*
> *strange generation, in their musty corner of a foreign town with these*
> *illustrious letters as their most precious possession.*

What fascinated James most of all was the obsessive collector and connoisseur, another figure increasingly visible in Florence. James himself, accumulating anecdotes, characters, and museum-grade gossip at dinner parties, salons, and teas, was in the same mold. Having gathered the threads of Claire Clairmont's story, he spun it into the tale called *The Aspern Papers*, the masterpiece of his shorter fiction. For purposes of atmosphere, he moved the locale to a damp and decaying Venetian palazzo, but contemporary Florence—the epitome of the "visitable past"—had provided him the specimen of the pursuer of beauty who, not content to visit the past in the manner of tourists, is compelled to possess it completely.

*B*ernard Berenson was another man on whom nothing was lost. He knew everyone and made everyone his supporter. Henry James's brother William and Ruskin's friend Charles Eliot Norton had been his teachers at Harvard; his budding career as a man of letters was being underwritten by Isabella Stewart Gardner, the Boston socialite and fanatic aesthete (known as "Mrs. Jack" after her millionaire husband); and he would have known Ruskin if Ruskin weren't by then insane. Soon enough he would come to know the London art dealer Joseph Duveen, with whom he would become the great authenticator, the provider of the scholarship that underwrote Duveen's hustling and his clients' vanity and greed. No one could ever quite say if Berenson was culpable in anything: he was adept at covering his tracks going back to the moment when he had gotten himself baptized an Episcopalian and changed his name from Bernhard to Bernard to ease his passage into the beau monde, to stymie the snobs and, not least, the anti-Semites.

But in 1889, when he first came to Florence on a stipend from Harvard and Mrs. Gardner, Bernard Berenson was all of twenty-three years old, a very young man in a very old city. Just then, the city engineer Giuseppe Poggi's improvements were reaching their climax with the gutting of the old central market at the city's core and its reconstruction as the Piazza della Repubblica. Berenson arrived in March, in time to see the last remnants of the "complex of bulk and shape in free-stone, in marble, in bronze, in glazed terra-cotta the like of which Europe had never seen."

He mourned that loss later—the impossibility of visiting that particular past—but he did the things people always did in Florence, that they still do, imagining themselves in the footsteps of Claire Clairmont, Ruskin, Elizabeth Browning, Henry James, or perhaps, today, Bernard Berenson: he took a room on the Piazza Santo Spirito, sat in the *caffè*, and watched the fountain spill and flood; walked to the Piazza del Carmine and the Brancacci Chapel and its Masaccios; bore down the Via San Agostino in the opposite direction to the Boboli Gardens and the Pitti Palace; then across the Ponte Santa Trinità and to the churches of Santa Maria Novella, San Lorenzo, Santissima Annuziata, and, not least, Santa Croce; and then, day after day, hour after hour, the Uffizi.

He was more than busy, he was inundated, swamped and overwhelmed by artworks and history, by the originals of the objects he had only heard about at Harvard. He felt he had no time to write his underwriters, who supposed he still planned to become a literary critic or novelist, but now there was nothing that interested him but art. Mrs. Gardner let her irritation be known—she wanted intelligence, information, news from abroad—and with that she cut off their correspondence. But within a few years she came back to him and, being Mrs. Jack, she would want much more.

Ruskin had pressed himself to the limit trying to "see things—as they Are." He was a visionary, but Berenson had an "eye": he didn't see what Ruskin might see, but he looked with rare, dispassionate acuity. Where Ruskin couldn't recollect whether Cimabue's dove wings tended up or down, Berenson could soon claim to differentiate the merest stroke of one Florentine studio from another. He loved art, but perhaps not "what she mirrors better." Just a painting, preferably a masterpiece, would do nicely.

O ther people had an eye too. They scrutinized rather than contemplated. For example, the story of the Borgo Allegri and Cimabue's Rucellai *Madonna* had always seemed suspect: Charles of Anjou came through Florence in 1267, when Cimabue was an unknown whose work would scarcely occasion a royal procession. Then in 1889, the year that Berenson arrived in Florence, Franz Wickhoff, an Austrian archeologist and historian, suggested that the *Madonna* wasn't even by Cimabue. He'd found an archival document of 1285 showing that a painter from Siena named Duccio di Buoninsegna had been commissioned to paint an altarpiece for Santa Maria Novella that could only be the Rucellai *Madonna*. Cimabue's masterpiece was, it seemed, no longer a Cimabue. Within a dozen years another art historian, R. Langton Douglas, concluded that, given extensive and dubious restorations, the poor state of the paintings, and the absence of documentation, there were no works at all that could be attributed to Cimabue: "to scientific criticism Cimabue as an artist is an unknown person." He might be no more than a Florentine legend.

B ernard Berenson decided he must stay in Italy at any cost. Without quite intending to, he'd run away from Harvard and America and found himself in the Shangri-la of art. Of course there would be no more support from Boston and Cambridge, so he went to London and more or less conquered it. His charm and brilliance brought him into contact with Bernard Shaw, Oscar Wilde, and, most intimately, with Frank and Mary Costelloe, a young couple nearly as witty and art-obsessed as Berenson. They traveled through Europe together (largely at Frank Costelloe's expense) and let one masterpiece after another wash over them, and at some point Bernard and Mary fell in love. Being together would involve enormous pain, difficulty, and sacrifice, and the stakes were high: "I want you to realize that beauty is scarcely less than duty," Bernard wrote Mary from Florence. "You do naturally, I am sure, otherwise I should scarcely have become your friend." They would be lovers, perhaps even marry, but, most important, they would devote themselves to art. The Uffizi would be their "workshop," the Pitti their "parlor." Mary and Frank Costelloe's children would remain with their father.

While Mary negotiated her separation and divorce in England, Bernard pursued his latest quarry, the work of Giovanni Bazzi (known as Sodoma), to the monastery of Monte Oliveto Maggiore near Siena. He took a room in the cloister and listened to the monks chant and pray as he read his Vasari. Four days passed and it came to him that he ought to become a Catholic: Mary had converted in order to marry Frank; he would convert in order to wed—or at least be closer to—Mary. A few months later, in February 1891, he made his first confession and was received into the Roman church.

Mary secured her separation from Frank the following year and joined Bernard in Florence, albeit in separate households to avoid further scandal. Still, there remained the question of how they would support themselves. Berenson had finished his first book, *The Venetian Painters of the Renaissance*, but writing art history was scarcely lucrative. Then, in the spring of 1893, he was asked, almost by chance, to give some advice to a group of wealthy Americans looking for art to buy. "I made a lot of money out of them," he wrote, and "they are likely to prove a pretty constant source of income." The following year Isabella Stewart Gardner reentered Bernard's life. Seeking to mend fences, he'd sent a copy of his Venetian book to her together with an apologetic, not to say fawning, letter. She replied and, after scolding him for his long absence, expressed an interest in acquiring a few paintings.

Unlike his first trip to Florence, this time Bernard now wrote back frequently and at length. But he got to the point quickly enough: "How much do you want a Botticelli? Lord Ashburnham has a great one." It seemed that Mrs. Jack would like one very much, and so began Bernard's thirty years of service to her as adviser and broker. She insisted on acquiring "only the greatest in the world" and he obliged. He had a knack for making her feel an insider of the highest order for whom he would sweep aside the mystic curtain of lost masterpieces and reveal finds and opportunities that only she was privy to and worthy of: "And now I want to propose to you one of the most precious works of art. It is a madonna by Giovanni Bellini, painted in his youth after his wife, as I have every reason to believe." And after a sale was made he never forgot to congratulate her on her wisdom and good fortune: "Brava! a hundred times brava! I cannot tell you how happy it made me to think of your possessing the most glorious of all Guardis."

Mrs. Jack and, increasingly, her other millionaire friends enabled Bernard and Mary to live on in Florence, to begin building their own collection of masterworks, and to research and write. In 1896, Bernard published his own magnum opus, *The Florentine Painters of the Renaissance*. It was a capaciously authoritative work and an immediate classic whose success made him an even more sought-after adviser and broker. It also took his scholarship beyond history and connoisseurship into the realm of theory. Art does not transcend reality, but distills it to its visual essence, "giving tactile values to retinal impressions," and it is this to which the viewer responds in a masterpiece: "It lends a higher coefficient of reality to the object represented, with the consequent enjoyment of accelerated psychical processes . . . hence the greater pleasure we take in the object painted than in itself."

To illustrate his point, Berenson compared two Florentine paintings of roughly the same age and subject, an enthroned Madonna, or *Maestà*. The first *Maestà* was by Cimabue, the second by his pupil Giotto. "With what sense of relief, of rapidly rising vitality we turn to the Giotto," Berenson opined, his disdain evident in writing Cimabue as "Cimabue," shrouded in quotation marks, as though the artist's existence were as dubious as his talent.

At the very end of December 1900, Bernard Berenson and Mary Costelloe at last became man and wife. With marriage came a home, and not just a house but a villa worthy of masterpieces. The sixteenth-century I Tatti, on seventy acres outside Florence in Settignano, was vast and beautiful. The grounds spilled down the hill in the direction of the river and the light was like water and oil: Samuel Clemens, who met the Berensons at lunch, marveled "to see the sun sink down on his pink and purple and golden floods, and overwhelm Florence with tides of color that make all the sharp lines dim and faint and turn the solid city to a city of dreams." Its rooms called out for beautiful artworks and decoration, which would require even more money than the considerable sums Bernard was now generating.

I Tatti also had its own chapel and it was there that Mary and Bernard were married—though both were now lapsed from Catholicism—by a priest. Their patience with Catholic morality had been exhausted during the almost decadelong scandal of their love affair and the Costelloe divorce. And once married Bernard's view of his vows would be rather more elastic than the Church's. He would collect sexual liaisons much as he did miniatures and objets. In that, he was culpable, but he came by his avarice innocently, for good and exalted reasons, because "beauty is scarcely less than duty."

*A*s the Berensons were settling at I Tatti, Edward Morgan Forster was finishing his last year at Cambridge. He was a diffident boy, a little oppressed by his mother Lily. What he would do with himself next was unclear, so in the mode of other such young men, he traveled, joined, of course, by Lily. They would go to Italy and they would go, naturally, to Florence. They spent their first three days in a hotel midway between the San Lorenzo market and Santa Maria Novella, but, as Edward wrote a friend, "my mother hankers after an Arno view," so on the fourth day they transferred to the Pensione Simi on Lungarno delle Grazie, with the river before it and Santa Croce and the Biblioteca Nazionale just behind.

Lily was pleased by her view, but as far as Edward was concerned they might as well have been "in Tunbridge Wells" as in Florence. The landlady was English with a Cockney accent and the other guests were English ladies all of a piece with his mother, clutching identical editions of the Baedecker guide. At dinner they recounted their identical days spent trawling the Uffizi, the Academy, the Pitti, and the rest. Edward's own days were filled with magnificence punctuated by squalor: "Yesterday I went to San Lorenzo. I had got ready all the appropriate sentiments for [Michelangelo's] New Sacristy and they answered very well. More spontaneous perhaps were my feelings at seeing the cloisterful of starved and maimed cats."

Florence, he supposed, was not exactly a disappointment: it did not fail him; rather, he failed it. He could not quite summon up a feeling commensurate with the city's beauty and greatness, his own responses numbed and muffled as though by a thick and clumsy pair of gloves: by the accumulation of previous responses of renowned writers, critics, and culture heroes; by the guidebooks and their checklists; by the mob of women like his mother. Later, he would write up the experience in a novel from the point of view of a girl named Lucy Honeychurch on a visit to Santa Croce:

> *Of course, it must be a wonderful building. But how like a barn! And how very cold! Of course, it contained frescoes by Giotto, in the presence of whose tactile values she was capable of feeling what was proper. But who was to tell her which they were? She walked about disdainfully, unwilling to be enthusiastic over monuments of uncertain authorship or date. There was no one even to tell her which, of all the sepulchral slabs that paved the nave and transepts, was the one that was really beautiful, the one that had been most praised by Mr. Ruskin.*

Edward and Lily were in Florence five weeks and at some point he did find a refuge from the legion of English ladies. The art historian R. H. Cust held a salon each Sunday—exclusively male—for young art historians. Cust was an expert on the art of Siena and a friend of Berenson's, having recently served as his stalking horse in a feud with Langton Douglas (the erstwhile debunker of "Cimabue") in an exchange of vituperative reviews and articles in *The Burlington* magazine. Cust appeared in the character of Mr. Rankin in an early draft of Edward's Lucy Honeychurch novel:

> *"It is inconceivable,"* concluded Mr. Rankin, *"how Alesio Baldovinetti can have been so long neglected. This alone"—he pointed to the Botticelli-Rafellino-Baldovinetti-Lippi-Goudstinker Madonna, which hung behind them on the wall—"would be sufficient to make his reputation enduring."*

Like Lucy in Santa Croce, Cust and his young men were less interested in art and paintings than in reputations and attributions. And well they might be: at around the time Edward was in Florence, Berenson was in London concluding an arrangement with Joseph Duveen whereby he would receive an annual retainer of $50,000 plus a percentage of each sale he facilitated. One could, it seemed, reap a considerable income while simultaneously enjoying "accelerated psychical processes."

But after a few afternoons at Cust's, Edward came to feel that the art historians were but a more polished version of the English ladies; that their smart talk and handsome profiles were only another aspect of connoisseurship and collecting for Cust, who "delighted to fill his rooms with viewy young men and hear them talk on art." The men were "viewy," forever appraising and being appraised. His mother wanted a view of the Arno in order not so much to see Florence as to possess a postcard of it. The whole pathetic, frustrating, and comic business would become a novel called *A Room with a View* six years later, in 1907. And it would be misunderstood: perhaps people confused the title with a work of his friend Virginia Woolf, *A Room of One's Own*, but the phrase came to represent not folly but a further piece of the legend of the epiphanies you might experience in Florence. And how could it be helped? Even Lucy was not so benumbed by her Baedecker and her provincialism to escape seeing it:

> *Evening approached while they chatted; the air became brighter; the colours on the trees and hills were purified, and the Arno lost its muddy solidity and began to twinkle. There were a few streaks of bluish-green among the clouds, a few patches of watery light upon the earth, and then the dripping facade of San Miniato shone brilliantly in the declining sun.*

O n November 4, 1903, more or less simultaneously with Forster and his heroine Lucy Honeychurch, a young Englishwoman named Dorothy Nevile Lees arrived by train in Florence:

> *It looked little like what my imagination had pictured, and yet the dull, badly-lit station, tumultuous with shouting porters and aggrieved tourists bewailing lost luggage, was indeed Florence, Florence the beautiful, the birthplace of Dante, the City of Flowers, the goal of a thousand precious hopes.*

Dorothy was twenty-three years old, the daughter of a once-wealthy Staffordshire family now reduced to fending for herself. She was an Italophile on principle and a devotee of Shelley, Byron, and the Brownings in particular, and if she was forced to eke out a living why should she not indeed do it where they—the poets and the artists—had done it?

She took a room in a cold, damp, and dark palazzo and shivered through the long winter studying Italian. The following spring Dorothy found work as a governess to a wealthy Italian family with a palazzo on the Arno and a villa in the hills, tutoring three children in English and French and taking them on cultural walks in the city and strolls through the country. It was an agreeable position with time to spare for reading, writing poems, and cultivating vistas and views. She might, for example, rise at dawn and render what she saw into poetical language:

> *Towards four o'clock the thunder died away in the distance and, as I looked out from my window, the grey light was stealing, and torn masses of white cloud lay among the hills. The river was in flood, and the swirling torrents of brown water rushed down under the bridges, roaring like some tameless and infuriated beast. The mountains were purple, almost black, and the jagged clouds hung low above them, but in the midst, serene and unshaken, rose the great tower of the Palazzo Vecchio . . .*

As she accumulated such impressions, she ceased to feel herself a tourist. But, unlike many artist/expatriates, neither did she become a snob in the mode of *A Room with a View*'s pretentious belletrist Miss Lavish, who proclaimed that "the narrowness and superficiality of the Anglo-Saxon tourist is nothing less than a menace." Dorothy's curiosity, energy, and independence of mind were inexhaustible. She wondered what it was that drove people to Florence, and especially, "what it is which brings the Americans, above other nations, in such numbers, to the Holy Land of Art?"

Sometimes, like other expatriates, Dorothy felt that the natives were not quite equal to their heritage. She jettisoned Shelley and Byron in favor of St. Francis as her patron and muse—"he who was the poet, not of the love of the women but of the love of God"—but lamented the "dirty and commonplace" monks she found in contemporary Franciscan monasteries. Instead, like Francis, she immersed herself in "the green cathedral" of the Casentine Forests, "the altar of the hills, the dwelling place of God," among Dante's "green angels."

In the city, Dorothy haunted the churches, not from any religious impulse—she had an English aversion to the "errors" and superstition of the Roman church—but in search of art. A year and a half after her arrival in Florence, she spent an evening in Santa Maria Novella contemplating the Rucellai *Madonna*. She knew there was a controversy regarding its attribution, but she favored Cimabue and his studio in the Borgo Allegri: "For my part, I love the story of the Merry Suburb, the jubilant city, the triumphant painter, the glad procession . . ."

And although at one time she might have marked it a distraction, she liked to watch people pray before the Madonna, lighting their votives and leaving their gifts, and Dorothy imagined that the Madonna, too, liked it: "Ah, Madonna, how much happier are you, with your candles and flowers in your dim chapel, than your many sisters, torn from their seclusion and set in rows in the great bright galleries, where only the critical eyes of strangers rest upon them, and no one burns candles in their honor . . ."

That evening in May at Santa Maria Novella, she watched a young woman, bareheaded and dark-eyed, pray before the Madonna. Dorothy knew that "young girls came to pray for their lovers" but grief and trouble hung over this woman, the double solitude of a pregnant girl on her own. After some time "she rose at last, laid a bunch of violets below the picture, and, leaning forward, kissed the frame." It seemed just then that Florence was infused—as much as by art and beauty— by prayer "articulate or inarticulate, and everywhere goes up, night and day, conscious or unconscious, the cry of the finite to the Infinite . . ." Or perhaps this was the art the Italians still excelled at, the seizing of expectation or at least hope, of the possibility of something rather than nothing as a form of beauty.

For that little time Dorothy, although not precisely a believer, became preoccupied with prayer, the least lucrative of occupations. She may have put her hand to it as she did to poetry. But then, like prayer, she wrote books no one seemed likely to read.

She sent off two rather similar manuscripts of her impressions of Italy to London, one called *Scenes and Shrines in Tuscany* and the other *Tuscan Feasts and Friends*. That autumn Dorothy went to work with another expatriate woman and set up the "Literary and Foreign Office," which offered translation services as well as typing for the last survivors of Henry James's old literary set in Bellosguardo. She also freelanced for the expatriate newspapers *The Italian Gazette* and *The Florence Herald*. Then, much to her surprise, she heard from London: both books had sold. Both would be published the following year.

With two books appearing in 1907—issued by major firms, Dent and Chatto & Windus—Dorothy suddenly found herself a professional writer. True, she'd managed to sneak only one of her poems into the books; and true, a reviewer had compared her prose style to that of Miss Lavish in *A Room with a View*, which had also been published earlier that year. But against that, in the new year she received an offer for a two-book contract from yet another prestigious publisher, Methuen. And she met and fell in love with Edward Gordon Craig.

Craig was entirely a creature of the theater, of acting, directing, and stage design, the last being the métier of his indubitable genius. His mother was Ellen Terry, the greatest English actress of the late Victorian age. He had just ended an affair with Isadora Duncan in Paris and was now collaborating with Eleonora Duse (herself the biggest star in Italy and the lover of the flamboyant writer and dramatist Gabriele d'Annunzio) for a production in Florence. He liked women: over his lifetime he would father ten children by five different mothers.

Craig was no mere craftsman: he was not only an artist but a philosopher, a theoretician, and a prophet. His aim was to set aside all the previous "Laws of Art . . . , to transform and make the already beautiful more beautiful." To that end, he would found a journal called *The Mask*. Dorothy would be his largely anonymous collaborator— he was the genius—but Craig made a wood-block image of her as a rough-hewn Etruscan deity to adorn the cover.

The first issue of *The Mask* appeared in 1908, filled mostly with articles penned by Dorothy and Craig under an assortment of assumed names. Over the twenty years of its life *The Mask* would be much admired if not often purchased or subscribed to. Dorothy sold her jewelry to keep it afloat. As for her own work and royalties, she'd declined Methuen's offer lest it interfere with Craig and their mission to transform beauty into still greater beauty.

They did not marry nor did they live together: as with Bernard Berenson and Mary Costelloe a few years earlier, that would have been a scandal neither expatriate bohemianism nor Italian tolerance could allow for. Instead, Dorothy took a room of her own—without heat or water and lit by candles—in a tower by Ponte Vecchio. There was a single chamber, a window and shutters, books and bookcases, a writing table with a vase of lilies upon it, and an *Annunciation* on the wall. It would be her home for the next thirty-five years.

Dorothy and Craig met at the office of *The Mask* and, otherwise, where and when they could—hotels and borrowed apartments and villas—usually away from Florence. In her diary she referred to Craig as "Signor," and recorded their encounters—"magical," "exquisite," "precious"—in shorthand. Nine years into their collaboration, early in 1917, Craig proposed a rendezvous in Rome, specifying not only food but dress:

> *Dine first—dine well and have a good bottle of vino for the sake of me—capito?*
> *You know I like things loose . . . Veiled is best.*

That September, Dorothy's son, David, was born. Several weeks before her due date she quietly left Florence and settled into a hotel room Craig had found for her in Pisa. On the page for the date of his birth in her diary she copied a line from Dante: *Incipit Vita Nuova,* "Here begins a new life."

There being no father of record, David was given his mother's last name and he also became, by default, an Italian citizen. There would be no ties to England: Dorothy's family, shamed, cut her off and disowned her. Craig had meanwhile left Florence for France—for other veiled women, other transformations of the beautiful—and the mother and the boy lived together in the tower. She reported on Italian affairs for the better class of English and American newspapers and periodicals and resumed work on her own books, finished, titled, but ultimately unpublished: *Life Goes On, Living in a Tower,* and *A Small Boy in Tuscany,* the last a heroically fictionalized tale of her own David. In fact, they were both very brave. They lived alone in a foreign country on very little and at a very great altitude. David was strong and of stern enough stuff to swim in the Arno.

Dorothy tried to prevent David's becoming estranged from his father. Perhaps, she wrote, "by-and-bye you may go and be with him a while. Papa is so wonderful and I love you both so much. All your life you can be proud of your father for he is one of the great artists of the world."

When David was about twelve, Dorothy gave him a camera, a caterpillarish thing with bellows, and now he too was an artist. Dorothy herself took on a life of contented forbearance: the life of a secular St. Francis, of unconscious but perhaps not unheard prayer; of the Madonna, candles, and violets.

I n 1926 *The Last Supper* of Giorgio Vasari was moved from its chapel at Santa Croce to the refectory. Its condition was recorded as being *molto guasto*—"very damaged"—but that was no one's concern. The refectory was considered the backwater of Santa Croce's artworks, and there Vasari's painting joined a *Crocifisso*, reputed to be by the dubious "Cimabue," that had once, in better days, hung over the high altar itself.

But regardless of the condition or reputation of particular paintings, connoisseurship flourished. At I Tatti Bernard Berenson was, as his biographer put it, "afloat on a golden flood." His yearly income exceeded $100,000 and he had an additional $300,000 in investments. He began to give some consideration to his estate, and met with an official from Harvard, who agreed that the university would be pleased to take over I Tatti at Berenson's death and operate it as an institute for the study of art history.

But then came the Great Depression. In 1932 Berenson's dealer, Joseph Duveen, wrote to inform him that henceforth his annual retainer would be reduced to $10,000 and he would receive only a ten percent cut of sales. Under present circumstances, the millionaires they had both depended on no longer had the means or the inclination to expand their collections. Still, it was Duveen who kept Berenson afloat, who paid for I Tatti and its maids, cooks, and gardeners, its rare books, its motorcars and, of course, its paintings. And it was Berenson who provided the guarantees that made Duveen's deals possible. They were in too deep together to part.

Five years later Duveen asked him to confirm an attribution of a *Nativity* generally believed to be by the Venetian master Giorgione. Berenson thought the painting was an early work by Giorgione's compatriot and student Titian. But Duveen had already lined up the banker Andrew Mellon to buy it at a record price of $300,000 on the understanding that it was a Giorgione. Apprised of Berenson's opinion, Mellon told Duveen, "I don't want another Titian. Find me a Giorgione."

But Berenson was unwilling to reconsider his attribution, or, rather, unwilling to do so without a return to his previous financial arrangement with Duveen. Negotiations stalled, Mellon died in the interim, and the painting was sold as a Titian to Samuel Kress, the department store magnate. Duveen and Berenson never spoke again. On Kress's death the *Nativity* passed to the National Gallery in Washington, D.C. It is today almost universally ascribed to Giorgione.

Berenson now felt pressed from every side: the art market was stagnant and the collectors that might have bypassed Duveen and come directly to him for advice had stopped traveling due to mounting global tensions. Moreover, he was an American citizen and a Jew living in a country increasingly allied with Germany. It seemed wise to transfer the deed for I Tatti now rather than at his death and to take an annuity from Harvard in exchange. He did not entirely trust Harvard. He feared they would turn I Tatti over to the academics and theorists who did not love painting as he did. But he trusted Mussolini less: Mussolini was a philistine. He didn't care about art. He was said to like modern art, which was even worse.

Dark Water

※←

*B*y 1938, Dorothy Lees was, among her other literary endeavors, "our correspondent in Florence" for *The Times* of London. She was not exactly a reporter, but she sent the paper short features, anecdotes, and information and tips for tourists. She was also often able to arrange for David's photographs—he'd begun entering photography competitions when he was still a high school student at Florence's Scuola d'Arte—alongside her own work, credited simply "David—Firenze." Now twenty years old, he was serving in the Italian army but still billeted in Florence.

On May 8 one of her items appeared under the headline "Brilliant Display for Herr Hitler." The German Führer was coming the next day to Florence, escorted by Benito Mussolini. Banners and decorations would be erected and a state apartment in the Palazzo Pitti redecorated for his stay. But above all, Dorothy wrote, "in Florence another side of Italian life will be displayed before Herr Hitler—the domain of art and culture." David too was caught up in the Führer's visit: with the permission of his superiors, he posted himself along the route of the motorcade and tried, unsuccessfully, to photograph the two great men.

Adolf Hitler was scarcely a passive dignitary being shown the highlights of the city: he had an appetite for art. At his specific request, Mussolini took him to the Uffizi. They went into Room 2, the new home of Giotto's and Cimabue's respective Ognissanti and Santa Trinità *Madonnas*, recently removed from their churches so that they might be better seen by the public. Here, as in the other galleries, it was clear that what people said was true: Mussolini gave not a fig for masterpieces. Journalists accompanying them noted Hitler's scarcely disguised shock at this realization.

The Führer inspected every artwork microscopically and four hours passed inside the Uffizi. Mussolini grew bored and exasperated (*Tutti questi quadri*, "All these paintings," sighed Il Duce). Hitler meanwhile listened contentedly to the explications of his guide and interpreter, Friedrich Kriegbaum, the Italophile (and secretly anti-Nazi) director of the German Art Historical Institute of Florence. When Hitler stopped for a long time before a Titian and expressed his admiration, Kriegbaum steered him on to another, lesser work, fearing that Mussolini, given to impulsiveness and looking to ease his boredom, might decide to offer it then and there as a gift to the Führer.

Kriegbaum was also an authority on the architecture of the bridges of the Arno, and in particular on the Ponte Santa Trinità, in which he'd proven Michelangelo had a role. He took Hitler to a window overlooking the river. But Hitler was less impressed with the Ponte Santa Trinità and its magnificent statues of the four seasons than by the Ponte Vecchio. When Hitler had been an art student in Vienna before the First World War, he'd specialized in illustrations of the most winsome and characteristic spots in the city. He hadn't lost his eye for the picturesque. He'd toured Rome with King Victor Emmanuel III at his side, but later confided that "those moments of joy passed in front of the Arno exceeded anything in Rome." He knew a view when he saw one.

Afterward, atop a hill in Fiesole overlooking the city, the Führer rhapsodized to the press corps: "The greatest wish I have would be to go incognito to Florence for ten days and, at leisure, study the unparalleled masterpieces of the Uffizi and Pitti galleries. I'd put on a false beard, dark glasses and an old suit, and comb my hair a different way. Then I'd spend that ten days in those art galleries of Florence worshiping as an artist at the feet of the old masters."

As Hitler prowled the galleries and the loggia overlooking the Arno, Ugo Procacci was at work in the Gabinetto dei Restauri, the Uffizi's restoration laboratory. The Gabinetto was Procacci's own creation, then Italy's first and only dedicated art conservation studio, founded four years before. He was scarcely twenty-nine then, and he might have been called a prodigy but for his evident humility. His brilliance took the form of curiosity, and that was unstoppable.

Only a year after he'd joined the Uffizi staff fresh from graduate school, he removed pieces of an altar in the Brancacci Chapel in the church of Santa Maria del Carmine and uncovered two spectacular fragments of early fifteenth-century fresco by Masaccio and Masolino. These works along with the rest of the Brancacci Chapel were considered the bridge between the dawn of the Renaissance and its full flower in the later 1400s and the 1500s—from Cimabue and Giotto to Botticelli, Leonardo, and beyond—and Procacci's discovery would lead to their full restoration over the next fifty years.

But Ugo Procacci was not simply an earnest young art historian but also a committed anti-Fascist. To have Mussolini plus Hitler inside the Uffizi seemed both an outrage and a sacrilege. Procacci's mentor and teacher Gaetano Salvemini had been dismissed from his university post and sent into exile for his anti-Fascist activities two years into their collaboration. Procacci subsequently served in two other anti-Mussolini groups, but by a combination of luck and a grasp of the precise level at which to keep his head down—the authorities did not in any case consider art history a breeding ground for subversives—he clung on in his laboratory and the galleries and moldering churches Il Duce so disdained.

Despite that, when Mussolini declared war on the Allies in June 1940, Florence immediately began to pack away its art for the duration of hostilities. Among his other responsibilities, Procacci was now second in command in the Superintendency—the agency with overall responsibility for Florence's museums and cultural monuments—and took charge of the evacuation of artworks to refuges in the country-side. With his customary energy, he emptied the Uffizi in ten days and then went to work securing the remainder of the city's art. What could not be moved to rural villas and caves was covered up with timber and scaffolding, cushioned with sandbags, or barricaded in masonry. It was an impressive effort: each of Della Robbia's tondi on the front of the Ospedale degli Innocenti sheltered in its own bombproof shed and in the Accademia Michelangelo's *David* was enclosed in an enormous silo of bricks.

That autumn Hitler returned to Florence. He was angry with Il Duce, who had just then invaded Greece against his wishes. But the Führer had earlier expressed an interest in acquiring a painting by the nineteenth-century Austrian artist Hans Makart for a museum of art he was founding in his hometown of Linz. The current owners, relatives of the Rothschilds, had hung it in their villa in the Florentine hills. Mussolini had it confiscated as matériel essential to the war effort (in the possession of Jews no less). A whopping seven-foot-long triptych in the late Romantic style, it was presented to Hitler by Il Duce in the Piazza della Signoria. Its title was *Die Pest in Florenz*, "The Plague in Florence."

To this and other travesties, indignities, and evils, Procacci could only resign himself and do what he could to keep the Gabinetto afloat: "Every day, another piece of good news," he wrote a friend archly. Despite shortages of money, supplies, chemicals, and even paint, he managed over the next two years to restore works by both Botticelli and Titian.

In the autumn of 1943 Mussolini had been deposed and Tuscany and northern Italy were under direct German administration. The Allies commenced bomber missions against the occupiers, focusing on installations like the Campo di Marte railway yards not far from

Procacci's home while taking special care to avoid hitting the historic city center. They were by and large successful in this, although 217 Italians died, as did one German, Friedrich Kriegbaum, of whom Berenson would later remark, "He was one of the most thoroughly humanized and cultured individuals of my acquaintance, gentle, tender, incapable of evil."

Kriegbaum was having a drink at a friend's near San Domenico, the village of Fra Angelico, when the raid began. His host fled to the cellar, but Kriegbaum remained upstairs. He'd seen much, much worse on his trips back to Germany, and he was confident the Allies would continue to be careful with Florence: *Chi potrebbe distruggere una tale bellezza?* he'd asked recently. "Who could destroy such beauty?"

*E*leven months later, in the summer of 1944, the Allies were closing in. Among them was a thirty-year-old American army lieutenant with a degree in art history from Columbia named Frederick Hartt, an owlishly intent young man rendered still more owlish by round spectacles. His eye landed him a posting as a reconnaissance photoanalyst and when victory approached he was assigned to the Allied Commission for Monuments, Fine Arts, and Archives. Fluent in Italian and familiar with Tuscany and its art—he'd written his thesis on Michelangelo—he was charged with following just behind the troops to locate and secure artworks and other culturally important property.

Hartt had reached Siena on June 30 in a jeep called "Lucky 13," ironically so in light of its shattered windshield, concussed body, leaking radiator, and lame shock absorbers. But his goal was Florence. Hitler had promised that Florence would be considered an "open city," treated as a no-combat zone on account of its beauty, history, and art. But there had been no further confirmation from Berlin that Hitler would honor his previous assurances. On July 20, when the Allies were perhaps ten days away from Florence, a group of Hitler's own generals had attempted to assassinate him and the Führer disappeared from public view.

Allied intelligence had in the meanwhile surmised that the Florentine museum authorities, believing Hitler's assurances, had begun or were about to begin moving their artworks back into the city. But given the actual state of affairs in Germany and on the battlefront—now perhaps twenty-five miles from Florence—this would be disastrous.

On July 31 Hartt, moving forward with advance troops from the U.S. 8th Army, reached a hilltop several miles short of Florence. He could make out the city, the hills on either side lit by German and Allied artillery flashes, the Arno a dark swath between them. But his goal, although in sight, was still out of reach: it seemed unlikely the Allies could take control of Florence for at least another week. Meanwhile, there was no telling what damage might be done, particularly if the Italians naively began moving things back to the city.

For Hartt, who knew the art intimately, the worry and frustration were overwhelming. He could reconnoiter the countryside south of the city in Lucky 13, scour likely villas, castles, and farms, and perhaps locate and secure artworks in storage there, assuming there still were any. But the most crucial thing he most needed to do was, for now, impossible: to get inside Florence and locate Ugo Procacci.

*H*artt would have found Procacci just then neither at the Gabinetto dei Restauri nor at his home (that had been bombed) but living and working in the Palazzo Pitti, now the headquarters of the Superintendency. During the last few days he'd received several inexplicable requests from the Wehrmacht: first, on July 29, the Germans asked for a detailed map of the Arno riverfront, and then an unidentified officer called him to ask if the four statues representing the seasons on the Ponte Santa Trinità could be removed on short notice. Procacci doubted it—not without damage, in any case—and the German hung up before he could ask why this might need to be done.

Later that day, a proclamation was issued ordering all persons living or working within three blocks of either side of the Arno to evacuate their homes and businesses by noon on July 30. With no place else to go, a significant portion of the Oltrarno moved into the staterooms, halls, courtyards, and gardens of the Pitti. Procacci assumed that at a minimum, the Germans wanted civilians out of the way while they made their retreat or, worse, that they planned to use the river as their battlefront and defensive line.

Two days later, August 1, Procacci sneaked through the Corridoio Vasariano, the elevated passageway designed by Giorgio Vasari to connect the Palazzo Pitti with the Uffizi by way of the Ponte Vecchio. From a window just short of the bridge he saw German soldiers kicking in the doors of abandoned houses and businesses, lobbing a hand grenade into each vestibule, presumably to flush out any stragglers. One of the soldiers glanced in the direction of the Corridoio and Procacci ducked down, fearing he'd been seen. When he was certain the patrol had moved on—when the sound of the grenades echoing out of the doorways began to fade—he looked out onto the deserted street again and now he noticed a series of rather elegant black, bell-shaped devices connected in succession by strands of cable fastened to the walls of every edifice standing near the Ponte Vecchio and those on the streets extending away from it.

Procacci realized these were charges of some kind, perhaps to stop an assault by the Allies by bringing the buildings bordering the riverbank down on their heads. Procacci's guess was close, but the actual German plan—code-named *Feuerzauber*, "fire magic"—was to withdraw from Florence but make the Arno impassable to the Allies. To that end, the Wehrmacht was installing bombs on all six Florentine bridges, including the Ponte alla Carraia, Ponte Santa Trinità, and Ponte Vecchio in the historic center. But that same day, as the Allies pressed within twenty miles of Florence, a telegram arrived from Berlin. Someone—at the very highest levels—had revised Operation *Feuerzauber* in a very particular way:

> *By order of the Supreme Commander Southwest, no military measures are to be taken against the Ponte Vecchio, not even antipersonnel mines and the like. Measures already taken are to be immediately canceled. Confirm that this order has been executed.*

*T*wo nights later, on the evening of August 3, Ugo Procacci and his wife were outside taking the air at the Palazzo Pitti. After five days of occupation by thousands of refugees from all over the Oltrarno, food and water were running short and the sanitary facilities overwhelmed. The atmosphere was stuffy, humid, and, not least, foul.

A little before nine, there was a series of explosions, vastly louder than those either of artillery or Allied bombing runs on the Campo di Marte. Glass shattered throughout the palace and dust and smoke rained down. The Procaccis, seeking shelter, found themselves crushed among the panicked mob huddled between the courtyards. A second, fainter set of explosions thundered from the direction of the river, and then it was quiet.

The first group of detonations had in fact come from the area Procacci had secretly reconnoitered two days before. Now all the buildings on either side of the Oltrarno end of the Ponte Vecchio extending several blocks in every direction were reduced to rubble. The second set marked the same process at the other end of the bridge. Four hours passed. Then, between two and four in the morning on August 4, the remaining charges were ignited. There were dozens of explosions and Florentines, whose telephones and electricity had been cut off at the same time, imagined that the entire city was being razed in some new and unparalleled kind of air and artillery attack. Pieces of the Ponte alla Carraia landed a quarter mile away from the river in the San Lorenzo market and segments of tram rail from the Oltrarno fell in front of the post office in the Piazza della Repubblica. It took the Wehrmacht engineers several attempts to destroy the Ponte Santa Trinità, so the explosions continued well into the morning, after which the Germans salted the debris with mines. Farther away, the percussion of the bombs shattered windows and sucked open doors. On each Lungarno, the twin avenues bordering either side of the river, landslides of shattered stone, brick, and debris had cascaded into the Arno. A miasmic inferno of dust and smoke, the afterglow of the *Feuerzauber*, hung over the heart of the city until midday.

In the morning Ugo Procacci leaned out his window, straining for a view that might reveal what had transpired the previous night. He spotted two armed partisans of the Italian resistance coming toward the palace from the south. Where were the Germans? he called out. Gone, was the response, but they were still holding positions on the other side of the river. And the bridges? All blown up—except the Ponte Vecchio, answered one partisan, and then the other shouted *Viva l'Italia!* Procacci responded with the same cry, a little weakly, he felt.

He should be overjoyed that the Germans were in retreat, but his thoughts were on the demolition of the night before and of the destruction of the Ponte Santa Trinità in particular. He was stunned and near tears: he half feared that something in him—perhaps a little inhuman, a little too in thrall to beauty—loved a work of art more than the liberation of his own people. Then, that afternoon, the first British troops arrived, and, as he would recall later, "a sort of delerium seized me—the abjection of twenty years, the agony of the last months, were over. I was a free man again."

The view that met the Allies who reached the Arno later that day was bizarre: the Ponte Vecchio stood untouched, intact but surrounded by acres of rubble, an island of the picturesque in a sea of devastation. To Paolo Sica, an architect later involved in rebuilding the other bridges, this lone act of preservation seemed perverse, almost pathetic: the Ponte Vecchio was saved, he said, a little mystified, "by a romantic scrupulousness of an exquisitely German kind."

A few days earlier, on August 1, Frederick Hartt received a report that a cache of artworks had been discovered in an abandoned villa near the battle line south of Florence. The British soldiers who'd stumbled across it were scarcely versed in art but someone seemed to think, crazily enough, that they'd seen Botticelli's *Primavera* among the stacks of paintings.

Dodging German shells in a borrowed jeep, Hartt arrived at the Castello Montegufoni the next morning. Inside, he passed through Baroque doors into a pitch-dark *salone* that had apparently not been entered for months, perhaps even years. He ordered the shutters swung open—there was, of course, no electricity—and in dust-spiraling light he slowly made out not only the rumored Botticelli but also dozens of other works evacuated from Florence at the beginning of the war, not least the Giotto *Madonna* from the Ognissanti church, Cimabue's Santa Trinità *Madonna*, and, alone and immense, the Rucellai *Madonna*, each slumped against the wall in this derelict ballroom in the Tuscan hills.

Hartt made sure guards were posted and returned to his headquarters. Apparently, contrary to intelligence reports, the Superintendency had not been returning evacuated art to the city. Meanwhile, there were other country estates where refugee artworks had been hidden and Hartt wanted to secure them as quickly as possible. But in some cases the Germans had gotten there first and were now making off with a booty of masterpieces as they retreated. From another villa, the Montagnana, they'd removed some 297 paintings—by Botticelli, Lippi, Bellini, and Tintoretto among others—plus a set of Lorenzo Ghiberti's bronze doors from the Baptistry of Florence.

The Wehrmacht continued to shell Allied positions on the edge of Florence during its withdrawal north (bogged down in the Appenines, the Germans had to abandon the haul from the Villa Montagnana), so Hartt wasn't allowed to enter Florence for another week. He continued searching out caches of art in the hills, in churches, chapels, cellars, and villas. He found masterpiece after masterpiece incongruously set down in empty countryside, and, in counterpoint, the piles of human excrement the German soldiers habitually deposited on tables, sculptures, and altars. On August 9, in a basement of an abandoned castle, he found an *Annunciation* by Filippo Lippi, and a little farther down, in the darkness, an enormous *Crucifix* by Cimabue; not the Santa Croce crucifix, but its earlier cousin from Arezzo, now crazily inverted in a wine cellar, the dolorous Mary on the left-hand extreme of its horizontal gazing up tenderly from the damp floor.

&—

*F*our days later, he finally reached Florence. He descended down the road from Siena past the placid monastery of Certosa that he'd first seen ten years before, innocent of everything but art and beauty. That was how all the world seemed then, but nowhere more than Florence.

But here, even at the edge of the city, there was the devastation and squalor caused by broken water and sewage lines, shelling, and bombing, the shuffling, tawdry misery of a hungry and homeless population. His first stop was the Allied Administrative Headquarters near the Porta Romana, where he had to obtain passes for himself and, absurdly, he felt, for Ugo Procacci, this unknown native of Florence who'd spent the last five years imprisoned inside the city.

When Hartt reached the Pitti, among the six thousand displaced Florentines he found Procacci, tall, birdlike, formal, intense. Procacci hadn't been able to see any of the destruction except what was visible from the high places on the palace grounds and he felt strongly that this was what he and the American ought to inspect first. He and Hartt had to approach the Arno like mountain climbers, using a ladder to ascend to the Corrodoio Vasariano and then out through a window and down a thirty-foot talus of rubble to the Ponte Vecchio. From halfway across they could look up and down the Arno, at the devastation on the banks, the stumps of the piers that had once supported the bridges, and the temporary span the Allies had quickly erected near the site of the Ponte Santa Trinità. Stopping the Allied advance for scarcely a few days, Operation *Feuerzauber* had been as pointless as it was destructive.

As they reached the end of the bridge and turned right to the Uffizi, chalked below the statue of Dante in Vasari's colonnade was a typically Florentine graffito—unsentimental, wry, faintly bitter—of the kind that instantaneously appeared within days of any flood or disaster: *In sul passo dell'Arno, I Tedeschi hanno lasciato il ricordo della loro ci-*

viltà, "On this stretch of the Arno the Germans have left a memento of their civilization."

Hartt and Procacci were perhaps softer-hearted. When Procacci let them inside the deserted Uffizi (there was scarcely any need for locks and keys) and they walked through the galleries—carpeted with dust, plaster, and broken glass—and up the stairs, each saw that the other was weeping. They went out into the loggia, where Hitler had taken his view of the Arno six years before, and gazed again at what seemed to sum up not the pity of war, or even the evil of war, but a dark mirrored analog of beauty; not mere ugliness or desecration, but an urge that went beyond destruction; a furious negation, annihilation aimed at absenting altogether what was most fully—in beauty—present.

*H*artt found a room on the shattered Lungarno by the ruins of the Ponte alla Carraia. He and Procacci took Lucky 13 back out into the countryside and checked and secured the remaining artworks Procacci had relocated in 1940. Then Hartt went looking for another missing monument, Bernard Berenson. Berenson had last been seen at I Tatti a year before, and since then the villa had been empty except for a caretaker. When Hartt arrived in Florence, I Tatti was still behind enemy lines and had sustained damage from shell fire. But Berenson was gone, as was most of his art.

Hartt made inquiries that led him to Giovanni Colacicchi, the director of the Accademia. Colacicchi had it on good authority that Berenson was still in Florence, but had been in hiding ever since the collapse of Mussolini's regime and the subsequent German occupation in September 1943. He'd been sheltered by friends in a villa in Careggi, on the northwest outskirts of the city then still technically under German control. During the first week of September Hartt finally reached the villa. Outside, there were two Wehrmacht corpses in the garden. He found Berenson upstairs, reclining on a chaise longue, shell holes in the wall above his head, surrounded by his paintings which he'd swaddled in blankets and cushions to protect them from shrapnel. He was seventy-nine years old, shaken, unsteady, and slow of speech, but his collection was unscathed.

Unhappily, Berenson had consigned about a quarter of his artworks to a friend's house on the Borgo San Jacopo abutting the Ponte Vecchio, and these were buried in the debris along the river. But Hartt took extraordinary pains to recover them—he found twenty-seven in all—and each week he came with one or two more, combed from the mud, dust, and rubble, and laid them before the old man as though an offering. And with that, Berenson seemed to come back to life, and with him the life of I Tatti, the guests and fine conversation, and then, with Hartt in the vanguard, an initiative was launched to restore the ruined parts of Florence in general and the bridges in particular. The mission statement insisted on both verisimilitude and art historical accuracy: *Dov'era, com'era*, "Where it was, how it was."

The most important but most difficult restoration would be the Ponte Santa Trinità, which was less a construction of stone than a sculpture surmounted by statues. The Four Seasons were now in pieces among the debris of the Lungarno or deep in the Arno, not just underwater but buried beneath tons of other stone. The sculptor Giannetto Mannucci was put in charge and he personally undertook the recovery dives into the Arno. In the dark and mud of the river bottom corpses were mingled with pieces of the statues: diving in October in search of the head of Caccini's *Autumn*, Mannucci was shadowed by a decollated corpse spinning in an underwater eddy.

Through luck and persistence, most of the statue fragments had been found by the end of October. But on the second day of November—

they always came during the first week of November, like a saint's day or a shift of constellations—the biggest flood since 1864 poured down the channel of the Arno. Hartt could hear the river from six blocks away. The tint of the water transited the spectrum from milky to ocher to brown to deep gray, and then came the tree trunks and "whole patches of earth with squashes growing on them" from farms upstream. Inside Hartt's apartment in the Palazzo Corsini on the Lungarno the noise was deafening, the gyre of black and gray that was the river and the downpour from the sky above it consuming all.

It would have been a minor flood, but the German demolition had rendered it something larger. Because of the debris under and along the river the channel was narrower and shallower, which raised the water level and increased the flood's velocity while decreasing the river's capacity. Water lashed and sprayed over parapets of the Lungarno like a ship's gunwales in a gale, and then the parapets were broken and breached. Water poured across the Lungarno and into the alleys perpendicular to it, the water pressing northward as though in pursuit of the retreating Wehrmacht. Four floors below his room, mud and water filled the cellars of the Palazzo Corsini as Hartt tried to read another inventory or to make out the details of an antique architectural plan.

Cleaning up after the flood became just another chore in the postwar recovery of Florence, which proceeded more quickly than anyone could have imagined. The city also began to regain much of its traditional social character, fomenting with complaint, blame, and backbiting as reconstruction of the Trinità and the other bridges stalled and seemed sometimes to languish altogether. As for the head of *Spring*, the last unrecovered fragment of the Trinità statues, there had been persistent rumors going back to the end of the war that she wasn't in the river at all; that she'd been seen amid the rubble on the Lungarno and had been stolen and sold for a pretty sum to one or another collector or museum, doubtless with civic connivance. In the rush to placate public opinion, ill-considered projects—half modernist, half a melange of traditional elements—went up on the sites of the dynamited buildings adjacent to the Ponte Vecchio.

Certainly, it wasn't Berenson's *Dov'era, com'era* approach: he abhorred modernism and some might have said that if he had his way, Firenze would be no more than a museum of itself, a replica of "Florence." Berenson—now universally known as "BB," the grand duke of Florence, if not of Firenze—was a monument that often seemed to overshadow the art he'd built his career and fortune upon. BB knew best, not only in his own opinion but in that of his successor art historians from America, Britain, and Germany. And both knew better than the Italians, who it sometimes seemed were not quite to be trusted with their own patrimony. Of course in some sense it belonged to the entire world, to all civilized peoples—Italians would be happy to concede that the art of their forefathers was that important—but didn't that mean that the world had some claim upon it in terms of rights and perhaps even control? In defeating Hitler the world (in the form of the Allies) had rescued Italy, and it had taken measures to ensure that Italy's art was protected as well, even if in the form of so humble and selfless a figure as Frederick Hartt.

In any case Italy could not afford to refuse the help, interest, or cash of the outside world and its art experts. When Berenson established (with funds from the Parker Pen Company) a reward of $3,000 for the return of the head of *Spring*, Firenze could scarcely turn up its nose at Florence's largesse, however much it might catch an aroma of condescension. Firenze and Florence shared a mutual love of these masterpieces, but love could be jealous and possessive. Possession, after all, was the essence of connoisseurship and of museum curating and accession, an enterprise the Italians were now as deeply implicated in as anyone.

Dark Water

⌘

rederick Hartt packed his bags for America in August 1945. Hostilities in both theaters of World War II had ended. Hartt had been awarded a Guggenheim fellowship to study Michelangelo and then would complete his Ph.D. dissertation. He also wrote a memoir of his year recovering art in Tuscany and the devastation on the Arno. Of the Ponte Santa Trinità, he wrote, "The design for this masterpiece . . . has been revealed by a recently discovered letter to have been corrected by Michelangelo himself." It was still too soon to say—the wounds were too fresh—that the discovery was made by Friedrich Kriegbaum, a German and, like all Germans, complicit.

Like Hartt, all across Europe everyone was going home, or headed somewhere to make a new home. The continent teemed with human traffic, the unrelenting movements of refugees, displaced persons, veterans and freed POWs, camp survivors, collaborators, black marketers, political criminals, orphans, widows, and, everywhere and nowhere, the missing.

David Lees had been gone seven years. Now twenty-eight, he'd served with the Alpine regiment (he was a skier and mountaineer as well as a swimmer) in Albania and France. After the overthrow of Il Duce and the transfer of Italy's allegiance to the Allies in August 1943, he'd escaped from the Germans over the Alps into Switzerland, where he waited out the duration in an internment camp. He found his mother, Dorothy, living outside the city walls in Bellosguardo. Her tower adjacent to the Ponte Vecchio had been destroyed by the German demolitions on the Arno of August 3, 1944. And now, in this new state of things, it seemed wise that his own photos of the Uffizi in 1938, however innocent in motivation, should disappear too.

But photography would remain his métier. He photographed the ruins around his old home by the river. He also got a job assisting a *Life* magazine photographer who was in Italy shooting a story on the masterpieces of the Renaissance. David was the ideal assistant, perfectly bilingual, cognizant of Italian art, and happy to deal with the exigencies and lapses caused by his boss's excessive drinking. He knew, of course, a fair amount about photography and, more crucially, he had an "eye." He went to the south of France and at last photographed his father, still an outsized character in his seventies, given to large straw hats, elaborately knotted cravats, and vast gesticulations with both cigarettes and a pipe. In David's acute, black-and-white photographs, he plays the genius, the master, at leisure, effortlessly amused by himself and the world that pays him court. Or rather, the photographs seem to tell, he overplays it. David lets Craig, the double betrayer of lover and son, hang himself. But Dorothy's admiration remained indefatigable. Shortly after David's visit, she wrote Craig to tell him, in effect, that he needn't ever write her back: "Your time is too necessary, too precious to *yourself,* to *EGC* [Edward Gordon Craig] *ARTIST,* to spend in many letters . . ."

With his boss incapacitated by drinking, David increasingly found himself doing *Life* setups and shoots on his own. Over the next four years, he consolidated his position and, by 1950, he was *Life*'s chief photographer in Italy. His work—art, human interest stories, royalty, tycoons, and popes—was now appearing regularly in the preeminent photojournalism magazine in the world.

Nick Kraczyna, Polish by citizenship, Russian by blood, and in 1945 all of five years old, would reach Florence by a most circuitous route. His birthplace, Kamien-Koszyrski, had been under three different jurisdictions since his birth in 1940: prior to the war, it had been part of Poland, was ceded to Russia under the Hitler-Stalin pact, and was occupied by Germany in 1942 during Hitler's invasion of Russia. On August 10 the Germans rounded up every Jew in the town—Kamien-Koszyrski contained a substantial Jewish community in what is today Ukraine—marched them to the cemetery, and slaughtered them in one of the most notorious massacres of the war.

Nick's family was gentile and survived. His father had been an officer in the suicidal Polish cavalry charge against the German invasion in 1939, but now he learned to live among the Nazis. Perhaps he and his family lived well enough to be suspected of collaboration. In any case, when the Russian counterattack of 1943 neared Kamien-Koszyrski, Nick's family fled just ahead of the retreating German troops and continued westward to Brest, then Warsaw, and finally Berlin. At the end of the war, in 1945, they'd pressed on southwestward into Bavaria, finishing up ten miles inside the American zone of occupation. Had they been on the other side of the line, in the Russian zone, they would have been deported back to the east and, at a minimum, Nick's father executed: it was an ironclad law of Russian logic that if you had survived as a Pole—never mind a Pole of Russian extraction—in Germany, you were a collaborator.

Nick spent the next six years in refugee camps. In the barracks with his family he spoke Russian, at school Polish, and around the camp German. Otherwise, nearly always, he was drawing.

In 1951 a church group from New Haven, Connecticut, agreed to adopt a family from Nick's camp. The family was Nick's and on May 2 they arrived in New York. In New Haven, he was put into the fifth grade at the local elementary school. Nick spoke not a word of English, but when his classmates found out he spoke Russian at home— it was the era of Senator Joe McCarthy—he was named "the dirty Commie." He had been a Pole, a crypto-German, and now, although he was supposed to be an American, he was a Soviet. Of course for most of his life so far he had been a refugee, a stateless person, and he might as well have just flown away, for all anyone would notice. But he drew like an angel, or at least like Icarus. He threw himself headlong into his art.

*T*hree years after the end of the war, the Uffizi was fully restored to its position as one of the world's two or three greatest museums of art. In 1947 Ugo Procacci staged an exhibition centered on the art that had been evacuated during the war, and a year later he added the Rucellai *Madonna* to Room 2, reunited with the Giotto and Cimabue *Madonnas* it had taken refuge with in the Castello Montegufoni where Frederick Hartt had found them. And to complete that ultimate proto-Renaissance collection he obtained the Cimabue *Crucifix* from Santa Croce.

Just then, it seemed that "Cimabue" might become simply Cimabue again and get some credit in the bargain. Roberto Longhi, perhaps the most eminent Italian art historian of the day, asserted that "Duccio was not only the pupil of Cimabue but [was] almost created by Cimabue." Like Giotto, Duccio had been Cimabue's student and had worked with him on the Assisi frescoes that had been Ruskin's epiphany. Cimabue had been the means, the inspiration, by which Duccio came to "see things—as they Are." Now, here they were again, almost touching, in Vasari's Uffizi. But, to Procacci's disappointment, the amalgamation was short-lived. The brothers of Santa Croce wanted the *Crucifix* back. Truth be told, it was the least important work in Room 2, in art historical terms significant as a way station to greater things, more an emblem of Franciscan piety than a true masterpiece.

Amid these triumphs, Procacci also acquired a protégé the following year, 1949, the kind of apprentice a master can only pray for. Umberto Baldini was twenty-seven and had done his art history graduate work on Giotto under the brilliant Mario Salmi. After graduation, he'd worked as a volunteer for the Superintendency, and Baldini had so impressed Procacci that he made him director of his Gabinetto dei Restauro, leapfrogging him over other long-standing candidates.

Taking on Baldini was a sign of Procacci's power and position, but at heart he remained an art historian who still thrilled to the chase, the discovery, and the consolidation of knowledge. Shortly after his appointment, Procacci raced into the Gabinetto breathless and exclaimed to Baldini, *Ho appena visto i morti,* "I've just seen the dead." Collapsing into a chair, Procacci explained he'd been at Santa Maria Novella and had conclusively discovered the original location of Masaccio's *Trinità,* replaced by Vasari's *Madonna of the Rosary* four hundred years earlier.

Baldini was, of course, also pleased, but he was of a more dispassionate, self-possessed nature, brilliant but efficient, his considerable ambition directed with remarkable accuracy and success to the objects and goals that appeared to him just then most needful. Unlike Procacci, he would have taken off his hat before sitting down.

On Baldini's first day on the job, he went to the Salone dei Cinquecento in the Palazzo Vecchio to inspect one of the Gabinetto's current projects—now one of *his* many projects—restoration work on Vasari's *Battle of Marciano,* said to be overpainted on Leonardo's *Battle of Anghiari.* Baldini might have regarded Vasari's tiny, cryptic inscription *cerca trova,* "seek and find," and seen the future before him: the beautiful acquisitions, prizes, promotions, boons, and women; reputation, fame, and glory, the accouterments of a great man.

*T*here would be no more floods, it was promised after the war. In 1956 construction began on a dam upriver on the Arno at Levane and the following year another was started at La Penna, works worthy of Leonardo. If the rains came as they had in 1844 or 1864 or 1944, the water could be held back, kept at bay in the mountains, in the high wastes of poplar and oak. That would be despite the simultaneous and "abrupt acceleration of sediment mining and channel bed intrusion" hydrologists would note looking back some years later. The Casentine Forests were indeed returning to health, but the Arno itself was now a tributary of postwar industry, agriculture, and modernization, more and more a greased sluice, a gun barrel bored for maximum velocity and capacity.

In the spring of the following year, 1958, the restored Ponte Santa Trinità was reopened, complete in all its parts except for the head of *Spring*, unrecovered despite Berenson's reward. And in the autumn of 1959, at the age of ninety-four, Berenson himself died, the Jewish Yankee with an eye who had taught the world how to look at Florence.

*T*wo years later, in 1961, a steam shovel dredging the Arno a little downstream from the Ponte Santa Trinità recovered, quite by accident, a lump, a stone skull that proved to be the head of *Spring*. No one had stolen it: it had been in the Arno all the while, buried within the collection of mud, rubble, and bones in the riverbed, the accretion of visions and views, of ambitions and lusts, and of losses and betrayals all touching one another, the water touching them running by, tumbling them together.

Vasari's *Last Supper* remained in the refectory at Santa Croce, moldering: *Non ha mosso molto l'interesse, né tanto meno l'entusiamo*, "It excited not much interest and even less enthusiasm," said one art historian. The same might have been said of the Cimabue nearby, the massive and forlorn *Crucifix*. Forster's Lucy Honeychurch hadn't been to see it. It wasn't in the Baedeker or Ruskin or Berenson. Perhaps it wasn't so much a work of art as a ruin, a remnant of a previous world. Or it was simply a man hanging on a tree, dead or dying; a wingless Icarus waiting for the west wind, for the deluge to ferry him away with the 54 billion.

Four

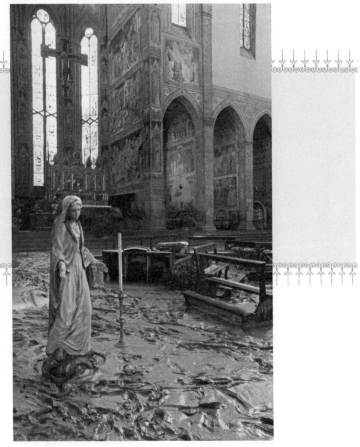

About suffering they were never wrong,
The Old Masters . . .

—W. H. AUDEN,
"MUSÉE DES BEAUX ARTS"

Interior of the Basilica of Santa Croce, November 6, 1966 *(Photograph by David Lees)*

*N*ick Kraczyna had read W. H. Auden's poem "Musée des Beaux Arts." Now he was looking at the painting that had inspired it, Pieter Bruegel the Elder's *Fall of Icarus*. It was a beautiful day, the plowman plowing, the shepherd shepherding his sheep, ships heading out or making for harbor, and in the middle distance the speck of Icarus, a plummeting teardrop, falling to his death. In the great world with its myriad preoccupations, Icarus is too small to notice, if not to see. The winged exemplar of the artist is lost in the vast and implacable beauty of the day, the disaster of his passing swallowed without a trace.

Nick was in the Galleria Doria Pamphilj in Rome. He was twenty-one years old and this is how far he had come from the nameless and temporary outposts of his childhood. He'd been given a place at the best art school in America and been sent abroad to study the Old Masters, to learn the things about which they were never wrong. Just now, in front of this painting with Auden's poem in his mind, he'd been given his métier, the overarching theme of his life's work. All he had to do from here on out was paint.

In the spring of 1962 he'd moved on to Florence, to a room near the church of Santo Spirito, the Oltrarno masterpiece of Filippo Brunelleschi. Nick decided he needed to spend the rest of his life here, to finish up as rooted in art and Florence as he'd been homeless and stateless in the camps, torn from Kamien-Koszyrski by Europe's self-immolation. His compass points would be the Masaccios in the Brancacci Chapel just west of Santo Spirito and the Pontormos at Santa Felicità to the east. He went to one or the other almost every day until his year abroad was over in June. Before he could come back to Florence he'd have to go back to the Rhode Island School of Design and then to one of the American graduate programs that were eager to have him, one last camp on the way home.

*T*hat same spring David Lees was following the path of Percy Shelley, the track through Italy of his foolish, glorious ascent toward martyrdom for art's sake. The events of the last few years—the death of Pope Pius XII, the election of John XXIII, and the start of the Second Vatican Council—had increased his prominence as *Life*'s man at the Vatican as well as its specialist photographer for European art, royalty, and fashion. Closer to home, a series of his portraits of Bernard Berenson—still squinting hungrily through his magnifying glass in his nineties—formed *Life*'s obituary when BB at last passed away in 1959.

But the Shelley project was smaller and more impressionistic, a portfolio of quiet, elegiac landscapes, shadowed, languid villas, and mossy statuary. It was also more personal, a search for what Dorothy had sought in coming to Italy, lured by this very poet; and so, at bottom, a quest for the source of David's own identity, the reasons and passions that caused him to be born an Anglo-Florentine rather than an English boy, or—if you took away whatever it was that Italy set loose in Dorothy—that caused him to exist at all.

The photographs were exquisite but, in the opinion of *Life*'s editors, neither newsworthy nor very compelling as a human interest story. David pushed for a year before *Life* agreed to run them in the international edition in 1963 and finally, the year after that, in the main American printing. The title of the photoessay would be "The Fatal Gift of Beauty."

But Lees found himself more and more in the role of photojournalist rather than art photographer despite a moving series of portraits of Ezra Pound clinging to life and to poetry in his final Venetian exile. There was the death of John XXIII, the election of Paul VI, and—in a photograph that circulated around the world—the historic embrace of Paul and the Patriarch of the Eastern Orthodox Church after a schism of nine hundred years.

In the autumn of 1963 Lees had to race to another breaking news story. On the night of October 9 the Vajont Dam in the mountains north of Venice was breached and two thousand inhabitants in the valley below it were killed. Vajont closed off a gorge nine hundred feet high, making it one of the tallest dams in the world, but for all the audacity of its construction, residents had been assured that both the engineering and the geology of the mountain behind it had been microscopically studied and found safe.

But that night 260 million cubic meters of mountainside sheared off in a landslide into the reservoir. It in turn displaced 50 million cubic meters of water in a wave that crested the top of the dam at seventy miles per hour. The force of 60 million tons of water fell on the valley below in a matter of minutes, wiping out the entire town of Longarone and four neighboring villages.

When David Lees arrived there was nothing to photograph. The dam, strangely, stood intact, towering over the valley. But everything in front of it was gone, scoured away. Even the water was gone. Lees took pictures of figures—an old woman, a priest clutching his rosary beads behind his back—gazing out onto the great empty plain delimited only by mountains in the distance.

Before a public inquiry could be launched, the chief dam engineer committed suicide, and perhaps, more than the actual official findings, that said all there was to say about the disaster. The ambitions of great men, ascending on pride, delusion, and lies, ended in tragedy for the many and, for the great men themselves, in the melted wax of their vain self-immolations. When the inquiry was concluded five years later, the surviving accused were sentenced to a collective twenty-one years, which was subsequently overturned on appeal for lack of evidence.

*B*y the time of Vajont, Dorothy Lees was eighty-three years old and had left her house in Bellosguardo for a convent run as a *casa di riposo*, an old folks home, by Franciscan nuns. Dorothy liked to sit with the sisters as they prayed their novenas, and on St. Francis's feast day they brought her carnations. She in turn bought candles for the church and she confided to her diary that she would like the Mother Superior all "to myself."

David—now living in Rome where *Life*'s bureau was located—came to see her as often as he could, and he came on St. Francis's day in 1964. He took her on a little tour of the city: "We went to Piazzale Michelangelo, where I had not been for years and looked down at the city, all lighted up." They came down the hill into Oltrarno, down to the Ponte Vecchio, and "I saw for the *first* time the site of my old tower and what they have built up in its place." It was more charitable not to say what she thought of the postwar reconstruction, and so she wrote nothing more.

She was to have one more St. Francis's Day, in 1965, with her David. He'd been in Florence for some time that year, shooting a color essay on Dante for *Life*: the editors had accepted his Shelley piece, and now one on the maestro himself, and wasn't that a fine and fitting thing? After all, the day she'd given birth to David, she'd written Dante's words, *Incipit Vita Nuova*, in her diary.

The next winter, on February 19, 1966, Dorothy died. On the page for that day in his journal where he kept track of his expenses and travel mileage, his spools of Ektachrome and tips to porters and lighting men, David drew a cross in blue marker and beneath it wrote, "Mamma."

In Dorothy's own diary, another hand, not her own, wrote on the same page, "Santa Dorotea." And so perhaps she was: certainly her life seemed to have been devoted half to prayer, if only for David. It must have been one of the nuns who wrote it—one of those women you see at shrines with their candles and violets—sorting her things, her relics and billets-doux from Gordon Craig, after they'd buried her.

Later that year, in summer, David shot a photoessay on the Arno for *Life*. He spent a lot of time in the Casentine Forests of the Arno headwaters among the monks at Camaldoli and still more at St. Francis's hermitage at La Verna. He couldn't stop photographing the monks and the pattern they made: dark, identical shafts against the huts and cloisters, the rocks and trees, anonymous persons, veiled in their habits, each one of whom was a lick of candlelight in the wilderness.

His attraction to these images sprang from no detectable religious impulse. He was no Santa Dorotea. In Rome he had a wife and two sons with whom he did not live. He had a separate apartment, a mistress, and other women besides. At some point David had become

Gordon Craig, his father. He was, if not a genius, an artist. The photographs of Camaldoli and La Verna certainly proved that much. But the photoessay never ran. By the time it was ready to go to press the following winter, it was not what people wanted to know about the Arno.

*F*rom Dante's celestial vantage point you might have seen it all: not Florence or Tuscany or even Europe, but the clouds, their peaks and chasms illuminated by starlight, turning endlessly like constellations and nebulae. Beginning in September and all through October the North Atlantic cyclone, the sun around which other weather systems spun, grew to immense size, in turn driving two high-pressure zones—one hot and one cold—like cogs and wheels. South of these, over the Mediterranean, trapped between the Alps and Africa, was a mass of cold air pressing down over an equally large concentration of warm, moist air. For six weeks, nothing moved, the clouds and gyres of vapor as fixed and motionless as Dante's Heaven: the sky shimmered down in streams of wind and gray water.

This did not seem remarkable: it rained as often as not in Tuscany this time of year. But the rain accreted, insinuated itself into the soil. Perhaps four inches fell in September and that much again in October, a little more each day. By the first of September, the ground in the Casentine was saturated and would begin, unobserved, to slide. Higher up, Dante's plaque at the head of the Arno was buried in snow and then, as the stratum of warm air bore down on the mountaintops, the snow began to melt. Falterona and the Gorga Nera, or rather the waters they could no longer contain, were creeping toward Florence. On November 2 alone, it rained seven and a half inches in twenty-four hours, and seventeen inches in the mountains. But by then it did not seem like so much. At the Ponte Vecchio the Arno could accommodate 32,000 cubic feet of water per second, a veritable deluge. And what was that—an inch of rain here and an inch there—compared to a thousand years of history, of beauty, and of simply persisting so magnificently in one place?

*U*pstream thirty miles from the city there was a place called Valle dell'Inferno, "the valley of Hell." No one knows if this is a literary allusion to Dante, or simply a bald statement of circumstance. In any case, on November 3, Lorenzo Raffaelli had had it with the sirens. The rain was bad enough. He and his wife, Ida, lived in the village just below the La Penna and Levane dams, good enough neighbors as such modern installations went. But at seven that evening the siren started up and, just as you gathered your nerves, began to wail again like a penned dog.

There was a sequence—though no one could remember how it went—of wails that was supposed to precede the opening of the floodgates by the dams' operators, ENEL, the Italian state electrical utility. But tonight, nothing was happening, nothing but rain. The siren must be a test, or a piece of stupidity by a dam worker. *Questa poggia è insopportibile. Vado a lètto*, Lorenzo told Ida. "This rain is just too much. I'm going to bed."

Two hours later, the damnable siren—no wonder they'd called this place Hell—started up again. Lorenzo dragged himself out of bed and went to the window. There was a roaring outside, or rather a roaring with the sound of a breeze laid over it. He opened the shutters. It was dark and he realized there were no lights anywhere. So it took a few moments for his vision to adjust, to see that water was racing by a few feet below his second-story window; that objects were being ferried past his house; his neighbors' things, pieces of their houses, tree trunks; then empty bottles and a chair, a chest full of gloves, and a piglet, its trotters bent skyward, masts on a white-and-black banded dory.

And strangest of all—ENEL must have opened the gates, or the whole thing had come down, all 500 million cubic feet's worth of it— were the stones. Rocks and boulders coursed by, big ones that might have fallen off the mountain. But stones couldn't float. Yet these rolled by, tumbled past, on the surface of the water a dozen feet above where the ground was supposed to be. So if they weren't floating, they must be flying. They were a flock of birds and the water was the sky.

*D*own in the city they had finished putting up the green, white, and red bunting for the next day's holiday, Armed Forces Day. There were Union Jack flags mixed in here and there: it had been "British Week," a merchandising celebration of swinging London. The 1960s were approaching their apogee: in neighborhood trattorias, the Beach Boys and the Beatles fizzed from the radio, and at the cinema *Il Viaggio Allucinante*, "Fantastic Voyage," was playing. There was a wet, lashing wind outside. In another movie theater John Huston's *The Bible* was playing with Huston himself in the role of Noah.

In the Palazzo Vecchio the mayor of Florence, Piero Bargellini, was to be the guest of honor at the American Chamber of Commerce banquet. Bargellini was late, preoccupied with the survival of his center-left administration, which was due to face a vote of no-confidence the following week. After his arrival they entertained him with a documentary on the Mississippi River, its beauties, perils, and spectacular floods. In his remarks at the end of the evening he joked, "Don't imagine I was fazed by your movie. Florence has never been afraid of competition: if it keeps raining like this, tomorrow morning the Arno will beat your Mississippi."

It was a jest, although Bargellini was a serious man, bookish and devoutly Catholic, for whom politics was the exercise of humanism and charity. He went home to the family palazzo in Santa Croce that night to his books and his prayers, knowing no more than anyone else. There was, as yet, no knowledge—never mind an alarm—to be aware of, to take hold of and take action upon. Upriver, of course, the flood was already a fact, but as the water reached a village it also cut the telephone lines. The river was covering its own tracks, for all its noise and roiling flotsam, proceeding by stealth.

Nonetheless, by eleven o'clock the fire department in Florence had received calls complaining of flooded cellars and garages. But a damp basement was scarcely an emergency. At the Brigata Friuli barracks near Santa Croce, a soldier went outside for a cigarette and returned to say that the sewers weren't working properly. But he was from Naples, and what could somebody from Naples know about the public works facilities of a great city like Florence?

Romildo Cesaroni worked as a night watchman for the syndicate of jewelers that had shops on the Ponte Vecchio. As was his custom, he made his patrols back and forth across the bridge on his bicycle, taking breaks at either end. But around one o'clock he dismounted midway across. The noise was tremendous—it was raining hard with what felt like a gale-force wind—but what struck him as he stood for a while on the pavement was a palpable vibration emanating from the stones, from, it seemed, the arches of the bridge itself, a vibration on the verge of becoming a throb. He went back to the phone at the far end and began calling his employers one by one. He was from northern Italy, born in a valley called Vajont. They'd better come quick and collect their gold.

A few other communications did get through. Bruno Santi, an art history student living in San Niccolò on the Oltrarno side of Florence, was asleep when his father got a call from his brother-in-law, Bruno's uncle. The uncle's village ten miles east of Florence was about to go underwater. Bruno's father got in the family car and began to drive upriver. When he got to the first bridge he needed to cross to reach the village, he saw water lapping the roadway, skimming across the bridge deck. Even if he got across, he'd be unlikely to get back. There was nothing he could do for his brother-in-law. He drove back to San Niccolò to secure his workshop and get his family to high ground. He woke Bruno, who was due to take his final graduate exam on quattrocento panel painting the day after next. That would have to wait.

Later, around three A.M., a journalist working the night desk at Florence's leading newspaper, *La Nazione*, got a call from a shift worker, Carlo Maggiorelli, upriver at the Anconella pumping station of the Florence aqueduct. Everything was underwater. He'd shut down the pumps, not that that mattered. The journalist urged him to flee. "I can't abandon the plant. It's my shift." Besides, he had a sandwich to eat. He had a thermos of coffee. He had ten cigarettes. He would manage. Two days later they found his body embedded in mud inside a hydraulic tunnel. Carlo Maggiorelli was reckoned to be the first fatality of November 4, 1966.

On Monte Falterona, the snow on Dante's spring had washed away. At nine o'clock an inch of rain was falling every sixty minutes. Snowmelt and downpour were massing in the riverbed, and in about nine hours 120,000 cubic feet of water per second would begin reaching Florence.

*A*t three in the morning Nick Kraczyna was just finishing. He painted every night while Amy and Anatol slept. He and Amy had gotten married in the spring of 1963, the first year of his master's degree program, and left for Italy the following year, crossing the Atlantic on a Yugoslavian freighter. Amy had been seven months pregnant.

That was two years ago. Now their son, Anatol, was eighteen months old and everything had gone more or less as Nick had envisioned: they were living a block from Santo Spirito, he was painting Icarus, they were happy, and they were poor. The apartment had no bathroom and no hot water, and for heat they used *scaldini*, the traditional Tuscan pots that held hot coals obtained from the wood and charcoal merchant. You cradled it in your lap, set it under the table by your feet when you ate, and put it in your bed for a while before you went to sleep.

That night it was 50 degrees outside, not terribly cold, although the stones of their palazzo a half block from the Arno held the cold far past dawn and, in weather like this, nearly sweated with damp. Before he went to join Amy and Anatol in the bed, Nick went to the window on the terrace. He could see the more substantial palazzi on the other side of the river illuminated by spotlights. At the edges of the light, he could just make out the water. It was high and moving at tremendous speed, like gray clouds stampeding before a strong wind. He could hear the river, or rather, the friction of the river on its banks, the parapets of the Lungarni and piers of the bridges, the Arno grinding against the city.

It was something to see, or because the light was so poor and the atmosphere so murky, to imagine; to seize the blanks in the picture and fill them, extrapolate the contents of what was now invisible; launch a winged visionary out the window to explore the hidden interior of the maelstrom. Nick went to bed, the rumble and pulse in his ears.

*T*he first dead inside Florence were seventy thoroughbred horses. The Mugnone, a tributary of the Arno, cuts down through the hills northeast of the city and then, by means of a chain of man-made canals, swings west around the perimeter of the city to join the main river by the low-lying Cascine city park, a recreation complex that contained tennis courts, soccer fields, a small zoo, and a racetrack. The horses, locked in their stables, drowned, thrashing and screaming, as though *impazziti*, driven mad. A custodian heard them in the distance at one-thirty in the morning.

At three o'clock, the city was asleep. Except along the riverfront, there was no sound but the patter of rain on rooftops. The waters of the flood, however, were running not just through the city in the channel of the Arno, but under it through sewers and storm drains. In most neighborhoods the flood first appeared not through breaches in the riverbank, but oozing up from manholes and drains. As the night went on, pressure within the system lifted and floated off manhole covers. Later, they would rocket into the sky, propelled on jets of floodwater.

In most of Florence information, like the water, only seeped into the city. There were no alarms, sirens, or radio and television bulletins. Only at the river, by the trembling Ponte Vecchio, was there unmistakably a flood, and soon you would not even be able to say how big it was. At three o'clock in the morning the city's flood gauge on the Lungarno Acciaiuoli between the Ponte Vecchio and the Ponte Santa Trinità recorded 8.69 meters—twenty-eight-and-a-half feet—and was then ripped away by the water and carried off down the Arno.

As often happened in Florence, what you got depended on who you were and whom you knew. The jewelers of the Ponte Vecchio had been informed, as, by sheer luck, had Bruno Santi's father. Mayor Bargellini had been awakened and returned to his office around two o'clock, just before the water in his Santa Croce neighborhood got too deep for anyone to leave. He would not see his home for many days to come.

In Rome, the telephone of the Florence-born director Franco Zeffirelli rang near dawn. It was his sister who lived on Via dell'Oriuolo east of the Duomo: there was water in her street toward the Santa Croce end and, she suspected, still more near the church itself. At 3:48 A.M. there had finally been a radio news bulletin referring to the flooding upstream, but nothing about Florence itself.

But Zeffirelli's sister was emphatic about what was taking place below her window and, once he seized on an idea, Zeffirelli was himself a force to be reckoned with. He phoned the president of RAI, the Italian state broadcasting network, and asked for a film crew and a helicopter. Shortly after dawn, Zeffirelli was filming in Florence, long before any other news agency (including RAI's own) was on the story.

Around five o'clock the Arno finally burst its banks within the city walls: water from still small breaches in the Lungarni met water coming up from the drains and flooded Via dei Bardi and Borgo San Jacopo on the Oltrarno as well as Corso dei Tintori between Santa Croce and the Biblioteca Nazionale on the north bank. At 6:30 A.M. the Franciscan priest Gustavo Cocci left his cloister at Santa Croce to say a seven o'clock mass at a neighborhood church. It was dawn, and he was the first person to pass through the gates of the basilica into the outside world that day. He opened the *portone*, the great door, and saw the piazza, the water moving upward on a gentle swell, a Galilee he might walk across holding his robe just above his waist.

*A*ll at once, at seven in the morning, there was news. Trapped in his second-floor studio, an announcer for RAI radio in Florence lowered a microphone out the window toward the torrent running down the street: "What you're hearing," he said, "is Florence between the Duomo and Santa Maria Novella station."

Even more extraordinarily, *La Nazione* managed to produce a morning edition headlined *L'Arno Straripa a Firenze*, "The Arno overflows at Florence." The last item had gone in at 6:10. The typesetting room was underwater a half hour later, the pressroom a little after the print run was finished at seven.

By then most of the quarters of Florence and its suburbs that were not already underwater were cut off from the rest of the world. The *autostrada* and other highways in and out of the city were inundated, bridges and causeways washed out, and most railways severed. The Santa Maria Novella station, well above street level, continued to function, even if its trains had no destinations to reach. Telephone lines had been cut for some time and gas lines shut down. The pumps that drove the city's water supply had been switched off in the middle of the night by Carlo Maggiorelli before he'd drowned in mud. Trucks and automobiles couldn't be driven or else stalled out as they took on water. And soon enough car after car began to float away. The city, except for the water and the things that floated upon it, was motionless.

Not only movement in space but, it seemed, time halted: At 7:29, with the last electricity cut off, hundreds of clocks stopped all over the city. That instant corresponded with what was later calculated as the moment of the flood's maximum violence and force. On the faces of Florence's clocks, it would remain 7:29 for many days. If time did not actually stop, neither did it seem to move forward into days that were like those before November 4, 1966. Perhaps, like the water, time receded, rolled backward into oblivion, Florence's great sea.

*I*t was not long after dawn when Nick was awakened. A neighbor was calling up the stairs: they should collect as much water as they could, in pans and empty *scaldini* and jugs. The pressure was giving out. In a minute the taps would dry up. There wouldn't be any water at all.

That was absurd. They had nothing but water, had had it for weeks, but Nick understood a moment later: the lights cut out. They were going to be roughing it, at least for today.

While Amy filled the last few pots they possessed, Nick tried to get a better sense of what was happening. He clambered across the roof to the terrace of Pensione Bartolini and descended the stairs to its entrance on the Lungarno Guicciardini. To see the edge of their side of the river from here, Nick would normally have to walk over to the parapet and look down twenty feet below him. But today the surface of the Arno was level with the top of the parapet, four feet above the street: the river channel was now higher than the level of the city, an elevated aqueduct whose sides were formed by the Lungarni.

Nick had brought his camera. He had sensed this was history. The water was splashing over the top of the parapet, and he started taking pictures. This, he was certain, was the crest of the flood, as high as the water would go, and he was capturing the definitive moment. He went back upstairs to help Amy.

&<

*U*go Procacci was at the Uffizi by dawn. The night watchman had called him and now there were a dozen people to clear the whole ground floor of the museum of any artworks in harm's way, which, it had to be presumed, meant all of them. Umberto Baldini had been called by Procacci about the time the clocks stopped and arrived soaked to the skin. He'd come in by way of Via della Ninna, which sloped down from the Piazza della Signoria to a level below that of the Lungarno at the front of the museum. The water there had been chest high. Within an hour the Lungarno would be breached, and the Arno would rush into the declivity, driving a forty-foot-long oak before it, which lodged like a battering ram behind the museum.

Luisa Becherucci was the director of the gallery, but it was Baldini who worked at Procacci's side. He was neither precisely Procacci's apprentice nor his right-hand man, but—despite his subordinate rank in the Superintendency—almost an extension of him, a co-Procacci, a free agent who still gave the formal appearance of being a junior partner. As an art historian and manager of the Gabinetto (now, as fitted its larger status, known as the Laboratorio), Baldini was perhaps less strictly brilliant than brilliantly competent, with a preternatural gift for detecting consensus and then shaping it to his own aspirations. He was not a genius, but slogging through Vasari's Uffizi that morning, he was in his element.

It would have been impossible to save the collection—the Uffizi housed more than 110,000 works of art—but for the fact that the actual galleries were almost all on the second and third floors, and these, as well as the vast portrait gallery housed in Vasari's Corridoio over the Ponte Vecchio, were high above the river. But that still left a large number of works on the ground floor and still more either undergoing or awaiting restoration in Baldini's lab across the court, among them pieces by Giotto, Mantegna, Filippo Lippi, Botticelli, and Vasari himself. Some were easily portable—two saints by Simone Martini from Bernard Berenson's personal collection—but others were in perilously fragile condition (a detached fresco by Giotto) or, in the case of Botticelli's *Incoronazione*, too large to move without disassembling their panels. In total, there were about two hundred paintings to be relocated, and twelve people to do it before the Arno crested and surged inside.

Nick thought he had caught the river at its apogee, although by the time he got back upstairs, the water was slopping over the parapet and down his street. But the ground to the east toward the Ponte Santa Trinità was still dry, and he gathered Amy and Anatol and brought them downstairs. They needed to see this stupendous thing— epic, biblical, apocalyptic—not from the window or the rooftop, but from dead center, from inside. He led them out onto the Ponte Santa Trinità, Amy carrying Anatol, to the midway point. He noticed his neighbor Antonio Raffo's Fiat, parked there, incongruous and alone.

The water was still several feet below the apex of the center arch where they stood, and as it emerged from beneath the bridge, it seemed to fall away, breaking into rapids, cascades, and cataracts, surging back against itself, forming chasms and whirlpools steep as thunderheads. The bridge—only fully rebuilt eight years previously—vibrated beneath them and Nick took pictures. Upstream, the Ponte Vecchio sat almost stolidly, like a dam, the water lapping the tops of the arches. In the opposite direction, to the west, the water seemed to spread and flatten before it reached the Ponte alla Carraia, and slid under the bridge with perhaps two feet to spare. Beyond that Nick and Amy could make out the shadow of the third downstream span, the Ponte Vespucci, disappearing under the Arno.

They'd been alone until now, but then they saw a man with a camera approach the bridge, walk out to mid-span, and begin taking pictures. "Look at him," Amy said, holding Anatol as the torrent seethed by. She was four months pregnant with another baby. "He's crazy to be out here."

That must have meant they were crazy too. But they were not afraid, and Nick least of all. He was twenty-five years old and felt nearly immortal. As for the bridge quivering beneath them, it might have been a roller coaster or a surfboard he was riding. Suspended above the river, the entire world racing away beneath him, he could have been hovering over the earth as it surged by, being made and unmade in one motion. Wasn't it incredible—like watching a galaxy being born or coming apart; wasn't it really the most beautiful thing you'd ever seen?

*B*y eleven o'clock, it seemed to almost everyone that the Ponte Vecchio was going to collapse. The water was still rising, and in addition to its own force and pressure—thousands of tons moving at perhaps forty miles an hour—was throwing enormous quantities of debris against the face of the span. Whole trees, forty and fifty feet long, had shot through the shops on one side of the bridge and out the other, lodged like spears. On the second story in the Corridoio Vasariano, the floor shuddered and glass trilled in the window frames.

It was there that Ugo Procacci decided he needed to go, alone. The portraits in the Corridoio needed to come out, and because he could not in good conscience place his staff in danger, the paintings would be taken out one at a time, each carried by him and only him. That was an official instruction, an order. He ran off down the Corridoio, scarcely able to keep his footing as he reached mid-span. By then Baldini, the first to disobey, was coming up behind him, and then the ten others. They formed a human chain, handing back portrait after portrait as the bridge shook below them, as trees and, now, a floating car and then a truck thundered into it.

When the job was done, all of them were trembling. Some wept while others were overcome by nausea. They needed something to eat, something to drink, said Procacci. They pulled themselves together once more and broke down the door of the museum snack bar.

*F*ather Cocci hadn't gotten to his mass that morning. He retreated inside the cloister of Santa Croce with his brother monks, or rather into the upper story of the cloister: by eight o'clock the ground floor was underwater. In fact, all around the Basilica—from Vasari's house to the south to Borgo Allegri to the north—the water was higher than it had ever been before, even in 1333, and it would go higher still.

To the west, the former Murate convent—the one-time home of Vasari's *Last Supper* before the painting and the nuns had been dispossessed by Napoleon—was half submerged. At dawn there had been men huddled on the roof, but by mid-morning most of them had clambered onto large pieces of floating debris or simply swum away. They were men of the most adaptable sort, accustomed to surviving by their wits. After Napoleon, the Murate convent had been converted into the Florence city jail. It still was. In the early morning hours, the guards realized that if the convicts remained in their ground-floor cells they were going to drown. After turning the locks, they abandoned the jail and left the eighty-three prisoners to fend for themselves. Some disappeared, their old identities and histories carried off by the flood; others were said to have performed heroic rescues and pitched in at soup kitchens and first-aid posts before giving themselves up. One, found clinging to the top of a traffic signal surrounded by twelve feet of water, was pulled to an upstairs window by neighbors using a rope of knotted sheets. They dried him off, put him in a warm bed, and fed him *ribollita*, only realizing who their guest had been some days later when the police came by.

By ten o'clock, the BBC World Service in London had broadcast the first international news of the flood and a few hours later the American television networks would report it on their morning bulletins. In Rome, the nation's capital, apparently no one knew anything: neither President Saragat nor Prime Minister Moro had any comment. RAI was broadcasting cartoons. But by noon Mayor Bargellini had made his way to a radio microphone and announced—to whoever might have been able to listen—"The water has arrived in the Piazza del Duomo. In some neighborhoods it has reached the second floor. I ask everyone to remain calm." There'd been an explosion, a real thunderclap, of a gasoline storage tank near Piazza Beccaria that had terrified half the city, but caused only one fatality. Bargellini added, "Those of you who have boats, canoes, and skiffs, bring them to the Palazzo Vecchio."

On the other side of the river, in San Niccolò, Bruno Santi and his father had managed to move their family up the hill to a relative's house. But their attempt to remove chemicals and corrosives from the basement of his father's studio had failed: the water was up to the threshold of the first floor. The cellars and basements of Florence were full of such things, most innocuously wine and olive oil, but also—more than any other substance—heating oil. The tanks were full for the long winter ahead. All this was beginning to seep upward, into the floodwater.

Still farther up the hill, twelve-year-old Barbara Minniti from Rome was visiting "Zio Nello," her uncle Emanuele Casamassima, director of the Biblioteca Nazionale, for the holiday weekend. A little after breakfast, the telephone had rung and Barbara's uncle answered it. He stood in the hallway, stock-still, listening, striking the side of his head with the palm of his right hand. Then, in a great hurry, he left the house.

At noon Barbara and her cousins went to the Piazzale Michelangelo, which overlooked the city from the south. There were a lot of people gathered there, staring, holding black umbrellas, silent in the rain. Below you could see the towers, the rooftops, and the Duomo looming above them like a volcanic island. And between them and where Barbara stood was a valley full of water where the river had once been, a distended stomach expanding from the gullet of the Arno upstream. A little to the east, toward Piazza Beccaria, a plume rose into the air, maybe another volcano, this one spuming smoke or black steam.

Almost straight across, just in front of Santa Croce at the place where the riverbank used to be, Barbara could see Zio Nello's enormous *bibliotecca*, the Italian equivalent of the Library of Congress. It might have been floating, marooned in this new sea, but tethered at the back to Santa Croce, which depending on how you looked at it, was either an island or the deepest point in the ocean.

Either way, there was no chance that Uncle Emanuele was going there today. Even a ship, a big one, would get sucked downstream and crash into the Ponte Vecchio. After Barbara and her cousins got home, her uncle came back, wet and shaking. Sometimes you couldn't say if Zio Nello was being silly or serious. "Now comes the looting, the cholera, the famine," he had told Barbara's mother.

Dark Water

Giovanni Menduni had just turned thirteen years old and he and his mother were going out to buy a chicken. But his mother still treated him like he was twelve, a *bambino* instead of a *ragazzo*. They walked down the Via degli Artisti, which led from the Piazza Giorgio Vasari to the Piazzale Donatello. People were saying *L'Arno è andato fuori di testa*, a phrase that didn't quite make sense to Giovanni. A person could *andare di fuori di testa*—"have gone out of his mind"—but could the Arno? Then, when they got as far as Piazzale Donatello and saw the water, his mother made him go home.

Here he was at an epochal moment in history—or at least the start of an adventure—and he was missing it. Meanwhile his eighteen-year-old brother was in the thick of it, coming home in his muddy boots with tales of rescues and close calls and devastation. But for the next week, his mother kept him in. It was frustration piled on top of frustration. Just ten days before the flood he'd finally talked her into looking at a Hammond B-3 electric organ, which he coveted more than any other object in the world, the gold standard in jazz and pop keyboards. It wasn't just his heart's desire but the single thing upon which the outcome of his whole life was contingent.

The music store was just off the Piazza Duomo, and Giovanni waited outside while his mother went in. After perhaps two minutes she came out looking not simply unpersuaded but shocked, even stunned. It wasn't just that the B-3 was too expensive, but that the whole world it represented was beyond the pale: she'd seen the kind of people who hung around the store—the kind of people who played the B-3—and they were seedy, shiftless jazz and rock types of the worst sort, neither good company nor examples for a twelve—all right, thirteen-year-old. The only way he'd ever get a B-3 would be if someone just gave it to him, or if he waited forever, until he was old.

So that had been that and now there was this. He might as well just give up.

❦

*N*ick and Amy needed food and Anatol needed milk. It was Nick's job to shop every morning before lunch—they had no refrigerator—and around eleven he went out to see what he could find. The clearest way forward seemed to be across the Ponte Santa Trinità, where Antonio's car still sat perfectly undisturbed, a pert jalopy atop a Renaissance architectural masterpiece with a deluge running under it.

On the opposite side Nick turned left and walked west along the Lungarno Corsini. But then he began to worry—even finally realized the likelihood—that the bridge would be washed away and that he would be stranded on the other bank of the river, cut off from Amy and Anatol. So at the next bridge downstream, the Ponte alla Carraia, he crossed back over to the Oltrarno side. At the Borgo San Frediano he turned west again, toward the Carmine church and the Porta San Frediano. He slogged on, block after block, the water at best shin-deep in some places but up to his waist in others. Perhaps a mile from his apartment, he was able to buy some canned goods from a grocer who was hurriedly moving his stocks up to his second-floor apartment.

Going home, Nick found himself walking against the current in what was now almost entirely waist-deep water. To move forward without falling he had to brace himself against buildings with both hands, so he put all the cans into his pockets or stuck them inside his jacket. Looking toward the river, he realized that the elevation of the Lungarno was actually higher than the streets immediately behind it, which sloped up toward the artificially raised banks created by Giuseppe Poggi a century earlier.

Having moved up to the Lungarno, and pushing eastward again, Nick was able to wade down the middle of the roadway to avoid being immersed by the water that was slopping and, increasingly, surging over the parapet. But between the Ponte alla Carraia and his apartment, the street had been torn up for repairs. That meant Nick would either have to turn back down to the parallel Via Santo Spirito, which he knew was already inundated, or work his way directly along the side of the parapet.

He chose the shorter if more reckless course, rather than the deeper, more tedious, but safer slog down the Via Santo Spirito. On the Lungarno he was a tightrope walker, clinging to the parapet edge. He was being thrown off balance by the force of the water pouring over the wall, and, as the water level in the Lungarno drew even with the river, equally at risk of being sucked into the torrent and carried away downstream. The food in his pockets and inside his jacket had already long disappeared, and his clothes and shoes had become dead weights that threatened to pull him in and under. But he inched his way along the parapet, his fingers white and swollen.

Later, Nick could not quite say exactly when he realized he might be going to die—maybe time really had stopped, *flowing* but not passing—or if he realized it for more than an instant before the feeling passed. Because as he forced his way upriver, with the whole Arno pressing down on him, what he felt most of all was joy, sheer exhilaration. When he reached his apartment he went out on the roof and saw that the entire parapet that had been his lifeline had been washed away.

*A*t one o'clock, the Ponte Vecchio was still intact, thanks in part to a truck that had smashed through both sides of the center of the bridge, easing some of the pressure of the flood against the superstructure by allowing water to pass freely over the deck. But the river was continuing to rise—it would do so for the next five hours—and with each cubic meter of water came a still larger amount of debris and, increasingly, mud.

Inside the Uffizi, Procacci and his staff had been joined by Maria Luisa Bonelli, director of the adjacent Museum of the History of Science. Trapped in her apartment on the top floor of the museum, she'd escaped across the rooftops to the Uffizi carrying Galileo's telescope. They and, as the day went on, others would move artworks until five o'clock the next morning. At around mid-afternoon Procacci's old art historian friend Carlo Ragghianti turned up. They embraced and Procacci said, "It's like August of forty-four, remember?" They cried for a few moments and went back to work.

By now other parts of Florence's artistic and civic patrimony more distant from the Arno had been struck. To the west, in the church of Santa Maria Novella, water was washing up against the bottom of Masaccio's *Trinità*. In the cloister Uccello's *Flood and Drunkeness of Noah* was now truly inundated.

Closer to the Uffizi, the state archives were awash, as was the Palazzo dei Tribunali, the city courts. Transcripts, briefs, and writs drifted through the courtrooms. In the basement, titles, deeds, and contracts swelled, sank, or floated along the ceiling. Facts and promises—vital to some, best forgotten to others—disappeared.

In the afternoon Florentines began to *rendersi conto*—literally "to render or take an account" but in common parlance "to realize"—that they had been struck by more than an inconvenience. "The Arno sure loves Florence," said someone in the Oltrarno, and a graffito appeared on the door of a trattoria: "No roast chicken today—only boiled."

Another artist and writer in Nick's neighborhood, writing in his journal, wondered how people would deal with what was happening. He was not optimistic: "Florentines are too old, too bitter, too gray inside and out, to believe in the existence of a flood like this." Nor, he thought, would they believe that anyone would want to help them.

In the *salone* of a residential hotel near the Ponte Vespucci, a wizened octogenarian woman—a countess from a forgotten aristocratic line—complained when the electricity went out, "What has happened to the lights? It's very dim in here without lights. And all these persons are talking extraordinarily loudly. It's not necessary to talk so loud, is it?"

She would not be persuaded that the dark and the hubbub were the result of a flood. She didn't believe in floods, and she'd lived in Florence all her life, ever since she was a debutante. She finally allowed herself to be taken to the window overlooking the Arno. "But why don't they stop it?" she said. "What is anybody doing about it?"

Some things could not be explained to anyone, or not to some people. The water was crawling toward the San Salvi psychiatric hospital and the patients would not be reassured or calmed. Most of them already lived in one or another Hell. They screamed and beat the walls like the horses in the Cascine stables.

Below the city, where the plain of the valley broadened, the Arno too was expanding, if not slowing. The garden where Marina Ripari played was submerged in an instant. Her father reached her, grasped her for an instant, but then the water tore her out of his hands. Being three years old, she would at least know nothing of Hell, or of the great sea to which the Arno was carrying her body.

No one heard anything from Santa Croce. The water had covered the steps of the basilica some hours ago and was now making its way into the church. The statue of Dante stood like an iceberg in the piazza. Pigeons with no place else to land settled onto the cap shielding his hook-nosed face. Around him, for blocks and blocks, people remained on the second or third floors of their buildings, trapped, waiting for the water to subside. Just now, at three o'clock, it was ten and a half feet deep. But it only rose. Save for the dead, the inhabitants of the Santa Croce district would suffer more than anyone in Florence.

People were poor in Santa Croce. They had St. Francis, but most didn't have telephones or appliances, nor did they hold much interest for the larger world or even the rest of the city. So the water stole in among them even more unnoticed than elsewhere.

For example, Delia Quercioli had a narrow escape on the Piazza dei Ciompi. "I was sleeping and was sleeping well. I'm deaf. My cat was already dead. They broke down the door to save me." Vanna Caldelli lived right on Piazza Santa Croce and from her window she watched tables, chairs, doors, and manuscripts from the cloister and the Biblioteca Nazionale drift by. Later came the heating oil, a stream within the stream of floodwater, the smell so strong you couldn't breathe. "I said to myself, 'Maybe this is the Last Judgment.' "

Azelide Benedetti lived in a ground-floor apartment behind the basilica, in line with the high altar where Cimabue's *Crucifix* had once hung and Vasari's *ciborio* had sat. She was sixty-six years old and pushed herself around the apartment in a wheelchair. At first, the water began to drip in, but then to dribble and flow. She rolled to her window—grilled to keep thieves away—and began to call out. The nuns from the convent next door heard her and by the time they came back with Father Boretti from the parish church of San Giuseppe the water had nearly reached the bottom of Azelide's window. Soon it would be running over the sill.

Supplemented by the subterranean water that had already crept into the apartment under the bolted door, the cascade through the window quickly began filling Azelide's front room. The water was finding its own level. Inside, lighter objects—pillows, bottles, pots, cups, wooden Madonnas and saints—became buoyant, and then the furniture began to shift, to bob and lift free, and circulate around the room. It pressed around Azelide and then drifted back toward the door to the hall and the street. The door, of a piece with the grill, was barred from inside, and by the time Father Boretti returned with more men to try and break it down, it was blocked on the inside by a tangle of furniture.

The thing to do, the priest realized, was to get Azelide up as high as possible; the water couldn't rise indefinitely, and then it would recede. He passed her a sheet through the window and told her to thread it through the spokes of the wheelchair and the uppermost bar of the grille. Then, pulling up the sheet and lashing it to the grille, they were able to raise Azelide in her chair almost to the top of her window. She was well above the priest, the nuns, and the men outside, but they were already nearly up to their heads. Soon the water would be rubbing, catlike, against Azelide's numb legs.

There was nothing to do but pray that it would stop. After an hour only Azelide and the priest still remained. He couldn't hold her hand, raised up as she was, and she had a rosary in it, which she clutched, worrying the beads as the water worked its way upward. She must have made her confession—Azelide was very pious—but that was not something Father Boretti could speak of. Around noon, she did say, with her face pressed against the bars of the grille, just before he had to leave—the water was nearly over his head, closing the last of the cranny between them—"I'm crying." Or rather she whispered it, as though it might put her soul in danger.

By six o'clock that evening the water was receding, although it would be several more hours before people were sure of this. The Arno had crested around noon, flowing at a speed of 145,000 cubic feet per second with 2.5 billion cubic feet of water passing under the Ponte Vecchio. For the next six hours, it continued to run at a slower 106,000 cubic feet per second. But the maximum capacity of the river was 77,000 cubic feet per second, which meant that there were 30,000 cubic feet—225,000 gallons—of water entering Florence every second with no place to go except into the city. By midnight, finally, the Arno was able to carry as much water downstream as it contained upstream.

The sun had gone down a little after five, but no lights went on in the evening, there being no electricity. Not everyone slept that night. Perhaps almost no one did. The rain pulse on the roof had stopped, replaced by a stillness, a little breeze that might have been the sound of withdrawal, of an ebb, of a tide going out where there'd never been a tide before. Don Luigi Stefani, a priest who lived at the Misericordia across the piazza from the Baptistry and the Duomo, prayed and wrote in his journal, and although he kept himself free from despair—he'd brought the Blessed Sacrament from the chapel downstairs into his room for safety—the words in the journal might have been spoken by Job. The Arno had become a lash, flagellating the church and the city; the ribbon of heating oil now running through and over it was a black serpent that licked the altars of Florence. God, it seemed, had deserted the city.

More than once, Don Stefani wrote, *Signore, dormi?*, "Lord, are you sleeping?" The night wore on. He took comfort in his prayers. It was out of the sea, the tempest, the flood that Jesus had called his apostles and comforted them. But Don Stefani himself slept fitfully. Across the piazza, perhaps one hundred feet away, Ghiberti's great Baptistry doors of bronze, half-ripped from their frames, clanged with the flow and swell of the ebbing water, tolled like sad, infernal bells.

Later, near the dawn hours with the water down a few feet, you might have been able to make out one of those ubiquitous Dante wall plaques by the moon—a crack had opened in the clouds; the rain had stopped—scarcely a block toward the river from Azelide Benedetti's apartment. It read, *Per mezza Toscana si spazia / Un fiumicel che nasce in Falterona, / E cento miglia di corso nol sazia*, "Through the middle of Tuscany a little river spreads itself that's born on Falterona; and a course of a hundred miles is not enough for it."

*M*iraculously, again, the journalists of *La Nazione* brought out a paper the next morning. They'd sent their copy over the mountains to Bologna, where it was composed and printed on the presses of a Bologna daily, *Il Resto del Carlino*. The headline was "Florence Invaded by Water: The City Transformed into a Lake: The Greatest Tragedy in Seven Centuries."

No one could yet say how severe the damage was. By dawn, the river had fallen fifteen feet, but that still left a yard of water standing inside the Uffizi. The artworks inside had been saved, but the city was devastated: thousands of Florentines were marooned inside their apartments and hundreds trapped on rooftops. There was no drinking water, no milk, no fresh food or bread, no heat, light, or telephone. Happily, the city's hospitals were all outside the flood zone and there, as well as in more makeshift delivery rooms, twenty-four Florentines appeared who would be able to claim the historic date of November 4, 1966, as their *compleanno*.

But as on the previous day, Santa Croce suffered most, unheard and seemingly despised. At the neighborhood's heart, the market square of Piazza dei Ciompi, there was still fifteen feet of water. And for all the beauty of the art saved at the Uffizi, people here were suffering like Jesus and Francis. People were cold and tired; people were hungry and thirsty; people were injured or sick; some of them might be dying or dead. It would be late afternoon before a soldier from the local barracks could reach Azelide Benedetti. He had to dig the mud out of the stairs and break down the door. Inside, wading through the sump of her apartment, he found a kitchen knife and cut her drowned corpse free, still lashed to the wheelchair and the window, suspended. For lack of a stretcher, never mind an ambulance or a hearse, they carried Azelide out on a clothes rack.

Nick had awoken not as from a dream or from a nightmare, but with the internal assurance that today things would go back to being the way they had been. It was not that he did not understand the laws of the physical universe (at school he'd been nearly as talented in math and science as in art) but, intuitively, it seemed that when the water withdrew—like a cloth, like the tide—everything that had been there before ought to be there again. He had, after all, nearly been dead, and now he was back here, alive.

Yesterday, after losing everything on the Lungarno, he'd found something for all of them to eat. In the afternoon he and Antonio Raffo—today they'd have to see how his Fiat had fared on the Ponte Santa Trinità—had broken into their landlord's offices downstairs and hauled his account books and files upstairs. Later they were rewarded with a month's free rent. In the afternoon, they'd all looked out Antonio's window on the Via Santo Spirito and watched the flotsam sail by, not just junk and debris, but furniture and antiques, presumably valuable, from the shops up the street. There'd been a pair of sculpted wooden angels—nearly as big as Anatol—Amy had had her eye on in a dealer's window a few doors down. Now she imagined the angels might float by, and if they'd had a grappling hook, a rod and a line, they might have caught hold of them, those and all the lovely things Florence was full of.

Today the sun had come out for an hour or so, and where the water had withdrawn, there was an ochre sheen of mire that was the same color as the traditional stucco of the walls of Florence. It seemed to Amy that the whole city was lacquered in tints of warm earth and *az-zurro* sky, so beautiful, like pigments just brushed on and still moist. Amy, Nick with his camera, and Anatol of course—how did this look to him; was it just one more stunning everyday thing?—wanted to go out and see how the morning after looked.

Antonio's Fiat stood absurdly untouched on the Ponte Santa Trinità, the apparent sole survivor in a necropolis of battered, over-turned, heaped, and swamped cars. But the three of them continued onward, as anyone would, like pins to a magnet, to the Ponte Vecchio, and Nick began to take pictures. Amy held Anatol. He looked at his hand, about to put the knuckle of his index finger into his mouth, to give it a nip, a suck. Amy gazed sidelong—she was still beautiful and young; she'd managed to brush her long hair—as if emptied out; a vessel drained, a *scaldino* without coals. Alongside the exhilaration they'd all shared, a sense of the devastation was rising in her.

Behind them was the river and bridge, pinioned and shot through with tree trunks like Saint Sebastian, overhung with limbs, hanks of shredded furniture and lumber, the plaster, wood, and stone of its own flayed innards. The river didn't bear looking at: it was a mammoth roiling sewer, slithering away, shamefaced.

They threaded their way across the Ponte Vecchio through the thicket of debris. Nick stopped to make photographs: antique chests and chairs entwined in roots and branches; wall-less, windowless jewelry showrooms with their chandeliers still immaculately pendant.

And on the other side, where the Via Ninna comes up behind the Uffizi, quiet; and then a ghostly bark floating toward them, full of silent souls, ferried toward them by boatmen with poles. They were crossing the river of forgetting, from the land of the dying to the land of the dead. Amy understood, at last, that something truly terrible had happened.

But then there was shouting and chattering: it was Firenze after all. The boat held a contingent of rescuers and rescued. The skiff was beating its way—upstream, so to speak—from the depths of the Via dei Neri and Santa Croce to the Palazzo Vecchio, where the water was now scarcely knee-deep. Nick, Amy, and Anatol worked their way north, across the mud flat of the Piazza della Signoria toward the Duomo. There was a crowd, Zeffirelli's film crew among them, and in the middle stood the mayor in his gum boots, gesturing emptily, as though water were pouring through his fingers, then kneeling in the mud.

Everyone was standing by the Baptistry, at the east doors, Ghiberti's Gates of Paradise. Five of the ten gilded panels were missing: they used to tell the story—Adam and Eve, the expulsion from Eden, Cain killing Abel—of the things that led up to the flood, the Mosaic deluge, but now those images were buried somewhere in the mud. Monsignor Poli, the head priest of the Duomo, and some custodians were poking the mud with staves. So far, they'd found one panel.

Two more panels were missing from Pisano's south doors, which were hanging by a few tendons of bronze from their frame. Nick took a picture of one of the empty wells in the door where a panel had been sheared away. There was a crack from the upper left to the lower right clear through the metal; a fissure, a chasm, as though an earthquake had rolled right through the door.

Nick and everyone else, really, had thought that the flood was merely water, a liquid, not a solid; a substance that yielded, passed around obstacles, sought the gentle, idle path of least resistance. They hadn't reckoned with its power, energy, or force: the weight of millions of gallons of water at sixty pounds to a mere cubic foot. Still less had they considered its residuum, its spent remains, the skin it sloughed off as it oozed away—muck, sewage, heating oil, and soil gathered from here to Falterona—which resembled nothing so much as *merda*, shit. Inside the city walls there was now one ton of mud for every man, woman, and child in Florence.

Nick, Amy, and Anatol turned east. They had an expatriate friend, a sculptor, Art Koch, in Santa Croce. Nobody had spoken of Santa Croce. They passed along the south flank of the Duomo, right past Giotto's Campanile. People had said the foundations had been undermined; that the spindly, arrogant tower might fall. But Pisano's figure of Icarus, up there above the waves on the southeast corner, hadn't even gotten his feet wet.

On the bank of the Arno below the basilica, Emanuele Casamassima finally got inside the Biblioteca that morning. He'd come by boat with his two assistants, Manetti and Baglioni. They'd worked their way inside with shovels. The water had retreated from the ground floor, but the card catalogs were buried in mud. Of the books for which every card stood as doppelganger, no one could yet say. But there were 62,000 miles of shelves in the library and perhaps half of them were on this floor or the floors below it. At a rough guess, that would make three thousand tons of books: sodden, as they assuredly were, twice that.

The Basilica of Santa Croce was directly behind the Biblioteca; in fact, the library and the Franciscan convent overlapped, Santa Croce's original second, southern cloister being occupied by the Biblioteca.

And as was true on the Lungarni in the Oltrarno, the riverbank was higher than the ground behind it: at the Biblioteca, the farther north— away from the Arno—you moved, the lower the ground. So as Casamassima went farther back into the library—six million items constituting the nation's written patrimony, with which he had been entrusted—his horror and then despair deepened. At the cloister, water still covered the ground floor up to the top of the lower arcade, forming a pool a thousand feet square. Books were floating in it, surfacing like wreckage from the sunken stacks below.

Just on the other side of the common wall, in the primary northern cloister, the priests and brothers had finally been able to descend from their dormitory. Outside help had reached them from the higher ground of the basilica steps: a rubber dinghy had been found in a neighborhood sporting goods store (could bringing aid to a mendicant religious order be called "looting"?) and turned over to the brothers. Now Father Cocci was aboard it, navigating the flooded cloister to the refectory. The main church had already been checked: water had streamed around the high altar, spilled into the crypt and tombs of Michelangelo and the other great men of Florence, but had stopped just inches below the frescoes of the Bardi and Peruzzi chapels. The blessed luck of Giotto had held again: his fresco cycle of Francis was untouched.

But the interior of the refectory was a shallow lagoon: a foot of mud, four more of water, and along the surface, river carp flapping and gasping. The water was retreating very slowly, but what remained was too noxious to support life. Father Cocci may or may not have disembarked from the inflatable at this point, but he was joined in the refectory by Father Barsotti and Brothers Franchi, Collesi, and Renzi. Later, there were supposed to have been twelve brothers present, like the apostles. But disasters, like miracles, are amorphous and slippery; realities that are at once more persuasive than ordinary events, yet refractory. So no one can quite agree what happened next, and today all the witnesses are dead.

It's said that Father Cocci saw the floating paint and gesso flecks, some bright and gilded like tropical fish; that it was only then he looked up at the Cimabue *Crucifix*, looming over the waters of the refectory like the creator spirit. Or rather like God reduced to shreds. It was *un brandello, carni strappate fino al volto*, "in tatters, the flesh ripped off up to the face," Christ crucified and then drowned. Someone found a tea strainer or a pasta collander and began to scoop the scabs of paint off the surface of the water. Another version has it that Father Cocci was still in the inflatable and that the inflatable was equipped for fishing, so the priest angled for bits of gesso and pigment, leaning over the gunwale with a net on a pole. And a persistent story, one that would not go away even after forty years, had it that the *Crucifix* wasn't attached to the refectory wall at all; that it was found floating facedown in the lagoon, drifting.

How else, analytic minds contended, could all that paint have come off? Who knew what had gone on? Con men and looters were supposed to have been roaming around the church; and, in Firenze, how could it be otherwise—someone looking for an angle, grating a little profit from the wedge, or just helping lost things stay lost? But no one could even agree on when the *Crucifix* had been discovered. Most of the brothers thought it was in the morning, but the first layman to enter the refectory, Salvatore Franchino, said it was in the afternoon and that the only way in was through a window.

Regardless of what time it was, all the priests and brothers could do was continue to pan and skim with their various devices, and when that was done—when no more bright specks of paint were left—retreat back to the cloister and save the rest of the basilica, their home.

Word of conditions inside the refectory wouldn't reach the world outside the basilica until later. Meanwhile, around the corner from the

Crucifix, there was Vasari's *Last Supper*, unseen. The flood had immersed the painting, and even now water slapped against the bottom—perhaps Father Cocci's bark had left a wake that beat in wavelets down the corridor—lapping on Judas Iscariot's sandals.

*B*y noon Nick, Amy, and Anatol had reached Santa Croce, the most deeply flooded place in Florence. The epicenter was a point approximately equidistant from the market at Piazza dei Ciompi, the Borgo Allegri, and Dante's statue in the piazza, which was now half mud, half water, surmounted by haystacks of cars. They found Art Koch's Volkswagen, almost vertical, suspended on a rail outside his apartment. Art's apartment was uninhabitable—on November 4 he'd been driven from the first floor to the second and finally to the third floor of his building—and Amy and Nick invited him to come live with them. They slogged down the boot-sucking trail back to the Piazza Santa Croce, where an army truck that had just arrived was distributing bread.

The bread was gone in a few minutes, but a crowd remained thick around the truck. There was no more bread for them, and there'd never been any water. Just then, at noon, the sun broke through, clear and strong, and perhaps that was why there was no shouting, no raised fists, no effort to stop the truck rolling off back to that drier, better-provisioned place whence it had come. After all, this was Santa Croce, Saint Francis's country, where you had to beg. The Communists at the Casa del Popolo by the Piazza dei Ciompi would have put it differently, would have said that Bargellini and the Palazzo Vecchio would just as soon let people here starve, assuming they couldn't exploit them. That Bargellini lived in the neighborhood and yet did nothing simply proved the point. Largely surrounded by water, Santa Croce was now an island—under the protection of St. Francis, Karl Marx, or both—and would have to become the steward as well as the handmaiden of its own suffering. No one else was going to bother.

In fact, relief was being organized, even if no one could say precisely by whom. There was the mayor and Palazzo Vecchio; there was the army; there was the fire department and the various branches of the police; there were priests, nuns, and monks; there was the single *panificio* in the hill village of Meoste (with its own well and an overstock of flour) that had dedicated itself to baking for the most devastated parts of the city; and there was the Casa del Popolo in Piazza dei Ciompi, which had decided to found its own Paris Commune to save Santa Croce. From Rome there was silence.

It was almost as if the farther away you were the easier it was to hear and to act: the BBC had sent a film crew headed by the young art critic Robert Hughes almost as quickly as Zeffirelli had dispatched his. Of course it was less the cry of Santa Croce than of the Uffizi, the Baptistry doors, the David in the Accademia, and whatever other art might be under threat—Florence rather than Firenze—that was being heeded.

You could hear it in America, in Philadelphia. Professor Frederick Hartt had heard it, and in his morning art history class at the University of Pennsylvania—it was late afternoon in Florence; the sky was clouding again; Art Koch was getting settled at Nick and Amy's; he and Nick were hauling drinking water up the 103 steps to the apartment—Hartt told his students what had happened. Then he explained, in tears as often as not, what else would happen if some things weren't done, if certain measures weren't taken immediately; which was why he was leaving them to go to Florence tomorrow.

In the Palazzo Vecchio Mayor Bargellini was trying to conjure up loaves and fishes for the hungry multitude of his city. A central distribution center for food, medicine, and clothing was being established near Campo di Marte, at the city soccer stadium, through which supplies could be efficiently channeled, inventoried, and secured. In addition to being able to handle trucks and heavy equipment, it was big enough for helicopters to land in. They were already coming: at midday one arrived from Pisa, carrying a *Life* magazine photographer from Rome. He'd had to drive himself up the coast to Pisa, camp for the night, and cajole his way onboard.

David Lees would spend the rest of the day getting his bearings and planning how to cover and photograph the city under what seemed to be near-battlefield conditions. For starters, he had to find a pair of rubber boots, without which nothing was possible. Then he would plunge in and start taking pictures. There was no way to assess the damage or even to discern exactly what kinds of damage—inundation, drowning, burying, soaking, rotting, moldering; all of Leonardo's hydrological lexicon—had taken place or might still be happening. Of all people, his wife, the mother of his children, had been in Florence yesterday. They'd talked for a moment. She'd escaped without harm and now she would be going back to Rome, their paths crossing in passing, moving in opposite directions, as was their wont.

David found his boots, set off through the streets of the city of his birth, and learned what he could. By the end of the day of November 5, the following things were true, if not yet tallied up: most of the city's museums and churches were either still inaccessible or uninspected, but some 14,000 movable artworks would prove to be damaged or destroyed; sixteen miles of shelved documents and records in the State Archives had gone underwater; three to four million books and manuscripts had been flooded, including 1.3 million volumes at the Biblioteca Nazionale and its catalog of eight million cards; the rare book and literary collections of the Vieusseux Library in the Palazzo Strozzi had been completely inundated, with book covers and pages stuck to the ceiling; and unknown millions of dollars' worth of antiques and objets from Florence's antiquarian shops were destroyed, swept away, looted, or otherwise missing.

That is one kind of knowledge, but for the moment what most people knew was amorphous and fragmentary, evanescent, frayed, and fractured. Everyone seemed to be saying, for example, that it was just like August 1944; or worse than August 1944; or that, when the sun went down, that it was dark in exactly the same way it had been dark in the war. Or people saw things: someone carrying off the Ghiberti panel of Joseph and his brothers from the Baptistry in a wheelbarrow; through the gap in the doors themselves, Donatello's *Mary Magdalene* stained by heating oil up to mid-thigh, besmirched beyond any penance she might make; a Dominican in Santa Maria Novella seated at a table, its legs and the monk's feet immersed in water, selling votive candles for one hundred lire apiece; in the window of a pet shop, a cage of drowned songbirds.

Five

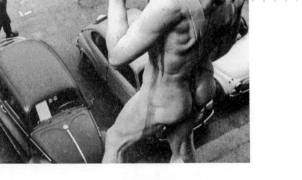

The intervention should happen!

—UMBERTO BALDINI,
*TEORIA DEL RESTAURO E
UNITÀ DI METODOLOGIA*

Moving paintings in the Piazza Signoria, November 6, 1966 *(Photograph by David Lees)*

*A*s of nightfall on November 5, Ugo Procacci had slept perhaps three hours in the last thirty-six. On the fourth he'd been up at dawn and had worked at the Uffizi until dawn the following day. That evening he'd gone back to his apartment in the Palazzo Pitti, where the telephone lines still worked, long enough to make some calls, and then washed and retired to bed, but one of Baldini's students, a twenty-year-old named Alessandro Conti, arrived breathlessly, saying Procacci was again urgently needed: there'd been a report from Santa Croce that the *Crocifisso* of Cimabue had been severely damaged, soaked from top to bottom, and was still shedding paint.

Now, at nearly midnight, there was no way to get to Santa Croce, and no light to work by, anyway. He gave Conti a note to take to Umberto Baldini in the morning:

> *Dear Baldini—*
> *They tell me we're in danger of losing the Crucifix of Cimabue; it*
> *seems that the head and body have already been badly damaged.*
> *Suspend any other work and get to Santa Croce immediately.*
> *Yours,*
> *Procacci*

Unable to sleep, Procacci got to the refectory at six the next morning. By then the water inside had receded to ankle depth over the mud. Only a little light reflected off the water, casting waves and glints onto the walls and, as Procacci began to make out, onto the *Crucifix*. It was a shadowy, immense gangling form among still more shadows, but as the dawn light slowly unveiled it, he could begin to make out its details, or rather, all that was gone: half the face, much of the right side of the body and legs plus the chest and the abdomen. Perhaps three-quarters of the image was gone, stripped down to the gesso or to the canvas beneath it. Procacci could not be sure—hearing the drip and slop of water everywhere, of things being sloughed off—that it wasn't continuing, in the dim light, to disintegrate before his eyes.

Procacci was not given to despair. But here there seemed to be nothing to save, regardless of what efforts he or an entire army or Cimabue's God might make. It was, at dawn, two days after the flood had coursed into Santa Croce, far too late.

By now—it was almost seven o'clock—some of the crew Procacci had sent for were turning up. They stood around uselessly, shuffling in the cold and the damp, watching Procacci standing before the cross in his mud-spattered raincoat, his face angular and weeping. Then, out of terrible audacity or raw frustration, someone said, "If you're crying, what are *we* supposed to do?"

When Baldini arrived a few minutes later—he'd dispensed with his customary suit and thrown on a blue pullover when Conti had turned up with the note—the light was stronger, strong enough for Baldini to see in seconds what Procacci had only made out over many minutes. He, too, wept, but Procacci was looking at him. And then, because no one else was saying anything, Baldini said, "We need to lay it down."

But how? The *Crucifix* was fastened to an iron support that was fixed to the wall, the entire assembly corroded. There were no tools. One of the workers found some scaffolding in an adjacent room that, once erected, allowed them to see what they were up against. The cross would have to be cut down like a tree. Someone went off to look for a hacksaw. He would be a long time: hacksaws were just then in great demand in Florence, along with buckets, pumps, winches, sponges, mops, and, most of all, shovels.

As they waited, Procacci and Baldini saw that the *Crucifix* was still shedding paint. Baldini's chief restorer, Edo Masini, began to fish through the water with a tea strainer and recovered about one hundred flecks of color, the largest perhaps a sixteenth of an inch in size. As Masini bent down, peering into the mire, tourist brochures and Giotto postcards from the gift shop floated by.

By late morning, a hacksaw and some other tools had been found and what Baldini would call the "deposition" began. Just then, David Lees arrived in the refectory. He was traveling light, shooting with his Nikon F and high-speed Ektachrome. As the workers sawed, he photographed the activity at the foot of the cross: Procacci stock still; Baldini gesticulating, a blur on the film; the others, waiting. The reflection off the muddy water overlaid by a sheen of oil threw up highlights here and there, the colors as lucid and deep as Cimabue's.

It took fifteen men and yards of rope to bring the *Crocifisso* down. Sodden, it weighed well over a thousand pounds (450 of that was the iron frame on which it was mounted). Cimabue had milled and joined the four-inch-thick planks of poplar to be strong, but no one knew how strong: struggling to maintain their footing in the slime or balanced precariously on the scaffolding, the rescuers feared the crucifix would come apart, fall, or collapse of its own weight, crushing them. Lees photographed the straining, grimacing men bearing the weight of the cross—itself bearing the weight of the world, Francis would have said—as a fury of labor, of suffering posed against suffering.

Afterward, David went into the basilica itself, the one-time home of the *Crucifix* (had it remained there it would have been safe), which was now a delta of mud. The mud was smooth in most places while in others it was banked and shoaled, rippled like sand after the tide's retreat. In the middle of it stood a wooden *Madonna*. To one side of her was a candlestick, lodged as though intended to be a votive offering; a little farther away lay the roof of a confessional and a tangle of pews and kneelers. She held her arms in the customary pose of Madonnas, her arms lowered but outstretched, the palms opened upward, as if to say, on the one hand, "Come—you're safe with me," or, on the other, "Behold, look," indicating her child in the manger or his body after his deposition. Now, with Mary shipwrecked, marooned here, both those possibilities were absent in the picture David took. Perhaps now she'd become the patron of mariners and sailors, *Stella Maris*, Mary, the Star of the Sea. She's gesturing outward, bidding David and us to look; blessing—it seems—the mud and the great tide that's just withdrawn from it.

*A*s the workers struggled under the cross inside, outside in the Piazza Santa Croce there was an even larger surge of activity. The president of the Republic, Giuseppe Saragat, was making a tour of Florence in an army truck, trying to demonstrate that Rome had reacted and did, in fact, care. He'd just announced that the government was releasing one billion lire—one million dollars—in unrestricted funds to the local authorities. This perhaps mollified some quarters of the city, but in Santa Croce it did not make much of an impression. People here did not believe in "unrestricted funds": they believed in bread, as they said at the Casa del Popolo.

Now Saragat was being chauffeured through the piazza, and perhaps contrary to his deepest wishes, it was here that the truck bogged down in the mud. There had already been a crowd, grumbling and launching jeers and epithets at the head of state, things you might hear anywhere but some uniquely Tuscan, involving pigs, swamp-dwellers, the Madonna, bottles, and anuses. Mostly, they simply shouted, "Bread."

When the truck stopped, immobilized and spinning its wheels, the crowd closed in. The truck began to rock and the president sat, smiling tightly, the color ebbing from his face as the interminable pitching and yawing continued. Then the truck was moving, waddling toward the Biblioteca Nazionale, and the laughter—it was mostly laughter now, plus a few imprecations so local as to be incomprehensible to people three neighborhoods away—fell away behind the greasy spoor of its tracks.

At the Biblioteca, one of the nation's preeminent cultural institutions, they'd cleared a path through the mud—where it wasn't an impasto of sewage it was a sort of dense black antimatter, snow heavy as lead, dark as bile—up the steps for the president's arrival. Or so he thought. Entering the front vestibule where the circulation desks stood piled with ten-foot-high stacks of sodden books, he was led to the library's chief, Emanuele Casamassima. Mud-spattered and bedraggled in a suit shapeless with damp and sweat, Casamassima seemed not to know who Saragat was. But then he said, *Presidente, ci lasci lavorare*, "Mr. President, leave us to our work."

It's said that Casamassima then handed him a bucket, but it's also said that Saragat managed to maintain his dignity and, despite everything, to meet these trials with a shy but palpable compassion. He was in the same mold as Bargellini, a good man inundated by the deluge of misery, anger, and despair that the flood left behind. People were prepared to believe the worst about everybody and everything. Earlier in the morning a rumor began going around that the Levane and La Penna dams, supposedly drained ninety-six hours before but now brimming again with water, were on the verge of collapse: another flood, equal to the first, was on its way. That story produced panic while others in circulation fostered bitterness or cynicism: for example, that on November 4, the dams were opened—or not opened, depending on the version—to save somebody's job or their money or to cover up a mistake or a bribe; another said that the jewelers and goldsmiths on the Ponte Vecchio had been warned hours and hours before the flood while everyone else was left to drown.

The atmosphere was rife with backbiting, suspicion, and calumny, and the air itself increasingly stank: as the water withdrew it left a mixture of mud, sewage, and heating oil to cure over a succession of warmer and sunnier days, an aroma at once fetid and acrid, a hybrid of tide flat, refinery, and cesspool. Now, forty-eight hours after the ebb, the things that had been submerged or drowned were surfacing: dead domestic and farm animals, foodstuffs (thousands of gallons of souring milk, wheel upon wheel of cheese, tons of fish, and hundreds of sides of butchered meat in the central market), and the effluents produced, hour after hour, by Florentines living on the street and in their now unplumbed homes. Among the resources that accompanied President Saragat north from Rome were army flamethrowers to incinerate the carrion in the streets, the horses in the Cascine, and, later, the monkeys, deer, goats, and a lone camel at the city petting zoo.

The Casa del Popolo had managed to find three hundred pounds of bread and four hundred candles that day. Sandra, Macconi, Federico, Carlo, Daniela, and the rest—their last names were irrelevant; they were young, they were politically committed, they were the vanguard—distributed half a loaf and a candle to whoever got to the Piazza dei Ciompi before they ran out. They were still waiting for water, and from farther afield, salvage equipment: the Casa had contacted its counterparts in the Communist Party in Perugia and bulldozers and backhoes were being sent. Based on friendship, commitment, and ideology, a network was forming and spreading in Santa Croce with no ties to the government or the authorities: people knew people and people worked together and shared what they had—a load of underwear and socks, cages of drowned chickens from the country—motivated by solidarity rather than profit.

While they waited for more supplies and equipment, all of them—Menzella, Luca, Beppe, Luisa, and more—shoveled or, because it continued to rain sporadically, bailed. The sewers were still full or blocked with mud and debris: with the smallest increment of additional water, they overflowed. Cellars all over the neighborhood remained full of rank standing water. Along with buckets and shovels, the emblematic tool—the hammer and sickle of the Santa Croce Casa del Popolo—was the *rastrello*, a wooden rake whose crossbar, with the teeth removed, could be used to push and plow through mud, water, or *melma*, mire and slime. Much more than with machinery—when and if it arrived—Florence was scraped and squeegeed clean with *rastrelli*.

Down the Borgo Allegri and across the Piazza Santa Croce at the Biblioteca Nazionale and its caverns of book stacks, only shovels and buckets would do, but even more they needed hands: there were almost one and a half million items to be moved—not just books, but newspapers, periodicals, manuscripts, pamphlets, and the written and printed ephemera that constituted the historical records of Italy. Conditions were appalling: wet, cold, and dark, everything stuck to everything, slime to sopping paper, boots to mud, books to one another or to their shelves. The bound volumes hadn't sat inert in the cases, but swelled: sometimes their sodden weight simply overwhelmed the shelves that held them, but they also expanded laterally, pressing against the sides of their bookcases until these gave way and the entire case collapsed. Where the verticals of the shelving were stronger, the books themselves distorted: with no space in which to expand, they pressed upward and downward to accordion into undulating curves like wave oscillations.

But that afternoon of November 6, books were nonetheless coming out of the stacks, emerging into the light of the circulation hall, hundreds per hour. It must have occurred to Emanuele Casamassima that he should be facing a labor shortage; that in a city without food, power, or transport, people should be too busy fending for themselves to be mucking about in his library. Yet they were, dozens of them, and he hadn't even asked them to come. Nor, it seemed, had they asked for instructions or equipment: the books just kept surfacing, bubbling up as from an inexhaustible spring. These workers weren't organized; they didn't have a party or a manifesto like the Casa del Popolo; it wasn't clear what they were against or what they were for, except perhaps books. You could call them volunteers, except they hadn't volunteered or been recruited: they'd simply appeared as though from thin air and set to work. Maybe they'd been sent by Francis or the Madonna; maybe they'd been thrown up by inevitable historical forces, by the dialectic operating at light speed. But they were some sort of miracle. Florentines came to call them *angeli del fango*, "mud angels."

In fact they'd been turning up since the day before, the day the water receded. At first they were Florentines, almost universally young, at loose ends with no families to feed or classes to attend. When Bruno Santi, for example, finished helping his father, he waded across the Ponte alle Grazie and rescued a Giotto with a group of soldiers; later he found himself working among the treasures and artworks in the church of Santi Apostoli, then in the Museo Horne, and finally, for many weeks, at the Limonaia of the Palazzo Pitti, which was being set up as a kind of refugee camp and hospital for flooded artworks. A near contemporary of Giovanni Menduni with perhaps less anxious parents, Cristina Acidini, turned up at the Biblioteca and was put to work and later moved on to the Museum of the History of Science. A pretty and energetic twenty-three-year-old art history student, Ornella Casazza, pitched in and finished up studying under Edo Masini.

Some became angels by coming home: Marco Grassi was the son of five generations of Florentine art dealers and restorers. Having studied with the magisterial Cesare Brandi in Rome, he now worked in the Swiss art collections of Baron Hans Heinrich Thyssen, the aristocrat industrialist and connoisseur. But on the morning of November 4, he'd jumped in his car and was in Florence by eleven that night. Joined by another young restorer, Thomas Schneider, he spent the next three weeks circulating between the Uffizi, Santa Maria Novella, and Santa Croce.

It was understandable that Florentines should be in the forefront of rescuing their own city, but over the coming days more and more *angeli* arrived from much farther away. A group of American college students saw the Franciscan brothers working outside Santa Croce and took up shovels and *rastrelli* on the spot. From as far away as Scandinavia, young Europeans simply dropped what they were doing and boarded trains or drove south. An extraordinary number came from England: a student from London's Courtauld Institute—perhaps the world's preeminent graduate school of art history—left the night of the flood, but not before going to his family's farm to round up all the pumps and hoses he could lay his hands on. Driving day and night across the continent in a Land Rover, he was at the doors of the Uffizi twenty-four hours later.

Luciano Camerino undertook a briefer but in some ways longer journey. Twenty-three years earlier, in his native Rome, he'd been seized by the Gestapo along with his entire family and deported to Auschwitz. Only he had returned alive. After the war he'd run a restaurant and started up a business that dealt in liturgical goods. He was good at all the things he did. Perhaps he was also lucky. But on November 6 he'd dropped everything and gone north to Florence. He'd heard there was a synagogue in Via Farina that held some 120 priceless scrolls of the Law plus fifteenth-, sixteenth-, and seventeenth-century commentaries—fifteen thousand volumes—of inestimable scholarly and antiquarian value.

Camerino arrived late that day and worked largely alone and almost continuously for the next seventy-two hours. The only way to save the 120 scrolls of the Law was to unroll each one—all 130 to 165 feet of it—and drape it over chairs, up and down the aisles, like drying pasta. He labored without food or rest or joy, as they'd labored in the camps. But he was saving the Word, the Law, and the Prophets. After the third day, he raised his palm to his forehead, staggered, and fell dead, of cardiac arrest it was said afterward. The flaw in the heart—his or the world's—that had been tracking him since 1943 had found him.

*T*he next morning, November 7, three days after the flood, a headline in *La Nazione* spoke of a "A Prayer Rising Up from the City," but at the Casa del Popolo in Santa Croce they entrusted themselves to scavenging and scrounging, stoked by need, solidarity, and anger. There had been talk of illness and even epidemic all day yesterday, a rumor abetted by the growing reek of sewage. Piero from the Casa tracked down fifty doses of tetanus vaccine. Graziella went to the barracks to ask if army doctors might come and treat sick people in the neighborhood but was told there was no process for allowing this; that the military, for apparently good constitutional reasons, mustn't encroach on the sphere of local government.

Nearby a group of neighbors from the Borgo Allegri had gone to the prefecture and refused to move until the city sent a truck and a crew to begin clearing their street of mud and filth. In their case the tactic worked, even as a block away on Via Pinzochere—where Mayor Bargellini's palazzo stood—residents went unaided: Bargellini had wanted to show that his home would be treated no differently than anyone else's in Florence, but the example served as another instance of civic neglect and incompetence. As with President Saragat—

another well-meaning figure who had the misfortune to be a good rather than a great man—the flood had the capacity to warp every intention, to muddy the most transparent virtue.

Saragat's tour of the city had occupied most of page one of *La Nazione*, but two other stories were given equal prominence: *Colpa alla Diga del Valdarno?*, "The Dams of the Arno Valley at Fault?," and *Semidistrutto in Santa Croce il Prezioso Cristo di Cimabue*, "The Precious Christ of Cimabue Nearly Destroyed in Santa Croce," with the subsidiary heading "Masterpieces of Art Lost or in Danger." Until now the press, like the public, had focused on the human and economic costs of the flood: even by very rough estimates, there were at least twenty people dead in the city, six thousand businesses wiped out, and 80 percent of Florence's restaurants and hotels—crucial to the city's tourist economy—out of commission. Arguably, the scale of misery had not decreased at all, or only by the smallest of increments, but art was pressing its way into the public consciousness. Regarding the Uffizi, *La Nazione* had assured its readers yesterday that "Dr. Baldini and the personnel of his laboratory are doing their utmost beyond the limits of human possibility," but now there was a sense that, as with other efforts to address the disaster, incompetence and a dearth of concern or will were threatening Florence's patrimony.

Florentines still had their dead to bury—there would be thirty-three, mostly drowned or suffocated by mud, but others killed by cold and lack of medicine—and their city to dig out, but its art was the larger world's preoccupation. Edward Kennedy flew in from a conference he was attending in Geneva and visited the Uffizi and the Biblioteca Nazionale. David Lees photographed him talking to the mud angels in a spattered trench coat. Lees had already decided to stay an extra day, rather than ship off his film and return to Rome. "This is history, not just news," he'd told one of the brothers at Santa Croce.

Frederick Hartt arrived from America that same day. Within hours he was standing before Franco Zeffirelli's camera in his own mire-flecked trench coat, explaining why the flood was not simply a catastrophe for Italy but for all of Western civilization. What was at stake here was, in some sense, our humanity, the traditions and artifacts that embodied our best aspirations, the things that gave us meaning.

In the space of the next ten days Zeffirelli's film, David Lees's photographs, and the example of the *angeli del fango* (now consecrated in their youthful and selfless idealism by one of the surviving Kennedy brothers) transformed the flood from a local disaster into a global tragedy. It coincided, perhaps, with a moment when people were especially prepared to respond to it. Their innocent, naive, and perhaps—from a twenty-first-century vantage point—even ignorant belief in human goodness and its capacity to change the world had been attacked at its heart, in the embodied idealism of art. Kennedy's words about the mud angels at the Biblioteca felt entirely true: "It was as though they knew that the flooding of the library was putting their souls at risk."

The *angeli del fango* phenomenon—a proto-Woodstock of high visual culture—gave the appearance of being a miraculous and spontaneous expression of youthful benevolence, epitomized that same night in Botticelli's *Magdalene* being transported from the Baptistry in a red Volkswagen Beetle (the archetypal student vehicle of the time), its harrowed face emerging from the sunroof. But for all the impromptu charm of the image—Procacci and Baldini would have been apoplectic (with good reason) had they known—the *Magdalene* arrived safely at the Palazzo Davanzati, where expert restorers of wood sculpture from Norway would join it in a few days.

In fact, coordinated decision making and planning was slowly taking shape: by the end of November 7, Procacci and Baldini had met with their counterparts at other museums, institutions, and monuments. A central office was established at the Uffizi to dispatch *angeli del fango* to the places and tasks for which they were most urgently needed. While the mud angels were amateurs in the best sense—lovers of art for art's sake—there was a surprising amount of expertise among them. Some like Marco Grassi and his friend Thomas Schneider were already professional restorers; others like Bruno Santi and the British volunteers from the Courtald Institute were graduate students in art history; and still others were working artists like Nick Kraczyna, people who knew something about the techniques and craft of painting and sculpture. Susan Glasspool had just graduated from the Slade in London and arrived in Florence on a graduate painting scholarship. Working among the mud-encrusted books of the Biblioteca dell'Accademia, she met another painting student, a Florentine named Giuseppe Bottaro, whom she married a year and a half later.

But if there was amateurism at the Biblioteca Nazionale and the other flooded libraries, it was entirely understandable: no one in the history of book conservation had ever dealt with materials damaged in this way and on this scale. In the course of recovering the contents of Florence's libraries, many volumes were further damaged by their rescuers' good intentions. As was also true with some paintings and sculptures, there was an urgent sense that things should be made dry as soon as possible with a concomitant failure to consider the damage that might result—cracking, splitting, and distortion—along with the overarching and pervasive problem of mold. No one knew whether books should be taken apart—disassembled from their bindings and sewn sections—or should simply be washed and dried, never mind whether this drying should be gradual or accelerated. For the latter purpose, by November 7, Emanuele Casamassima had secured not only the use of tobacco kilns in the Tuscan countryside but the powerhouse and heating plant of the Santa Maria Novella railroad station. The main thing was to keep pulling books from the mud, rinsing them off, and hanging them to dry. The rest would be figured out later.

Simultaneously Procacci, Casamassima, and their colleagues were meeting and calculating the extent of the damage to date: 321 panel paintings; 413 on canvas; 11 fresco cycles; 39 single frescoes; 31 other frescoes—32,000 square feet's worth—detached from their original locations; 158 sculptures; 37 miles of shelved materials at the Archives of State; and 6,000 illuminated manuscripts, psalters, and musical texts in the Duomo. In all, there were fifteen museums and eighteen churches described as "devastated." And at the Biblioteca Nazionale, despite the labors of the *angeli del fango*—whose numbers were increasing by a dozen per hour—in some places the mud was still twenty-two feet deep.

The ability of Procacci's staff and their counterparts throughout the city to make such tallies and summaries suggested that, if the worst was not over, the disaster was becoming comprehensible. But the mind numbs before the abstractions of figures, however impressive in magnitude: a body count, however massive, pales in impact beside the visible, terrible fact of a single corpse. It is from such discrete and tiny realities that meaning arises and can be grasped, from which the awful whole could begin to be sensed.

That was what began to happen to Cimabue's *Crocifisso* on November 7. Baldini had described it to the press in Vasari's terms, "the first page of Italian art," which was to say it was valuable and important. It was worth saying because, contrary to later impressions, the *Crucifix* was neither famous nor beloved: it hadn't been high on the list of must-sees in Florence; it wasn't, in fact, on the list to begin with. It was known, of course, to art historians, but less as a work of art in its own right than as a precursor of truly important work, the obscure Cimabue's half step toward what his pupil Giotto achieved.

Despite that, almost immediately the Cimabue became the preeminent symbol of the flood. But *symbol* wasn't quite the right word; it implied yet another abstraction rather than a particular but transcendent fact—which is, after all, what (in fact) art may be—a body that had suffered, a body that embodied much more than itself precisely in itself; a particular being that was also an essence. Here, it was wood and paint and brushstrokes that came to mean—that came to become—all of Florence: its beauty, its suffering, and its redemption.

And maybe there was one more thing that made the *Crocifisso* such a profound vehicle for meaning: it occupied a boundary between human suffering and the damage to artworks where the two seemed to blur or overlap. On the seventh and the following days, everyone in the media was listening to Frederick Hartt: he was an expert of global standing, he was perfectly bilingual, and he had, in a sense, been through all this before in 1944. And his love for the city and its art was tangible: he teared and choked up at the slightest provocation.

Talking of his first sight of Ugo Procacci that day, he said that Procacci "looked like a man ruined, used-up, destroyed by fatigue and covered with mud." And then Hartt was talking about the Cimabue *Crocifisso:* "It's a corpse, the paint is gone and it can only be displayed as a relic." Where did Procacci end and the painting begin? Where did a person—any person in all of suffering Florence—shade into Cimabue's image, now both luminous and besmirched, shading into the ruined Christ?

You might say all this, but the people at the Casa del Popolo in Santa Croce would only grow more impatient and angry. They had their own art. There was a large graffito outside in the Piazza dei Ciompi depicting male and female characters, "Mama Flood" and "Papa Deluge," standing in a puddle next to a building whose toppling wall is shored up by props. The text says they've "run off leaving sorrows, ruins, and tears behind them." Next to these are smaller figures of "the sons and daughters left behind": "Hope," "Streets," "Neighborhood," "The Arno Restrained," "Bracing for Houses," "The Help Twins," and, last, "The Promise Twins." Beneath them is the legend

"And we hope that someone wakes up in order to aid these orphans." It's an allegory of the Santa Croce *quartiere*, wry, facetious, and bitter, a black-and-white panel painting that found its way up the Borgo Allegri to this piazza.

No one in Florence thought that art was a luxury, a diversion from truly important things. But among all the troubles—shortages of food, water, and medicine, streets wedged with cars, trees, carrion, and yards of mud, and a mere 150 pumps in the entire city to drain thousands of rooms, courtyards, and cellars—these pleas on its behalf were a little troubling. An artist who lived down the street from Nick and Amy found himself writing, "Am I supposed to care about the Christ of Cimabue or the doors of Ghiberti before the reality of five people who could be my own family faced with darkness because they can't even scrape together three hundred lire to buy candles—assuming there were any candles?"

Don Luigi Stefani had other misgivings. Writing in his room above the Piazza del Duomo, looking onto the Baptistry and its shattered doors, he wondered if "perhaps it isn't true that the Christ of Cimabue has really been lost because of our indifference to every aspect of its religious and moral significance, retaining only the aesthetic? And when a 'Christ' ceases to speak to the soul, what are we to do?"

Both writers voiced their concerns as questions rather than statements. There was nothing to do but go on thinking, feeling, and expressing; nothing to do except to make more words and images. David Lees had taken another photograph inside the basilica. There was a brother working in the Chapel of Madonna delle Grazie with no more than a small broom. The *Madonna* that the chapel belonged to had herself washed up outside in the nave, where David had photographed her the previous day next to the candlestick. Inside the chapel mud inclined up the front of the altar like a snowdrift, the retreat of the water marked by undulating sidewinder ripples. And here, in the photograph, taking it all on—the ton of mud that buried the room—was this slight Franciscan with his little stick and its hank of straw.

At eight o'clock on the morning of November 8, the Casa del Popolo of Santa Croce officially opened as the de facto relief center of the *quartiere*. Food tables were set up on the right, clothing tables on the left, and an infirmary at the back. It should have been easy by then for the residents of the neighborhood to make their way there: the city had said that six hundred men would be out with shovels to clear the streets. But thus far perhaps a tenth of that number had turned up in Santa Croce. Butter, cheese, fruit, pasta, and meat had been promised, but only bread and milk appeared. Elsewhere in the city, it was said, cafés were already serving cappuccinos and croissants. Perhaps just as vexing to the Marxists of the Casa (who would have preferred that all the blame go to Bargellini and the Christian Democrats and their capitalist masters) was the report that the Seventh Day Adventists were distributing free copies of the Book of Revelation, St. John's Apocalypse, as the key to everything that had befallen the city and the *quartiere*.

Santa Croce, or at least the Casa, had had enough. The people took to the streets. Paolo and Menzella got a loudspeaker and a crowd gathered, urged on by the plea "What's there to lose?—the only thing you have is mud and water!" At 2:30, some two hundred persons marched on the Palazzo Vecchio, "united," the Casa assured, "not by ideology, but common misfortune." They were going to see the mayor and they wouldn't leave until he'd talked to them. Bargellini's deputy finally agreed that three delegates from the marchers could come in, which Paolo negotiated up to five.

The mayor met them seated in an antechamber and asked them

what they wanted. They wanted to know, Paolo replied, how things really stood; they wanted to know why Bargellini kept saying that Florence had met the flood with a smile on the lips, that its citizens were heroic, and that the city was now already on its way to recovery. That, Bargellini responded, had been said in the interests of morale; people needed hope, did they not? But how, he asked again, could he help them?

To start, they wanted the streets cleared. They wanted basements pumped out. They wanted the whole quarter treated with disinfectants. They wanted all the supplies they'd requested—food, clothing, tools, and medicine—and they wanted official recognition of the Casa. Bargellini tried, by his lights, to be kind and good-humored. But according to Paolo, Bargellini hedged and chuckled and then slipped away, having only agreed that his deputy would accompany the demonstrators back to Santa Croce for an inspection.

When they got to the Piazza Santa Croce, there were indeed some of the workers promised, a bedraggled squad that had been furnished with spades too small to penetrate the mud effectively (although by now some five thousand shovels had reportedly been delivered to the city); and even if they'd had the right tools, they looked too exhausted to lift them. The deputy made excuses and promised to look further into the matter when he got back to the Palazzo Vecchio. But before he could make his exit he was seized by a group of neighborhood women and, pulled by the arms, marched down the Borgo Allegri, bootless, his suit spotted with more and more mud as he was forced to *rendersi conto*—to take in and acknowledge—the extent of the chaos and misery. Then he was set loose.

Late in the afternoon, however, like a revelation, the heavy equipment the Casa had been promised by their fellow party members in Perugia appeared, not only bulldozers and backhoes but lights and generators that would allow them to work into the night. With the rose window on the front of the basilica illuminated by the spill from the lamps, Santa Croce was finally being dug out, overseen by the statue of Dante in the center of the piazza, beleaguered these four days and just now emerging from the underworld, blinking in the sudden glare.

*I*nside the basilica, in the refectory, people had been coming to visit the *Crocifisso* they'd been hearing about. Nick had come with his camera. Workers were putting up scaffolding on the west wall so that restorers could get a closer look at the damage to Taddeo Gaddi's immense *Cenacolo* fresco. The Cimabue still lay where Procacci and Baldini and their crew had set it down, lying flat on the cluster of benches they'd scraped together from the furniture scattered in the mud. To one side, there was a section of gold picture frame molding they'd used to wedge the cross into position.

Nick photographed the *Crocifisso* upside down, the head and the halo inverted, and from that position it was no longer clear that there'd ever been a face, or even a body. It was still recognizably a cross, awaiting, perhaps, a victim. He took another shot from the front, the *Crucifix* supine before the iron wall mounting that had once supported it, which itself looked like nothing so much as a gibbet, a cross upon which to crucify the *Crocifisso*. Anyone could come and look at it.

There were also still people from Procacci's staff at work. They'd turned from the Cimabue—no one quite knew what was going to be done with it yet—to the other artworks in the refectory and the rooms adjoining it. In addition to Taddeo's fresco, there was an important *Deposizione* by Francesco Salviati and another by Alessandro Allori, as well as a *Descent into Limbo* by Bronzino, all from the mid to late 1500s. A little later someone noticed a severely damaged painting from roughly the same decade in another room, *The Last Supper* of Giorgio Vasari.

That day, November 8, Marco Grassi and his friends Thomas Schneider and Myron Laskin—an international, polyglot group, as *angeli del fango* always seemed to be—were sent by the coordinating office at the Uffizi to Santa Croce. They were assigned to doing *velinatura*, covering damaged areas of paintings with Japanese rice paper attached with Paraloid, an acrylic resin. Each sheet of *velina* (tissue) covered about a square foot and was held in place with the fingers while the Paraloid was brushed over it. Like everything else associated with the flood, the process was sticky and smelly, although the aroma was synthetic rather than fetid. It was a stopgap measure, a way to put a painted surface in suspension, intact (including any dirt, oil, and mud) until restorers could begin working on it.

Velinatura, then, was the art conservation equivalent of sandbagging, ubiquitous and effective up to a point. It didn't make things better, but it stopped some of them from getting worse. Baldini's staff and the mud angels used up all the rice paper in Florence, Bologna, and then all of Italy in a matter of days, and when it was gone they switched to Kleenex tissues.

It fell to Marco and his friends to do the *velinatura* on the Vasari. The painting had been thoroughly soaked and at about eight by twenty feet it would be a long and tedious job, like pasting a billboard with handkerchieves. Swollen with water, the five panels had begun to pull apart: Bartholomew, James, and Andrew from Thomas the Doubter; Simon, Jude, and Matthew from Philip and James the Greater; the apostles dispersing, going their own crooked and various ways. The central panel of Jesus, Peter, and John was in the best condition, the one to its left, Iscariot's—performing his fey, devious pirouette— in the worst. While the Paraloid was still wet you could see the painting as through a veil, and then, as the resin dried, it slowly disappeared beneath the cloud of tissue. That was the last time anyone would see it for a long, long time.

Marco and the rest were at it for some hours, long enough to be photographed a half dozen times and to be caught in a panning shot by Zeffirelli's crew during its final hours in Florence. Marco himself remained for another two weeks daubing lesser masters with Paraloid before he returned to the Thyssen collection in Switzerland. The baron had telephoned to ask what he might do to help, and Marco told him he supposed clothing would be much needed and appreciated. Within a week box after box of slightly worn cashmere sweaters, tuxedos, velvet dressing gowns and jackets, and Charvet neckties arrived at the mayor's house. All but the most unprepossessing items went undistributed: what the Casa would make of handing out smoking jackets to the working folk of Santa Croce Bargellini could by now easily imagine. Instead, the mayor opened a depot to dispense more functional clothing on the ground floor of his palazzo. In exchange for donating a large part of her own wardrobe, he allowed his daughter to take a camel-hair coat from the baron's hand-me-downs.

Beyond the press and his political opponents (who certainly had no intentions of halting their own agendas during the emergency), Bargellini had to deal with sudden shifts in public feeling caused by rumor. The talk about the jewelers on the Ponte Vecchio wouldn't go away nor would the suspicions about the La Penna and Levane dams as well as fear of their potential for bringing another flood. That same morning *La Nazione* had published ENEL's denial of having any role in the disaster. But people would believe what they wanted to believe, and Bargellini was, in his optimism, his piety, his bookishness, and aristocratic humility, not entirely of the perennial Florentine temperament, even if he was a native son. He was not well equipped to sustain, on the one hand, cynicism about ENEL and the goldsmiths and, on the other, sentimentality about the survival of the pet boar Esmerelda in the Cascine zoo. But the classic Florentine—the one whose soul Dante had anatomized and upon whose governance Machiavelli prognosticated—could. All that, bound by the love of *quartiere, denari*, and *bellezza*—neighborhood, money, and beauty—was the Florentine's essential character.

And how could Bargellini or anyone know what was true in the midst of all this chaos in a city marked by deviousness at the calmest of times? It was true, for example, that there were still fifty-eight prisoners from the Murate unaccounted for, but it was false—so far—that cholera had broken out; and as to whether there were scuba divers salvaging gold under the Ponte Vecchio, you couldn't put it past somebody to have thought of it, not in Florence.

There were even rumors about art, about the *Crocifisso*. It was said—it even got into the newspapers—that when Procacci and Baldini arrived at the refectory, they found the cross drifting like a derelict raft in the mire and watched helplessly as it shed its pigment before their eyes. It was also said that the fragments the monks were supposed to have sieved from the *melma* had been left (for lack of any other receptacle) on a platter that a laborer, looking for something to eat his lunch from, subsequently scraped into the trash.

The next morning's edition of *La Nazione* extrapolated some anxious comments by Ugo Procacci into the headline "No Hope for the Cimabue Crucifix." A subheading on the prognosis for all the damaged art estimated "Twenty Years Needed to Complete Restoration Efforts." Another page reported, for the first time, the phenomenon of "Groups of Students Working on the Recovery of Artworks." Bargellini had already wondered, "Where will we put them all?"—there were now a thousand of them in Florence—and struck a deal with the state railway to bunk them in idle sleeping cars and coaches.

The mayor had to concentrate on these and other practical details, but by now other voices began making the case for Florence: in London, the *Observer*, echoing the global media from Paris to New York to Tokyo, insisted that to allow the city to fend for itself without "the entire world doing everything possible would be unpardonable." The paper had noted the dead, the ruin, and the homelessness, but it was "the finest fruits of the Renaissance . . . abandoned to decompose in the mud" that clinched the argument and would become the focus of the world's outrage and pity.

That same day, November 9, the weather turned against the city again. The sky lowered and grayed and the temperature fell. By noon it was bitterly cold. People said that the Arno might now freeze: it was already thick with the mud and refuse that was being dumped into it from every corner of Florence. There were still 18 million cubic feet of debris to be cleared from the streets, enough to dam the river to Leonardo's specifications. An old man with a pail, trudging back and forth across the Lungarno from the riverbank to the cellar he was bailing, chuckled, "It's a good thing we have the Arno" as he dumped another bucket into the stream.

Mayor Bargellini made his way on foot around the city that afternoon, past the lines of people queuing up for typhoid shots, and even down to Santa Croce, which was, after all, his *quartiere* too, despite the hotheads at the Casa. In the piazza, someone mentioned the *Crocifisso* yet again and, perhaps a little exasperated, Bargellini said, "Enough about Cimabue's poor Christ. Now we must think of the poor Christians."

Later, in his study, in his journal, alone in the night, he could still dream his Florentine humanist dreams: "We'll be free at last to remake [the city] on our terms, more beautiful than now—like it was once-upon-a-time! Like it was in our golden age."

A week after the flood, on Friday, November 11, young Giovanni Menduni's mother finally let him out of the house. She was going to the Casa del Popolo to volunteer on the breadline, one of a growing number of people from outside the neighborhood who wanted to help. That they did not come from the *quartiere* was not a problem, but that they did not belong to or support the Party often was. A debate was surging among the leaders of the Casa about whether the organization was losing its Communist identity. In the end Carlo and Daniela, who'd been putting people in positions of responsibility regardless of affiliation and who were now being criticized for it, walked out.

Giovanni and his mother were bourgeois, from the middle of the middle classes. Giovanni attended Florence's elite Pestalozzi academy—he was an able student if rather less well-off than most of his fellows—situated a few blocks east of the basilica. Cooped up at home and for days having had to listen to his elder brother's exploits in the disaster zone, he was eager to pitch in but also curious about the fate of his school. So Giovanni got himself a *rastrello*, propped it on his shoulder, and, leaving his mother at the Piazza dei Ciompi, set off for the Pestalozzi.

The Borgo Allegri and its adjacent streets were now cleared of mud although scarcely free of smaller debris—the Casa's own dented and mud-encrusted blue Fiat 500 had blown five tires in two days—but to Giovanni they looked like a battlefield, like Berlin after the war, not that he'd ever seen a war. One thousand houses in Santa Croce had already been condemned, and much of the rest were propped up with timbers, the walls plastered with mire and oil. He might have expected to smell powder and cordite, but the pervasive smell was sour where it was not sharp, a mix of dirt, petroleum, and rot. The army had succeeded in incinerating almost five thousand animal carcasses and tons of meat, but there was still the reek of rehydrated and now decomposing *baccalà*, the dried cod that was a staple of the Italian diet and of the poor in particular.

Giovanni traversed the mud-slicked steps of the Pestalozzi and made his way into the vestibule. Around the landing of the stairs he'd ascended each day for the last two years was a knot of furniture and enslimed jetsam, and standing nearby, as though presiding over it, a woman. Giovanni could not say if she was old or simply exhausted. Indicating his *rastrello*, he said he wanted to help. It had been his school after all. He'd come as soon as he could.

The woman spoke to him, flinging out her hands in irritation. "Can't you see there's nothing—nothing to do, to be done?" Giovanni thought he'd better leave. Outside the morning went on; the sunlight strong and cold, angling up the street from the east, past Azelide Benedetti's barred window two doors down from the school, the curtains hanging stiff with dried *melma*. He turned west, across the Piazza Santa Croce, and in the Via dei Benci found a shopkeeper who was willing to let him push some mud around the pavement with his *rastrello*.

Around lunchtime he went back to Piazza dei Ciompi. He and his mother walked toward the *centro*, toward the Duomo. Just beyond the Baptistry was the music store, hollowed out, the metal shutters over the windows and doors sucked inward by the water pressure; butted and nosed, perhaps, by the twenty thousand cars Giovanni's brother had told him were floating everywhere a week before.

Men were working inside the store, carrying sheet music and LPs out to the street. Giovanni went to look more closely, and he saw that, just then, four workers were wresting a mud-clotted crate out of the showroom. It was the Hammond B-3, *his* B-3. It was too big and too awkward to pass up the stairs and out the door easily, so the men simply shoved it through, battering the case, which was now split open. Giovanni could see inside it, see the ninety delicate "tonewheels" that gave the B-3 its inimitable sound, now sheathed in mud.

They got it outside and dumped it on the street, splayed with its wires and guts hanging out, alongside the other junk from the music store: horns and brass instruments plugged up with mud, guitars and violins swollen and split like melons. It was then that Giovanni understood the meaning of the flood: that this was how things ended up, this was how the world *is*. Never mind the money his mother didn't have: they could have just *given* him the Hammond ten days ago and everything would have been different, would have been better. This one beautiful object would have been saved and Giovanni himself would have been happy beyond measure. There still would have been a flood and of course that would still have been terrible, but this one small hope wouldn't have been lost, would have stayed true. It was a lesson in *lacrimae rerum*, the tears of things, that phrase Virgil had come up with for the *Aeneid* and taught Dante. They would be studying that in Latin at the Pestalozzi, if there had still been a Pestalozzi.

*T*he *angeli* were still pulling books out of the underworld of the stacks at the Biblioteca Nazionale, still removing the bindings, washing the pages, and hanging up the leaves on clotheslines in the boilerhouse at the railway station. Other *angeli* were stacking volumes and folios from the Archives of State under the arcade on the piazza of the Uffizi. You could hear music from someone's transistor radio—it was the Beach Boys, usually—and the angels needed music, just as they needed to stop and smoke a cigarette, not just to relax but to keep warm, heating themselves from inside out. It was always cold and always damp where they worked, and often where they ate and slept. There was, of course, a surfeit of Chianti dispensed from immense demijohns just as there was limitless talk and laughter. People fell in love: with art; with one another; with themselves, because how often did you get to be a hero, much less an angel?

For example, an art history student named Silvia Meloni was working in the Uffizi, wiping mud off pictures that had been set aside as insufficiently important to require expert handling. She swabbed at one for some time, and then she wiped it down until a bit more of the paint emerged, and then she exclaimed—perhaps only to herself, perhaps to the whole world—"This is the self-portrait of Velázquez!" And so it proved to be. Miracles were for the asking.

Across the river in the Oltrarno, Nick was counting his losses. He and Amy could manage without electricity and they'd never had heat. Their household and kitchen could cope with boarders like Art Koch and the usual passersby, even if their number seemed to swell each day. But Nick was supposed to have a show of drawings and woodcuts at the end of the month. It went without saying that it would have to be postponed, but there would probably be no work to show anyway: on November 4 most of Nick's art had been at the printer's being photographed for the catalog. The shop had been flooded up to the second floor, and even now the printer was still mucking out.

More likely than not, the work would be ruined, assuming it was found: he'd done half the drawings with a ballpoint pen on butcher's paper the previous year when he and Amy had been particularly short of cash. Last summer he'd managed to buy india ink and rag paper after he'd sold some work in America. Almost all the drawings were on the theme of Icarus. Nick had been dreaming about him, and in the dreams Icarus melded with other subjects and traditions: Annunciations, Depositions, and, most recently, Pietàs. Nick drew Icarus, dead and shattered, draped in the lap of a female figure, a mother, a lover, a god—you couldn't say. The image was only a shard of a dream Nick had had. But maybe it meant that Icarus wasn't just ambitious, foolish, or vain; maybe in his ruination Icarus's drowned and crumpled body warranted love, or at least pity.

A week after the flood the printer turned up with Nick's portfolio. He'd found it wedged between the ceiling and some pipes in his basement. The earlier drawings were indeed reduced to pulp, but the ones on rag paper were intact, albeit muddy. As was true of so much of the art that survived the flood, the Old Masters were never wrong about materials. Nick washed the drawings off, the mud lifted, and the images—perhaps a little depleted and weary—were still there.

In the drawings Nick had willfully mixed traditions—he was very big on the unconscious, the serendipitous chance or collision, the classical and the Christian swallowing each other's tails—and under the circumstances, who could object? Only the day before, Frederick Hartt had told another group of reporters that "there were two cities that occupy the most special place in the history of human civilization: Athens and Florence." So why not put Icarus and Mary together in a Pietà; why not make Icarus into the crucified Christ? Maybe that was precisely the art the moment called for, just as it called for the world's help. That was what Hartt had meant about Athens and Florence: "When something happens to one of them, all civilized people have a moral obligation to run to their aid."

With that final remark, Hartt flew home to America. He and Fred Licht, the art historian from Brown University who'd accompanied him to Florence, had been busy consulting with Ugo Procacci and when they arrived in New York they set about getting him what he needed most: expert restorers and money. Within two days, sixteen restorers headed by Professor Lawrence Majewski of New York University's Conservation Center were on their way to Florence. That same week they helped found a fundraising and coordinating organization, the Committee to Rescue Italian Art (CRIA), with Licht, his Brown colleague Bates Lowry, and Millard Meiss of Princeton's Institute for Advanced Study in charge in the United States and Myron Gilmore of I Tatti as their liaison in Italy.

Mayor Bargellini was meanwhile struggling with the third and fourth waves—he'd lost count—of the *angeli*, who now numbered well over a thousand: "What should we do with all these kids?" he pleaded, and found more railroad cars, dormitories, and spare rooms outside the city.

If there was no place to put the *angeli*, Ugo Procacci had found shelter for the art. He seemed to have recovered from the devastation so apparent to Hartt during the first week after the flood and was now marshaling the considerable wherewithal he'd exhibited when they'd met twenty-two years ago. Panel paintings would be sent to the Limonaia of the Palazzo Pitti; canvas paintings to the Accademia; sculpture and objets to the Palazzo Davanzati; and books to the Forte Belvedere.

Much had been accomplished in a little more than a week after the flood, and it had happened very quickly. Some people had done what they could and were moving on, or resting up before another tour of duty. David Lees had already left Florence on November 8, the Tuesday after the flood, to take a load of film and submit his expenses: 6,000 lire for high boots and 5,000 lire for cleaning his mud-spattered suit. The helicopter ride from Pisa had been free, courtesy of the army. He stocked up on film and returned to Florence on the eleventh and would stay for the rest of the month.

Franco Zeffirelli left for Rome that same day. He would edit, script, and score his film *Per Firenze*, "For Florence," in one week. To narrate it, he rounded up Richard Burton, with whom Zeffirelli had been filming *The Taming of the Shrew* at Cinecittà with Burton's wife, Elizabeth Taylor. Burton recorded the soundtrack twice, once in English for global distribution and again in Italian. He spoke no Italian but read from phonetically transcribed cards in a convincing accent and with visible, near wrenching emotion. Burton spoke of the recent landslide at Aberfan in his native Wales. Twenty-eight adults—almost as many as in Florence—had died. So too had over one hundred children. But Florence was worse, Burton said.

Such testimonies and appeals were, of course, just the beginning. Asked how much and how long the restoration of the artwork would take, Ugo Procacci estimated $32 million and twenty years. Conscious of the need to underline the gravity of the situation he allowed himself to be a little pessimistic. As it turned out, he was off by millions and by decades.

*I*n Santa Croce the disorder had taken on a certain order of its own: when supplies arrived, there was a flash of voices, a shock wave that went around the neighborhood, reporting that at this instant there was milk or bread or clothing or blankets. A line would form, like iron filings swarming around a magnet, and then when there was nothing left—there was never enough; someone always went without—the clot of persons would dissipate, and the quiet, the slow drip of Santa Croce would begin again until the next truck arrived.

And what of the river? By mid-November the level of the Arno had fallen back to normal, even a bit below average for the time of year; too low, in fact, to carry away the detritus that both nature and man had dumped into the riverbed. The Arno channel looked like a junkyard, heaped with mattresses, furniture, and tons of lumber, paper, and cars. Along the banks you might spy a rivulet of purses or shoes or a cascade of café chairs. All this was ugly or morbidly striking, even bizarrely beautiful: Dante's infernal ditch brought to life through a cornucopia of sullied consumer goods.

But it was also dangerous. City engineers repeated their earlier warning that dumping raised the floor of the riverbed and might cause the Arno to disperse the next flood even less effectively than it had on November 4. People rather than nature could make a deluge. Perhaps they'd even had a hand in the one that had just happened: on the weekend of November 13 the *Sunday Times* of London published an exclusive: "Our investigation has reached the conclusion that the disaster of the flood in Florence was made even more grave by a mass of water released from a hydroelectric dam." The newspaper claimed that at nine o'clock on the evening of November 3 ENEL opened the gates of the Levane dam "releasing five million cubic meters of water." It concluded that "this means that all the civic authorities knew that the flood would strike Florence at least eight hours before it happened."

ENEL had already done its own preliminary investigation and responded to the *Times* article the next day. You only had to do a little arithmetic, ENEL argued, to see that the charge was false: 250 million cubic meters of water had struck Florence, but the reservoirs had only ever contained 13 million, and even then the gates had never been completely opened. Moreover, there were now conflicting accounts about when or even if the supposed "mass of water" had been released. The residents of the village below the dams were a little fuzzy on the time they'd heard sirens or at what hour the flood first swept by.

Lorenzo, Ida, and the rest of the village would maintain they had every right to be a little confused on November 4: it was the middle of the storm, it was the middle of the night, and then it was total chaos. They were still picking up, not to say recovering their sanity. You could parse cubic meters until you were *impazzito*—driven mad—but they'd seen and heard what they'd seen and heard.

The villagers' story and all its kin, its vague but shapely logic and thrust toward tragedy and complicity, was more satisfying than the mathematics of ENEL. It was organic and whole. It possessed a kind of beauty. The calculations were something you could know, but the story was something you could believe.

It was the same with the rumors and recriminations about the jewelers on the Ponte Vecchio. Maybe they'd been warned early because the guard had been specifically instructed to issue a warning if the water rose any farther and had also been especially vigilant about floods on account of coming from Vajont. But it was also assuredly a conspiracy, conspiracy being one of the arts of Florence. It was a matter of smarts, information, and connections, the neural net of political economy. Capitalism Medici-style (and who was more a capitalist than a goldsmith or a jeweler?) was a higher form of awareness, the equal of religion and philosophy.

*A*lthough the streets were neither flooded nor engorged with mud, Florence was scarcely dry. The city had taken a soaking worthy of Noah and no one would quite shake the damp from their bones until spring, even as electricity and gas returned. An enormous quantity of the city's fuel oil had gone into the floodwaters, but most people in places like Santa Croce or Nick Kraczyna's neighborhood in the Oltrarno didn't have central heating anyway. You were better off, for once, with a *scaldino*.

Even then, much of Florence was literally moldering away. The pervasive damp fostered several varieties of mold, and within weeks walls all over the city were felted with white, green, and blue-gray spores. Mold fed on *melma*, rich in organic materials from the river and the sewers, and also on paint, especially the kind of colors and media used in traditional Florentine wall painting. Sustained by moisture and by the paintings themselves, the mold—it had a certain beauty, a soft, embracing patina—was eating artworks alive.

Nor would the water simply run off and the walls dry. A vast quantity had been absorbed into the ground (particularly in low spots like Santa Croce) and in the aftermath of the flood began to wick its way upward, carrying much of what was in the soil with it. Bricks and stucco were porous and behaved like a sponge. When underground water and damp surfaced under a building, they continued to rise through the masonry.

Moisture alone, together with the pervasive mold, could do tremendous damage to wall paintings. Fresco had an advantage in that the paint was part and parcel of the plaster to a certain depth, but in the presence of enough damp, the plaster surface itself would crumble. In the case of *secco*—color applied directly on dry plaster as Giotto had done in the chapels at Santa Croce—the paint simply blistered and flaked off.

The problem was exacerbated by dissolved salts, phosphates, sulfates, and nitrates: as the walls dried, these compounds migrated to the surfaces of both fresco and *secco*, forming crystals under the color that erupted and burst, carrying the paint away with them.

The problem was probably most grave in the refectory of Santa Croce, which, in addition to the *Crocifisso*, contained another major artwork, Taddeo Gaddi's immense frescoed *Cenacolo* on the west wall. Only its lower edge had been immersed on November 4, but it was now under a triple assault from moisture, mold, and salts, flayed from its wall by their crystallization. Santa Croce, in addition to being the dampest ground in Florence, was also especially rich in phosphates and nitrates: the soil beneath the basilica, the cloister, and the refectory were the repository of a seven-hundred-year accumulation of bones, the cadavers and skeletons of thousands of Franciscan brothers.

*A*t the Biblioteca Nazionale, Emanuele Casamassima had help, almost a surplus of it, and it was perhaps the most cosmopolitan volunteer rescue effort in history. But after nearly two weeks of excavating books and materials, Casamassima found himself in a position akin to Mayor Bargellini, puzzling out where he was going to find bed and board for the *angeli*. Thanks to Casamassima's own organizational skills and the seemingly spontaneous and unconscious efficiency of the angels, a tremendous quantity of items had been removed and relocated, and were now being washed and dried. All told, there would be around one billion leaves or sheets of paper to deal with, and the question of what to do with them next seemed suddenly to arise: Should torn and fragmented pages be somehow mended or sutured? Should oil and mud stains be bleached out, cosmetically restored, or left untouched? Should some or all of the millions of volumes be rebound? How did you balance the utilitarian needs of future readers and scholars against the integrity of books and manuscripts as aesthetic and historical objects? Assuming time and money were not infinite, was it more important to have a continuous collection of every newspaper published in Italy during the nineteenth century or a letter in Machiavelli's own hand? Casamassima realized that he simply didn't know. Nor did he have much time to consider the matter: mold fed even more eagerly on paper than paint.

No one knew more about paper, printed texts, manuscripts, and binding than a small group of experts in London and Oxford, and what the Americans were to artworks, the British would be to books. On November 25, three weeks after the flood, Casamassima called his counterpart at the British Museum, who in turn contacted Peter Waters of the Royal College of Art. The next day Waters, accompanied by the restorer Anthony Cains, arrived in Florence and they were later joined by Christopher Clarkson of the Bodleian Library, Oxford. They found Casamassima at the Biblioteca cooking lunch for the *angeli*.

The British spent two days watching and listening. The makeshift operation Casamassima had improvised worked much better than the British might have expected: books were being covered with sawdust and interleaved with blotting paper, which was good, but also, to their horror, with colored mimeograph paper, whose pigments leached into the pages the interleaving was designed to protect. Nor was it sufficient to let the interleaving absorb the moisture and then leave it inside the book: once it had blotted up water, it had to be replaced with a dry sheet, sometimes up to a dozen times. Otherwise the interleaving itself would turn the book into a sodden brick of pulp, which mold would quickly begin to consume. Fortunately, the weather had remained cold: warmer conditions would have fostered an epidemic of spores. But many books might decompose with no assistance from mold: the extremely fine-grained mud of the Arno had not only coated the pages but worked its way between the very fibers of the paper, abrading the leaves from both inside and out. Other books, impregnated and brittle with glue from their bindings, might simply crumble.

On the Tuesday after their arrival, the British had a meeting with Casamassima. They outlined all the problems they'd observed and suggested solutions. But at the end of the meeting they proposed something more radical. The entire salvage program of the Biblioteca to date consisted of washing, drying, and wrapping books in paper to await action to be determined at some future date, regardless of their condition. This was no way to run a library, Waters diplomatically suggested, backed up by the rather more acerbic, chain-smoking Cains. Why not aim to restore and rebind every book that needed it? Set up a kind of production line in which each volume would be disassembled, washed, dried, photographed, wrapped in fungicide-treated paper, and sent on to whatever specialist treatment it needed—repair or rebinding—and then reshelved as quickly as possible. Money could be found. *Angeli* could be taught the necessary skills. Waters would agree to stay not for a week but ten months, and then Cains would take over for what would prove to be three years. To the surprise of the British, Casamassima accepted the entire plan.

What was needed immediately was streamlining, organization, and more technical know-how. In short order the British devised and improvised forty stainless-steel washing stations, a program to chemically inoculate books against mold, and a visually coded card system—many *angeli*, for all their enthusiasm, spoke neither English nor Italian—to track each item and the treatment it required. The least damaged volumes needed washing—it took about four hours per book—but others needed their mud scraped away with surgical blades, one page at a time. A large number had to have each leaf pried apart from the next, stuck together by the dissolved and redried glue from their bindings, the entire volume now an impregnable block.

Drying was as problematic as washing, given the absence of electricity and fuel. Christopher Clarkson had taken charge of the railway station boilerhouse and its crew of *angeli* washing and drying pages. The ceiling of the building extended up several stories and ropes had been stretched across the vault in rows and layers, each a few feet higher in altitude than the next, folios of paper draped over them like densely packed Neapolitan laundry lines. When David Lees came to photograph the *angeli* in the boilerhouse for *Life*, the book leaves looked like an enormous flock of doves descending. Once, a door was left open, a gust of wind entered, and the papers did exactly that, sailing through the air and falling by the thousand.

In a week forty book restorers and binders were at work, backed up by several hundred *angeli*. Waters and his team were inventing the science and techniques they needed as they went along; they realized, for example, that it wasn't enough to sterilize a book and its wrapper against mold. The storage units and stacks in which it would be deposited also had to be sterilized, and so they sterilized the entire Biblioteca, not once but three times. The compounds and treatments for this and other problems were devised by Joe Nkrumah, a young chemist from Ghana by way of the British Museum. Nkrumah, his beard a nimbus of wiry hair, was as passionate about Florentine art and culture as any of the *angeli*. He would stay for almost seven years, working both in book conservation and in a lab funded by the Australian government to rescue and restore prints, engravings, and lithographs. He loved company as much as he did art, and soon he and Anthony Cains found their way to Nick and Amy's apartment in the Oltrarno.

To underwrite this and other projects the British would develop their own fundraising network: Zeffirelli's *Per Firenze* had premiered the previous week in London before Queen Elizabeth, raising $25 million. Meanwhile the American founders and organizers of CRIA were achieving extraordinary things—they would send Procacci his first check for $70,000 only twelve days after they'd established themselves. CRIA was freighted with *grandi signori*, drawn not just from the realm of art history and museums but from American business, politics, and high society: Jacqueline Kennedy agreed to serve as honorary chairwoman and Clare Boothe Luce and David Rockefeller were directors. CRIA was in a position to stage high-profile art auctions, fashion shows, and society galas and balls as well as secure bountiful media coverage, booking, for example, Marchese Emilio Pucci on the *Today* show to make a nationwide appeal on their behalf.

CRIA was officially launched with an announcement on November 28 in the *New York Times*, a full-page advertisement festooned with the names of the great, the powerful, and the chic (many of whom would be attending Truman Capote's legendary Black and White Ball that same night). For all their excesses—and how blameworthy were these if the result was the salvation of a large portion of Western culture?— they chose to place David Lees's simple image of Mary standing marooned on the mudflat inside Santa Croce at the center of their announcement. Lees and his employer, Clare Boothe Luce's husband,

Henry Luce of Time-Life, donated the rights to the photo to CRIA, and it, too, helped save Florence.

Or rather its art. The Paleys, Rockefellers, and Whitneys were not sending checks to the Piazza dei Ciompi and the Casa del Popolo. But the Casa was, in any case, winding down its activities. After a month, life was returning to normal in Santa Croce; to ordinary poverty, at least, where the basic provisions necessary to sustain life were in reach, most of the time. Sandra, Macconi, Federico, Carlo, Daniela, and the rest had done an extraordinary thing with no resources whatsoever beyond their sweat and passion, a small, briefly lived but transcendent work made *ex nihilo*. Now they could return to the perennial struggles of ideology and politics, capital versus the proletariat instead of the Arno versus the poor. The poor will always be with you, as the son of Mary—she of the embracing, futile gesture, blessing the mud—had once said.

*T*he Arno was running cold, cold enough to freeze. It had been nearly a month since the flood—the lights were on almost everywhere—but as happened every ten days or so, a fresh outbreak of rumors erupted, efflorescing throughout the city like the spores of the now pervasive mold.

On December 2 it began to rain and the river to rise. It never got any higher than ten feet below the Ponte Vecchio. But it was enough to make the rumors seem credible, even prophetic. By evening the roads out of town—some people already had their new Fiats—were clogged in response to a story that the dams had been breached, or were about to break, or one or another variant on the tale. Running alongside or under it—a bass line of dread as counterpoint to the hysteria—was the report that there'd been an outbreak of cholera.

The *angeli* had their own rumors, which tended to bear on the art they were rescuing. With tremulous conviction, an American student maintained that the floor beneath the *David* in the Accademia was buckling; that the towering statue was heeling over, on the verge of toppling. She'd seen it, or someone else had seen it and told her, or the superintendency knew it and didn't want anyone else to know it.

Perhaps these weren't mere rumors, loose words skylarking through the city or, more darkly, circling overhead like vultures. Maybe people, maybe even the press, were having visions and hearing voices, like madmen or saints. But almost none of these stories were true. David Lees had photographed the *David* twice since November 4, once a few days after the flood and again ten days later. The statue had stood impassively, the languid cocked wrist slack on the hip, the sling over the back, the whole body gathering itself to push back the flood by merely looming, depthlessly beautiful, over it. In Lees's first photograph there were only a few inches of water on the floor of the museum; in the second, a skin of tan dried mud.

In fact Procacci had arranged for a temporary reopening of Florence's museums on December 2, a kind of Christmas gift, as he'd described it, a return to normalcy designed precisely to militate against despair or panic. That afternoon, the Cimabue *Crocifisso*, supine in the Santa Croce refectory for four full weeks, was moved to the Limonaia of the Palazzo Pitti. People had been visiting it and photographing all that time, as though it were undergoing an extended lying in state. Now, after the deposition on November 6, would come the entombment. Twenty people carried the cross out to a flatbed truck and strapped it down. The truck set off, never faster than fifteen miles per hour. It crossed the river at the Ponte San Niccolò, and in the Piazza Ferrucci a woman dropped to her knees before it and made the sign of the cross.

The truck had to climb the hill to the Piazzale Michelangelo, past the viewpoint where Barbara Minniti watched her Zio Nello's library seem to sink into the Arno. Then it descended the serpentine slope to the Limonaia. The truck stopped on the road outside and the cross was raised up on grappling lines, almost silently. A meager rain fell. Procacci and Edo Masini, vested in their lab coats, sprayed the cross with Nystatin fungicide, sweeping up and down it like priests with censers.

They took measurements: the *Crocifisso* was still waterlogged, with a humidity level in the wood of 147 percent (normal would be about 18 percent), enough to almost double the weight and add three inches to its length. Then it was hoisted through the doors and laid down just beyond the chief restorer's office, glass-walled like a nurse's station in an intensive-care unit.

The Limonaia was a hothouse, constructed in order to furnish oranges and lemons to the Medicis and the grand dukes of Tuscany. It was one of those Florentine building projects that was less an edifice than a gesture, a demonstration that the mighty possessed the wherewithal to conjure up and enjoy citrus fruit in the dead of winter. Now Baldini had had the heat turned up for several weeks and the orange trees were dying or dead. That didn't bode well for the paintings, as it turned out. The whole notion of using the Limonaia was founded on its being potentially both a large, well-lit work space for the restorers and a kind of dehumidifying chamber for damp artwork. But even after improvements funded by CRIA, it was at once too hot and too moist, fostering excessively rapid drying on the one hand—fast enough to make panels crack and to harden Paraloid on their surfaces into an epoxylike varnish—and mold on the other.

Procacci's goal had been to move in everything destined for the Limonaia before Christmas, and he and Baldini managed it by December 18. More funds were coming from CRIA: in New York they'd auctioned off Picasso's *Recumbent Woman Reading* for $110,000 and the proceeds were on their way to Florence. In the New Year the real work of restoration could begin. Procacci and, more particularly, Baldini were still swamped, but soon they would be able to sit down and figure out how to proceed. The paintings, from the Cimabue to the obscure, unvisited Vasari *Last Supper*, were safe.

*M*ayor Bargellini was a devout Catholic, but he was not sure the Pope should come to Florence. The pontiff was a complicated figure for Italians, the beloved (or at least respected) head of their church but also the representative of an ancien régime that had crushed—often ruthlessly and cruelly—their aspirations to become a people and a nation. Even now, after Vatican II and the liberalizing pontificates of John XXIII and, now, Paul VI, the arrival of the Pope anywhere could have the quality of a state visit, the reception of a sovereign by a subjugated people.

So there would not be a Papal Visitation, but merely a visit by the Pope. He would look around, say a mass, and go home. But he would do it on Christmas Eve, bestowing an honor that normally belonged to Rome and St. Peter's upon Florence and the Duomo. The Pope wouldn't be deigning to honor Florence with his presence, but coming to pay tribute.

Christmas Eve was cold, almost bitterly so, but clear. Paul VI entered the city about nine o'clock, standing up in an open-topped black Mercedes. His first stop was at Santa Croce, where he was received by the mayor and the Franciscans of the basilica. He was then immediately to be driven to the archbishop's palace, but instead he descended into the crowd, shaking hands, patting cheeks, offering blessings, and in at least one case, exchanging a bear hug and a kiss with a burly laborer from the *quartiere*.

In those days there was little concern about the Pope's personal safety, but Bargellini didn't want things to get out of hand, particularly not in Santa Croce with its pride, resentments, and political volatility. Perhaps the Pope's instincts were surer than the mayor's: the crowd in the piazza swelled, almost pulsed, and there were boys hanging off Dante's statue at the heart of it all. It seemed they wanted the Pope, as much as they'd ever wanted bread, blankets, and shovels.

Finally they yielded him up, gave him back to the civic dignitaries and the Mercedes. At the Palazzo he and Bargellini exchanged gifts: a decorated copy of the Gospel of John for the Pope, a rare volume of Dante for the mayor. Then they moved to the Baptistry, where Paul VI put on his vestments and walked in procession to the Duomo, opened that night for the first time since the flood. At the end of the midnight mass, the Pope again departed from the agreed program. He asked to be brought the Gonfalone, the official city banner, the symbol of its independence, its emblem of defiance against outsiders, tyrants, and, yes, popes. Paul bestowed a papal medal upon it and then blessed it.

The Pope's last stop was supposed to be San Frediano, Santa Croce's Oltrarno twin in poverty. But after blessing the crowd there, he asked to be taken one more place. It was two o'clock in the morning and the Pope was due in Rome to say mass at St. Peter's at ten. But he wanted, he said, to go to the Limonaia, to see *la vittima più illustre*, the flood's "most illustrious victim," the Cimabue *Crocifisso*.

Ugo Procacci was located and brought to the Limonaia. The Pope asked him how the art was faring—what its prognosis was. They might have been standing in a hospital, in a ward crowded with lepers and cripples. Then Paul kneeled before the *Crocifisso* and prayed. He prayed very softly and in Latin, but Procacci made out the words *adoremus te*, "we adore you," the traditional prayer for Christmas, for the newborn Christ, offered to this broken Christ, this Christ not of the manger but of the tomb. He thought he saw the Pope weep.

Paul left Florence at about three in the morning, the coldest hour of the third shortest day of the year, fifty days after the flood. At dawn the city was sleeping. In an hour or so water would be boiled, *scaldini* stoked, Christmas dinners begun, bells rung, masses said. A little ice seemed to be forming on the margins of the river. The Pope was gone but the city was still blanketed with his presence, flocked and swaddled with his prayers and benedictions.

For all that, Florence would never be pious, at least not with the solemn, wizened-lipped piety of the morbidly devout. Of course Florence, being so lovely, was under God's protection, even after the flood, which itself must have been a mistake. God would come to his senses. Maybe he'd even apologize. And as for the river, some *vero fiorentino* had hung a stocking filled with charcoal on the Ponte Vecchio with a card that read *All'Arno che quest'anno è stato molto cattivo*, "For the Arno, who this year was very naughty."

When John Schofield was a boy in England, his father read him Vasari instead of bedtime stories. His father's father was Walter Elmer Schofield, the American Impressionist, and his uncle was Peter Lanyon, a leading member of Ben Nicholson and Barbara Hepworth's St. Ives artists' colony. Uncle Peter also knew Mark Rothko, Robert Motherwell, and Franz Kline in New York. John grew up believing that nothing—it went without saying; what else was there?—mattered more than art. In the manner of Vasari's Renaissance artists, John took up both architecture and the fine arts, and it was while studying painting at the Slade in London that he met Susan Glasspool.

Susan had just decamped to Florence on a postgraduate painting scholarship at the Accademia when the flood struck, and John wrote to ask what there was that he might be able to do there. She wasn't sure: the city was full of young people more or less like themselves, and they didn't so much get jobs or perform formally set tasks as simply turn up—crop up, really, like mushrooms. But John needed to go to Florence as some young men had once needed to go to war against the Kaiser or Hitler. It took him until December to organize the money and the time off, and he arrived the night before New Year's Eve.

Susan's place was full, and Susan herself was just then falling in love with an Italian classmate. They'd met in the canteen at the Accademia, where the authorities gave out free meals to the mud angels. So John found a room in Fiesole and, two days later, a bunk in a dank hostel. The other *angeli* were noisy, carousing at all hours, drunk and obnoxious. It was hard to believe they were serious about anything, least of all art and beauty.

After two days of trying unsuccessfully to volunteer his services, a girl he'd met told him she'd heard that help was wanted on the other side of the river in the Limonaia. She was going and John crossed with her to the Oltrarno. On the nether side of the Palazzo Pitti, they ascended through a gate, two doors, a vestibule where a group of laborers were tearing into lunchtime bread and wine, and finally through a sort of airlock. They'd arrived in an office overlooking an enormous hall, sheathed in polyethylene, threaded with shiny new air ducts, illuminated by a white, sterile glare, the whole place echoing, faintly thrumming, vastly empty.

This was the Limonaia, remade with a tenth of a million of CRIA's dollars, now sheltering some several hundreds of priceless—or, if you had to place a value on them, perhaps a hundred million dollars' worth of—artworks. Descending, John felt alone with them, entombed with them in this isolation chamber; and there, just down the steps to his right, was Cimabue's *Crocifisso*, a presence, almost a person, that it now seemed he had been brought here to meet.

In fact John was not alone, but merely blinded, disembodied, and aloft in a bubble of awe. The girl was talking to a man in an elegant suit—slight, wearing glasses, but formidable by virtue of a reserve of specialized knowledge of a very powerful kind. Maybe he was the attendant spirit, the magus, of the Cimabue, the keeper of the gate to its world.

He spoke no English, or deigned not to speak it. John and the girl came to understand that he was called Dottore Baldini, and that he might have something for John to do, and perhaps something for the girl—John noticed she was pretty—too. Baldini had lovely hands; he radiated *autorità*.

John was put on the mold detail. He couldn't say what had been done with the girl. His supervisor would be another *dottore*—they were all *dottori*, although it seemed that Baldini was the archdoctor—named Puccio Speroni, younger and much more approachable than Baldini himself. Only Speroni was allowed to work on the painted surfaces of the artworks, but John would apply something called alchyl-dimethyl-benzyl-ammonia to the back of the panels. He'd be doing it alongside an art history graduate student from San Niccolò, Bruno Santi.

John wanted (as he'd wanted for the last three days, since he'd stepped off the train) to get to work and he kept at it until the night watchmen made him leave. He and Santi talked: Bruno told him that his father's studio had been wiped out by the flood and there'd been no insurance; that he himself was still hoping to finish his study of Neri di Bicci, but maybe he wouldn't be able to; maybe he'd have to go to work for his father, to extricate them all from the mess the flood had made of their lives.

For those first hours and into the next day, John was agape: here he was, in the Palazzo Pitti, rescuing art he'd read and dreamed about since he was a child, working in a state-of-the-art restoration facility under one of the most eminent art historians in Florence. But then, sometime into the third day, he felt doubt, a sense that not everything was as it should or could be. He'd been dutifully tending the panel paintings he'd been assigned, waiting for a crack at the Cimabue, and it seemed to him incongruous that in most cases the backs of them were still encrusted with damp mud, a perfect medium for culturing mold. Why bother to lavish attention keeping the front of each piece free from spores when you were, in effect, letting mold run riot at the back? Why install an elaborate dehumidification system when the artworks were still swathed in the muck that had made them damp in the first place?

The next day John was allowed to work on the *Crocifisso*, or rather under it. Although the Cimabue was the showpiece of the entire facility—Baldini had it positioned at the front so the press could get at it more easily—it too was sheathed with mud on the back, not to mention carpeted with black, blue, and pink mold. The problems were exacerbated by the cross's steel wall mount, still fastened to the back of the panels, which prevented him and Bruno from applying their fungicides to large areas of its underside. John brought his concerns to Speroni, who he supposed reported them to Baldini, although Baldini made no mention of the matter. John took that as a kind of consent by default to proceed as he'd proposed: to get all the mud off the cross and then find a way to inject fungicide into the inaccessible spots.

From that day, John made himself at home under the cross, took shelter there in a clubhouse or camp where he was joined by Bruno

Santi and sometimes even by Speroni, who was proving to be an extremely easygoing supervisor, more a contemporary than a boss. They drank tea and smoked to keep warm and devised plans to save the *Crocifisso*, even to restore it. Speroni said the work would likely be done by Gaetano Lo Vullo from the Laboratorio, since he was the best restorer Baldini had at his disposal. Regardless, no one from outside was going to get their hands on it. There'd been talk of filling in the lost sections with white and then perhaps sandwiching a sheet of Plexiglas over it with the original details stenciled on it. John suggested that this was worse than no solution at all.

John could be a little zealous, *un inglese un po' impertinente*. But he worked as late as they'd let him, usually until eight in the evening. Sometimes he had the whole Limonaia to himself and he had the chance to look at the technical records and documents. The cross was indeed drying out, but in bursts, the humidity dropping precipitously over Christmas and then rebounding in the New Year. The treatments for mold had also been recorded, including those made by John.

The data were meant to indicate a kind of progress, proof that things were getting better; that the cross and its companions in the Limonaia were healing. But it didn't seem that way to John. The mold came back every day, not just on the back, but on the paint on the front, the precious remnant of Cimabue's brush that Baldini himself was supposed to be monitoring. The black mold in particular was almost impossible to eradicate: John brushed on his chemicals and twelve hours later it was back, invulnerable, mocking him.

Spending so much time around and under the cross, John knew it better than anyone; or he felt he did, felt its dampness, its swollen, twisted limbs, its leprous skin, the pain and shudders running through his own body. Now, after a week in the Limonaia, he saw the *Crocifisso* was cracking. Fissures were erupting upward through the wood. It was as though the Cimabue were shifting, flexing itself, imperceptibly flailing on its bed of scaffolding, tearing itself apart with the effort. And no one seemed to be noticing except him.

The cross, of course, received constant attention, but not the kind it really needed: reporters and photographers came almost every day, the office door flapping open with another gale of superheated air of exactly the kind that John believed was causing the damage. The week he'd noticed the cracks, an athletic-looking man—apparently English, but speaking Italian like a native—took pictures for two days. He was supposed to be from the most important magazine in America.

The day after the photographer left, Baldini came in to do his afternoon inspection, his rounds of the ward and its two hundred fifty patients. John steeled himself and approached the *dottore*. He spoke in stammering, childish Italian, explaining what he'd seen under the cross: the cracks, the mold he couldn't treat because he couldn't reach it. Baldini stood listening, unperturbed, steely in his faint amusement, not exactly imperious; or perhaps he was imperious, this being his empire.

John had an idea to get at the inaccessible mold behind the metal frame: he could buy a perfume atomizer from a *farmacia*, fill it with fungicide, and puff the vaporized chemical into the unreachable spots. Baldini told him to go ahead, and John pressed his luck a little further: he told Baldini about the cracking and proffered his theory to explain it. Every time the office door next to the cross opened, a blast of dry, hot air blew against it, defeating the steady, slow dehumidification process the cross was supposed be undergoing. What made matters worse, John pushed on, was that while the heating and dehumidification plant CRIA had provided was quite effective in the center of the room, the effects dissipated toward either end, at one of whose extremes the cross was now resting. John didn't say it ought to be moved—his Anglo-Saxon impertinence wouldn't go quite that far, not with Baldini—but the implication was clear. Baldini decided the two of them should hang a sheet of polyethylene between the office and the Cimabue to fend off the gusts from the opening of the door; and so they did, Baldini's suit seeming miraculously to evade any spot or crease despite the effort.

That night, at dinner at Ottavio's in the Via del Moro, John and Bruno talked politics. They agreed about everything, a consolation to John who a few hours before had despaired of being understood by anyone in Italy. All of them except Bruno, it seemed, were satisfied by half measures, a patch here, a dab there. For all their talk about their precious Cimabue, their tears and hand-wringing, John sometimes felt, under the cross, brushing, scraping, and spraying, that the weight of the whole thing rested on him.

*J*ohn Schofield had a week left in Florence. Then his money and time would run out. The weather had turned bitter and ice was edging farther out into the river channel. Downriver, beyond Pisa and the delta, Shelley's storming Tyrrhenian Sea was still pitching detritus from the flood up onto the beaches; trees, of course, but also the odd incongruous *natura morta*, still lifes: a shoe, a café chair, a demijohn filled with sand and red wine. Now too there was a final death toll: in the province of Tuscany, 121; in Florence, 33. There were also six people missing. In Florence, of course, no one believed any of this. It was worse: it had to have been worse.

Every day John came into the Limonaia and every day there was mold on the *Crocifisso*. It had been black mold for a while, but now the white mold was back. Maybe it was the weather; or maybe each mold preferred a different component of the cross—wood, gesso, pigments of one shade or another, a favorite color as anyone might have a favorite color. He was not optimistic about what would happen once he left, but he hoped his absence would only be temporary. CRIA was going to give Baldini grant money to hire people to do the work John had been doing: there would be no point in finding someone new and untrained when they already had him—he who'd spotted so many problems, who took such initiative. He'd spoken to Speroni several times about coming back, and he assumed he'd talked to Baldini; that they'd see what could be done and be in touch.

In that last week he and Bruno went to see some of the artworks John had always wanted to see in Florence, but until now had been too busy to visit. They went to Santa Maria Novella and Santa Croce, using Baldini's name to get past the guards. In the refectory at Santa Croce, he saw some mold at the bottom of the Gaddi *Cenacolo* that must not have been noticed. He'd remember to tell Dottore Baldini about that.

John looked at the place where the *Crocifisso* had hung, the sawn-off, rusting stumps of the iron that had supported it. He supposed they'd bring the cross back when they'd done whatever it was they decided on: leave it a ruin, fill in the lacunae with white or black, cover it with plastic, or even paint in the missing bits. Regardless, he imagined a lot of people would come to see it someday.

For all Baldini's asperity, hauteur, and rumored womanizing—John had heard reports from female *angeli*—the *dottore* arranged some special favors for John and Bruno that final week. The day before John was due to leave, Baldini gave them the key to a room in a far wing of the Pitti where Donatello's *Maddalena* was now being stored. The room was pitch-dark and unheated, and the *Maddalena* lay on her back in a far corner, a thread of light across her body from a crack in a shutter.

John and Bruno switched on the single overhead bulb and made their way toward her. Whoever was minding the sculpture (assuming anyone was) had put a swath of white paper underneath to catch the flakes of gesso, polychrome, and splinters falling off her. It looked—

the light was too poor to be sure—as if they'd gotten most of the oil off. From the waist down, she was swaddled in rice paper. Her thighs were cracked, cleaved in two places as though by a hatchet.

He knew he shouldn't, but John touched her. She was cold, colder than the room, cold as ice or damp stone. He put his hand over her hand. Her hands, unlike her face, were young; her fingers delicate, longer than his. There was a crevice where her collarbone met her neck and John put his fingers into it. That was colder still, the hollow where the sheath of her flesh met her old bones. Her eyes were blank and staring. She'd been ready for the flood: it hadn't fazed her. She'd drowned long before.

The next day Speroni let them put Nystatin directly onto the front—previously off-limits to nonprofessionals—of the *Crocifisso*. There was mold along the edges that no one had treated since they'd brought it here in December. Bending down close to work, John could see Cimabue's brushwork through the veil of the rice paper, the green-gold edge he and his assistant—Vasari had said it was Giotto, hadn't he?—had laid down around the body of Christ. Then he checked the back again: there was, of course, mold, as there was every day. He wondered who would take care of it after he left. He wondered if he was being derelict in leaving Florence. He couldn't imagine anyone else would bother.

His train left that night. At eight he'd met Bruno one last time on the Ponte Vecchio, and they'd walked to the station. John had done his bit for Florence. People in his family had even died for art's sake. His uncle Peter had taken up flying gliders, and the sensation of flight—silent, as though borne on his own wings—poured into his canvases until it seemed he surely needed to fly in order to paint. One day he crashed badly on the coast of Cornwall and died of his injuries, broken like the fellow in the myth.

Baldini never did get in touch with John about coming back. He had hundreds of artworks to tend, and Florence was full of young people who wanted to save one or another of them. But on January 17, the day after the boy had left, Baldini rechecked the data on the Cimabue. It seemed things were turning around: the humidity had dropped 7 percent since they'd last measured. The cross was finally drying, evenly and steadily. Why, just now, no one could say. But soon they could begin.

*B*y the end of January, Procacci and Baldini had sixty restorers working for them together with an incalculable number of *angeli*. Forty of the restorers were Italian, six British, and between two and four each from the United States, Germany, Scandinavia, Switzerland, Czechoslovakia, Poland, and Russia.

The British dominated the salvage effort at the Biblioteca Nazionale, but Joe Nkrumah, the Ghanaian—perhaps the only Ghanaian in Florence—was often the most visible and ubiquitous figure. At the railway boilerhouse, Nkrumah was supervising three binders and eight apprentices plus forty-two general workers and double that number of *angeli*. Even now, five truckloads of books arrived each day, and it seemed there would always be an infinite supply: Casamassima figured there were 1.3 million items to deal with, not to mention 8 million cards from the catalog, without which the Biblioteca was no longer a library but a chaos, a black hole of damp paper.

There was, for the moment, sufficient money: the British Art and Archives Rescue Fund had raised £115,000 to date, primarily through Zeffirelli's *Per Firenze*. But with the books, the issue was never just money, nor was it precisely labor. Book conservation, which up to now had consisted of a handful of artisan bookbinders in England and a few other places, was being more or less invented on the fly in the boilerhouse and at the Biblioteca by Waters, Cains, Clarkson, and Nkrumah. That in itself was a challenge, but the greater challenge had the features of a conundrum you might encounter in higher mathematics or physics: given a nearly infinite quantity of books—of pages and words—and a finite number of conservators, space, and time, would there ever be an end point, a time when the job would be done, or even a point of equilibrium, where input and output would be in balance?

Waters and his colleagues were at most forty years old, Nkrumah twenty-five. He'd begun his working life at the age of six in Accra, rising at three A.M. to go down to the beach to unload the fishing boats, afterward peddling newspapers in the street, and then selling yams for his mother. Between times, he'd go to the British colonial school. Work, he knew, was endless—that was life—but a single task was not; not until now, not until this one. He'd guessed it would go on for years, maybe a decade. The *angeli*—scarcely more than teenagers, for whom a short hitch like John Schofield's was a long time—couldn't even conceive of it.

The Florentines were used to thinking in centuries. Time passed very quickly, or seemed not to move at all, in the manner of trains rolling off from a station in opposite directions, the future stalemated by the past in a tug-of-war. It could make you take the longer view or render you shortsighted. In March Eugene Power, who'd made a fortune with University Microfilms in Ann Arbor, Michigan, offered to microfilm every single book in the Biblioteca Nazionale—the ultimate insurance policy against future disaster—gratis, for art's sake. Casamassima, who had been so receptive to the British book restorers, turned him down. There were mysteries in Florence that surpassed both reason and art.

On February 24 there was, however, some clarification of the role of the dams on November 3 and 4. Four ENEL employees were indicted for falsifying records, but ENEL itself continued to maintain that the dams had played no role in the flood. This was conceivable. The engineers and watchmen said they'd altered the logbooks to make sure nothing could be misinterpreted, not because they'd done anything that required covering up. It was a matter of appearances, of adjusting the ratio of shadow to light, of managing the chiaroscuro. Anyone could understand it and would have done the same.

*T*he *Crocifisso* of Cimabue was continuing to dry and shrink, and the mold had abated since January, almost miraculously. But the rice paper *velinatura* covering the painted surface had been applied when the cross was still soaked, and now the paint—adhering to the rice paper—was in danger of distorting or peeling away from the gesso and canvas underneath it as the dimensions of the cross shifted.

The cross was at war with itself, the wooden body wrenching and pulling away from its painted skin. From one point of view, it seemed imperative to save the painted image, with or without the wood underneath it, to amputate the afflicted part that was endangering the picture. Thinking aesthetically, in the mode of Berenson, Forster's "viewy young men," or many museum curators, the *Crocifisso* consisted essentially of its painted surface—or not even its physical surface but an essentially disembodied phenomenon, an impression received and reconstituted in the mind of the viewer. Yet the *Crocifisso* was assuredly physical, both a painting and a sculpture, a painting of Christ placed on a sculptural cross. On the raised tilted wedge that contained the head and halo of Christ, the painting erupted from its two dimensions to become three-dimensional, not quite panel or crucifix. Cimabue's creation was no simple canvas to be hung on a wall, but a large and heavy complex of different materials and media. As a restoration problem, it was formidable.

Florence had been dealing with the conservation of its own artworks for centuries and restorers had at one time taken extraordinary liberties with the pieces under their care, not just cleaning them but brushing on concoctions to brighten them up or, alternatively, to add "patina." They'd repainted both missing and even perfectly intact sections with an eye to "improving" them. Now such interventions seemed an outrage to the integrity of both the artist and the artwork, which surely deserved to survive in its authentic form, the one intended by its original creators and audience.

With that in mind, *restauro* had become a good deal more sensitive, perhaps at times to a fault. Under this newer approach the aim was not only to conserve the artwork but to keep it as close as possible to a hypothetical "mint" condition: its state as it left the studio, exactly as the artist intended, unaffected by subsequent change or mishap over time, save the natural accretion of patina. That meant, in many cases, not simply maintaining it, but undoing the work of earlier restorers: removing misguided "improvements" and any kind of overpainting that attempted to replace or replicate lost or damaged paint.

In some paintings, however, where larger areas—whole faces and bodies—had been lost and repainted, the removal of such accretions resulted in there not being much left to look at, a loss not just of detail but of recognizable figures and even subject matter. At the end of the process, you undoubtedly had an "authentic" remnant of the work, but not the work itself, whose original appearance had been lost to whatever mishaps and inevitabilities time had imposed upon it. This was perhaps good archeological practice—displaying the bones and broken pottery exactly as they'd been found at the excavation site—but what did it have to do with *art*, with seeing the beauty and transcendent value in these works that were supposed to make them worth looking at in the first place?

In fact the rationale for most of the art of Cimabue's and Giotto's time had not been aesthetic but liturgical, didactic, or devotional. The accretions in such work might have nothing to do with "improvement" but rather with allowing it to continue to serve the function for which it had been made. A crucifix or Madonna was, in the mind of Cimabue, Duccio, or Giotto, above all an aid to prayer and worship. *Restauro* in the name of aesthetics could conflict not only with historical truth but also with religious faith.

Procacci's counterpart in Rome, Cesare Brandi of the Istituto Centrale per il Restauro, was perhaps the first person to attempt a theory— a set of first principles—that might govern a more sensitive *restauro*, and in particular the problem of the "gap," lacunae or heavily damaged spots in an artwork in which part of the image had been lost. The gap both was and was not a part of the work: in one sense, it was a deficiency, a loss, but in another sense it became part of the artwork in the way that a scar does a body, a piece of its history if not of its original essence. To fill a gap was to falsify that history, but to leave it untreated was to falsify the work's soul, the artist's intent, the life of its meaning.

Brandi's solution was a kind of neutral inpainting, designed neither to hide nor to highlight the gap, called *tratteggio*, "hatching," the infilling of gaps with lines or cross-hatching in neutral tones based on the color of the intact surrounding painted surface. From a distance, the eye would fill what was missing, but close up the gaps would still be subtly but clearly gaps. The integrity of both art and history would be respected.

Not everyone was persuaded. Florence versus Rome was a perennial rivalry going back to Dante, and it would prove to be so in the field of art restoration. Ugo Procacci saw Brandi's point, but he thought the logic of *tratteggio* did a little surreptitious inpainting of its own. You couldn't simply dodge the whole engine of history or fudge the fact that Brandi's modern restorer, the "neutral" *tratteggiatore*, would always and necessarily impose his own personal, time-bound preferences—his brushstrokes—on the artwork. Brandi and Procacci had disagreements about both the theory and practice of *restauro*. But provided neither encroached on the other's realm—and if Italy contained half the significant art in the West and Florence contained half of that, there was plenty for both of them—they could coexist by ignoring one another.

Unlike Casamassima of the Biblioteca, where the British had been given much of the authority over the restoration work, Procacci and Baldini had complete charge of the rescued art. Americans like Frederick Hartt knew the history of Florence's art as well as anyone, but no one at CRIA could claim to possess similar expertise—never mind experience—in restoration. Hartt, it went without saying, both liked and trusted Procacci, and felt he had been to Hell and back to save his city's heritage, two times over. Hartt's fellow board members had no reason to doubt him, although for all of them Baldini remained an unknown quantity. But CRIA would adopt a mostly hands-off approach beyond insisting on an adequate accounting of the funds it was disbursing.

That bookkeeping included knowing which art its money was being spent on. There was an "adoption list" of artworks on which CRIA funds could be spent, and obviously not every piece in Florence could be on it. Aesthetic judgments unavoidably got jumbled up with financial ones, as they had since the days of BB: the larger the number of famous or prestigious works CRIA could claim to be rescuing, the more funds it could raise from the public. In theory this should have meant that the money raised by promoting the masterpieces CRIA was saving would underwrite their less celebrated artistic kin, but in practice it seemed only to increase the pressure to find and repair more masterpieces. People wanted their money spent on something important, on the work of certifiable geniuses.

CRIA's adoption list therefore had to be periodically trimmed of lesser, inessential, or unappealing art. The first deletions were made in April 1967, four months after the flood. Among the artworks that failed to make the cut was a "tavola, c. 1546, loc. Santa Croce: *L'Ultima Cena* di Giorgio Vasari."

On May 15, 1967, Nick Kraczyna finally got his show. It was hung at the Casa di Dante, a block off the Piazza del Duomo, the physical and symbolic heart of Florence. The night of the flood—the night he'd gone to bed at three in the morning, imagining that the roar of the Arno was no more than a strong wind—he'd been working on a Pietà of Icarus, and that too was in the show. So were the rag paper drawings the printer had found crushed against his ceiling.

Among those was Nick's *Requiem in D Minor for Icarus*. He'd made the drawing using an extremely fine nib to produce hairlines and a maze of cross-hatching—*tratteggio* in a different mode than Brandi's—more etched than drawn. The effect was of something woven, a fabric with a whorl of bodies and limbs at the center. It might have been an image of the flood—junk and flotsam, eddies and spouts, death and consolation—prior to the flood, in the mode of Leonardo's deluge drawings. But at the center of it, in the lap of the Madonna, there was rest: requiem, *requiescat in pace*; the promise that this was not the annihilation of death but mere sleep. Except for the fact it was drawn a year beforehand, you might have imagined this was Nick's commentary on the flood and the spring that was just now following it.

Amy and Nick's baby daughter, Anna—who had been with them, in utero, on the trembling Ponte Santa Trinità that day of November 4—

had been born just before the opening. Now they were moving house, from their cold-water aerie near Santo Spirito to a stone house up the hill beyond the Porta Romana, a long way from the Arno. They'd have to furnish it, and for a moment the memory returned of the flotilla of antiques they might have netted coursing down their street on November 4. But they'd found two nice leather sofas. Of course, like so many things in Florence, they needed a little help, some restoration. But Joe Nkrumah conjured up something in his lab, and, once it was applied, like everything he touched, the sofas were practically good as new.

*B*etween January and May 1967, David Lees had been back three times, first to the Limonaia—Procacci and Baldini's "Painting Hospital," as the editors in New York were going to call it—in January, again in February, and finally in May to shoot an additional feature on the restoration's progress to date. After he'd finished at the Limonaia, he went to the Palazzo Davanzati, where Donatello's *Maddalena* had been moved from its storeroom in the Pitti.

David found her laid on her back, tended by a sculptor named Pellegrino Banella. He was clad in a white coat, working under a spotlight, looking through a pair of microscope lenses with a tiny awl in his hand, bent over the *Maddalena*'s head in the manner of a dentist. Her face, set in its haggard rictus, seemed to be imploring the sculptor to stop; her left arm was raised, those long fingers John Schofield had compared to his own about to seize Banella's wrist.

Banella's work on the *Maddalena* would prove to be a situation in which the *restauro* would not only bring an artwork back to its preflood condition but perhaps even much closer to the way it looked when it left Donatello's studio. For as long as anyone could remember— certainly before Ruskin if not Vasari—the *Maddalena* had been considered a monochrome sculpture, the wood ranging in color from dark umber to ebony to black. But that assumption was washed away in the course of Banella's meticulous deep cleaning. The *Maddalena* was, in fact, a polychrome, scarcely gaudy, but undeniably tinted in a range of terra-cotta and flesh tones. The dirt and residues of seventeenth- and eighteenth-century restorers' chemical concoctions had dissolved to reveal Donatello's *Maddalena* rather than history's. She was still penitent but also redeemed. Life had been restored to her flesh as well as her soul.

When she was finally put on exhibition three years later, the *Maddalena* would be a triumph for both the Superintendency and for CRIA. And as things stood now, in May 1967, you might have imagined it would be one of many. CRIA's efforts were yielding both attention and cash; its chairman, Bates Lowry, curated a special exhibition, "The Italian Heritage," while Jackie Kennedy's favorite designer, Valentino, staged a benefit fashion show, and when they were done CRIA had raised $1.75 million to date. Such success redounded not only to the restoration work in Florence, but to CRIA's board. At the end of the year Lowry was named a curator of the Museum of Modern Art and six months later was appointed its director, the most visible museum post in New York.

The progress thus far had been splendid, and if you doubted it, there were David Lees's photos of white-coated restorers at work in the Limonaia in their "Painting Hospital." But while the Limonaia looked impressive, photographs could not capture all the details, nor record the gradual deterioration in its operations over the last few months. During the summer of 1967 CRIA's board received a confidential report that confirmed everything John Schofield had sensed earlier in the year about the Limonaia, and much worse.

To begin, the building was filthy and infested with crawling and flying insects. And while a technically advanced dehumidification plant had been installed the previous December, there was neither heat nor, with Florence's customary infernal summer weather coming on, air-conditioning. The artworks were suffering, but, through the winter and cool spring, so were the staff. Colds and respiratory infections had become almost epidemic, and aside from the man-hours lost to sick days, people didn't want to come in for fear of catching or aggravating something, not to mention plain dislike of the chill.

If they did come in, there was no guarantee they'd be paid. CRIA had been sending money for their wages, but the money wasn't getting disbursed: April's paychecks hadn't been issued until May 20. The pay was scarcely lavish to begin with: 700 lire (a little over $1) per hour for the laborers and the *angeli* who'd been hired on and up to 1,100 lire (about $1.75) per hour for trained restorers. As a final insult to almost half of the staff, foreigners were paid 200 lire less per hour than their Italian counterparts. Volunteers and restorers from abroad were expected to be not only *angeli* but martyrs.

Bad morale of such magnitude might have prompted a mutiny but for the fact there was rarely any senior personage present against whom to revolt. Speroni, whose easygoing manner John Schofield had found congenial, was nominally in charge, but pretended in effect not to be: when asked to make a decision or issue instructions, he demurred, saying he really knew nothing about restoration or art outside his own ambit. But there was no one else to go to: one much esteemed and experienced restorer had been told that he could not approach Baldini (whose visits were increasingly infrequent and brief) directly, but only through an intermediary. The *impertinente* Schofield hadn't realized quite how cheeky he really was.

The report laid the blame entirely on what it acidly called "the troika" of Baldini and his two chief restorers at the Laboratorio, Masini and Lo Vullo. There were further absurdities—one pair of tweezers and one lamp to be shared by three restorers—but one grave and overarching problem: art wasn't being saved or even being protected from further degradation. Staff were either sick, slacking off, or quitting, and no replacements would be hired who were not considered reliable and loyal by the troika. In any case, the word was out: the Limonaia was a dirty, cold, thankless place to work and no sane restorer in Florence would now willingly take a job there.

It might be imagined that Baldini, directly or through Procacci, would be told that this state of affairs was unacceptable and be made more accountable. But Baldini was a moving target, always one step ahead: the Limonaia, to be sure, was a disaster, but Baldini was already converting buildings at the Fortezza da Basso, the huge fortress near the railway station, using funds under his rather than CRIA's control. He'd shortly pack up the Limonaia and move the entire operation there, miles from the prying eyes of CRIA's office at the Pitti.

Throughout the autumn letters came from New York insisting that Baldini make the nature of what he called his "consulting" for CRIA clearer; detail his "moonlighting" on who-knew-what; list his hours more precisely; and generally make the full scope of his activities known. Again and again New York implored Florence to get Baldini under control through the intercession of Procacci, but Procacci couldn't or wouldn't do this. He and Baldini were, if not joined at the hip, comrades in arms in the rescue of Florence's art: that summer of 1967, *National Geographic* printed a fanciful, corny reimagining in pastel of the two of them salvaging paintings in the Uffizi as the rising waters swirled around them. They were a heroic and, now, iconic duo.

Not everyone was so impressed or malleable. Leonetto Tintori, perhaps the most eminent restorer in Florence, let it be known that if Baldini wasn't reined in, he'd stop cooperating with him and the Superintendency. But by the end of the year, Procacci, far from restraining Baldini, named him director of the new and largely independent Laboratorio at the Fortezza, with authority over most of the restoration in Florence, now even freer from anyone's interference, including Procacci's.

Procacci himself seemed to be losing his touch. His unself-consciously fervent love of art and Florence—an almost Franciscan compassion—that had earned and sustained his staff's loyalty and respect was wearing away. At a meeting held on the first anniversary of the flood to thank and salute the various *angeli*, workers, and restorers for their labor, Procacci failed to so much as mention the entire sculpture and polychrome team based at the Palazzo Davanzati. If it wasn't a snub—and conditions at Davanzati were at least as spartan as at the Limonaia—it was an extraordinary omission that was also utterly out of character. Who, of course, knew what the flood had really done to Procacci, especially in those first few days when he'd been so fragile, had seemed to be coming apart; who could say what it was still doing to him? On a normal day, before the flood, he bore the daily responsibility for what many people would say was the ark of Western civilization. And then there had been the flood to deal with. Maybe if you were humane enough to want to do the first job, you were insufficiently hardened to do the second. But somehow Procacci had found the strength—perhaps he found it in Baldini, for all of people's complaints—even if he'd lost a little of his instinct for weeping or saying thank you. Maybe that gap couldn't be restored.

8

*B*y June 1968 the humidity inside the Cimabue *Crocifisso* was down to 25 percent after almost a year and a half in the Limonaia. It had shrunk an inch across the foot of the cross. It was time to move it to the Fortezza, time to get down to business, or at least to begin to think about it.

At the Fortezza a room had been prepared in which the ambient humidity would be maintained at the same level as in the Limonaia, albeit at a higher temperature. But within three months of the move, the cross had shrunk a further half inch, faster than the wood could withstand without cracking. The paint too was moving. With its canvas and gesso ground still adhering to the wood at some points but not at others, the paint, although still attached to its protective covering of rice paper, was being pushed and pulled in every direction: breaking apart, crumpling, flaking, overlapping, or thrusting upward like arctic ice under compression.

No one had planned on that. Baldini had assumed that the *Crocifisso* would be allowed to rest until, like a hospital patient, its vital signs became stable; that a gradual drying process over several years with the painted surface held in stasis by the rice paper would end with the cross ready for whatever restoration had been decided upon. But this was an emergency, and the worst option—separating the paint from the cross—seemed to be the only option. The work, performed by a restorer named Vittorio Granchi, began in October 1968.

Although the painted surface of the Cimabue and its ground of gesso were laid down on canvas rather than painted directly on the wood, it was no simple matter to detach the canvas and slip it free from the cross. The canvas was, for one thing, not a single piece of fabric but a jigsaw of irregular parts, the result both of Cimabue's original construction and of splits and seams that had occurred over time, through previous damage, or from the previous interventions of restorers. In places, the floodwater had already dissolved the original animal glue; in others, Granchi could use a syringe to inject a neutral solvent between the canvas and the wood; and in some he simply had to pry the two apart with the thinnest of spatulas. It was nerve-wracking work.

But it was done in a month. No more difficult operation would be attempted on the *Crocifisso* than this *trasporto*, or separation, although Granchi was not much remembered when everything was finished. Credit, like heat, humidity, and glory of all kinds, tended upward. Dante, Vasari, even Icarus, could have told him so.

Now, what precisely were they going to do? There'd been talk around Florence—at least among the restorers—about what Baldini would decide. The practical and theoretical challenges were considerable, and perhaps given the Cimabue's status as *la vittima più illustre*, there ought to be some sort of larger discussion among the experts—not just from Tuscany, but from the rest of Italy, even from the outside world—or perhaps a civic commission. But that was not the way the fate of artworks was decided, not in Florence. A fiat would be laid down by someone secretly or, alternatively, maybe in the manner of a force of nature, like the Arno or a Medici. A joke went around that the Superintendency should turn what was left of the Cimabue over to a certain restorer in the Via delle Belle Donne, whose studio rather blurred the line between *restauro* and forgery. The artisan in question was good—a master. Let him have it for six months. Then Procacci could pull the curtain off. The cross would look as good as it had on November 3, 1966, maybe a little better. Procacci could say that after careful consideration the Superintendency had determined that in fact the Cimabue wasn't really so badly damaged after all. That would be the genuine, the classic Florentine solution.

Baldini doubtless had a plan, but he wasn't saying what it was. At this point he had a bare wooden cross that still hadn't completely dried out and that would need considerable repair when it finally did. And he had a detached canvas, or rather one large piece of canvas—the bulk of Christ's head, torso, and legs—and a number of smaller pieces ranging from near scraps to larger sections of the two arms. Edo Masini, his second in command, was working on the canvas's cleaning and consolidation, and Baldini himself might have been said to be consolidating the Fortezza; or, from CRIA's point of view, his own position.

Baldini was also enlarging his staff and recruiting and training new talent. One was a pretty, recently married twenty-five-year-old named Ornella Casazza. She'd been a graduate student in art history and, like so many of her fellows, worked as a mud angel. She was smart and willing, she could manipulate tools and brushes with skill, and she had the theoretical grounding to write scholarly papers. Ornella bore watching. Baldini put her to work directly with Masini.

Unlike some of their predecessors at the Limonaia, Ornella and the cohort she was part of were being paid regularly, if still scarcely handsomely. The staff of the Fortezza were officially employed by the government, but when they worked on "adopted" pieces, their hours (plus what one New York official referred to as the "so-called overtime hours of Baldini") were billed to CRIA along with more nebulous "administrative costs." The latter made up about a quarter of the amount invoiced, with Baldini's personal share representing about half of that. At various times during 1968 and 1969, in addition to paying the bills for work on its "adopted" art, CRIA effectively paid the entire payroll of the Fortezza when the authorities in Rome were disinclined to meet it.

CRIA kept the Fortezza afloat for six months. The fact that Baldini was presiding over an enterprise that some people might describe as technically bankrupt seemed to have no effect on his continuing ascent nor his amalgamation of other offices and institutions: within another year, he was not only running the Fortezza but had been appointed the director of the Opificio delle Pietre Dure, Florence's other principal restoration laboratory, which specialized in sculpture, mosaic, and decorative objects. It was a final benefice from Ugo Procacci, who retired from the Superintendency that year.

_L_ater in 1969 Ornella Casazza had been joined by another young restorer-in-training, Paola Bracco, and together they assisted Masini in performing a _trasporto_ on Allesandro Allori's _Deposition_ from Santa Croce. The _Deposition_, hung a few yards away from the Cimabue _Crocifisso_, had been severely damaged, and only detaching the pigment from its support could save it. Unlike the Cimabue, most of the paint on the _Deposition_ was intact: the group of _angeli_ and young restorers that had included Marco Grassi had secured it with rice paper and Paraloid at the same time as they had Vasari's _Last Supper_. Like the Vasari, the Allori _Deposition_ was painted directly onto wood, and as the swollen panels expanded and then began to contract back to their original size in the Limonaia, the paint underwent a microscopic but wrenching set of stresses. Now dry, the surface of the Allori was ridged and channeled, the pigments and their underlying gesso alternately bunched up and pulled apart like tiny parallel mountain ranges.

To be restored, the irregularities of the distorted surface would have to be flattened out, pressed back to their original dimensions, and only then cleaned and restored. But the painting's surface and its underlying wood panels were no longer the same size. (In fact, the dehumidification and drying process at the Limonaia often shrank the wood to dimensions smaller than its original ones.) The only way to save the paint was to sever it from the panel beneath it, placing the *Deposition* facedown and scraping and gouging away all the wood, right down to the gesso. The freed surface, almost tissue-thin, was now smoothed out and reattached to a new backing, in the case of the *Deposition*, a single piece of canvas that was then retouched by Casazza and Bracco.

By 1972 Baldini had enough pieces of restored artwork from the flood to merit a show. He conceived it as a public demonstration of his progress so far, a celebration of the fortieth anniversary of the foundation of the Laboratorio, and a grand parting salute to the Laboratorio's founder, Ugo Procacci. Baldini decided to house the exhibition inside the Fortezza: his laboratory would be, in a sense, the star of the show. "Firenze Restaura" opened on March 18, 1972, and was a triumph for Baldini, a deserved one. The entire enterprise had brought out the best in him: not just his energy and organizational skills, but a considerable knack for curating and structuring an exhibition. You entered through a series of rooms that laid out the history of restoration in Florence and of the Laboratorio and its beginnings as Procacci's Gabinetto dei Restauri at the Uffizi, then continued past a succession of works rescued from the flood, including the *Maddalena* and the Allori *Deposition*, and finished in a chamber holding the naked wooden spine and crossbeam of the Cimabue *Crocifisso*.

"Firenze Restaura" also revealed another aspect of Baldini's creativity. His theoretical and technical papers on restoration were inert and stuffy, but in the catalog for the exhibition—he wrote most of its 150 pages—he was a sensitive, even moving, writer. His descriptive entry for the Cimabue was a near meditation on art, spirit, and redemption. He imagined the *Crocifisso* at the moment when the painter began his work—"we see it as Cimabue first did"—but also as it was transfigured by the flood: "a leafless tree," "an enormous wooden machine," "the devastated body of Christ himself, denuded and wracked." Baldini's essay was a reverie in the manner of Ruskin. For all his empire-building, evasions, and pride, here was something Baldini seemed to love.

As for the Cimabue's restoration, there would be no half measures: "Nothing, absolutely nothing more will be lost of this extraordinary first page of Italian art," he wrote, paraphrasing Vasari. Nor would it become a "reconstruction," which would be no more than "a copy." Previous conceptions of restoration would be bypassed and surpassed by a new "mental reconstructive synthesis" that would take enormous quantities of labor and thought. But if they were successful, their work would cause "the sparse leaves" to bloom again on the reunified flesh of this wooden Christ.

Baldini was not promising the *Crocifisso* would be returned to its original condition. What, in any case, would "original" mean? Its condition the day Cimabue finished it; or just before midnight on November 3; or as it looked, dimly glazed with centuries of patina, when Vasari had it taken down from above the high altar of Santa Croce? Baldini wasn't going to falsify history with a replica of the cross at some reconstructed moment in its past, nor would he falsify aesthetics with an artwork that manipulated rather than moved the spectator. With the surviving remnant of the Cimabue—less than a third of the original painted surface—Baldini aimed to extract its essential artistic beauty and historical truth; if not a masterpiece, then something very much to be reckoned with.

When the show closed on June 4 the bare cross went back to its laboratory. It would be almost three more years until Baldini decided it was dry enough to proceed. In the meanwhile, there were other things to do—hundreds of artworks that needed attention—and it was perhaps then Baldini and Ornella Casazza began to notice each other, not that Baldini, with his fine eye, had not yet noticed Ornella. They were not unhappy people, but they had large aspirations and impulses to go with them.

They would not run out of art to occupy them, not now or ever. The Fortezza was crammed with potentially intriguing projects as well as works that were of less interest. *The Last Supper* of Vasari had been hauled over when the Laboratorio vacated the Limonaia, but was taking up valuable space at the Fortezza. That same summer of 1972 it was moved to a Superintendency storage room and then, twenty years later, another one. For three decades, no one would give it a thought.

On May 21 that year, Pentecost Sunday, a Hungarian armed with a hammer leaped over an altar rail in St. Peter's Basilica in Rome and attacked Michelangelo's *Pietà*. He battered Mary's face and shouted that he was Jesus. Afterward a good proportion of public opinion decried the vandalism, but others, recalling the "No more masterpieces" graffiti painted on canvases at the Louvre during the *événements* of 1968, interpreted it as an act of aesthetic radicalism, a protest against the twin repressive apparatuses of Christianity and cultural elitism.

David Lees was sent to photograph the damage. It was his last assignment for *Life*. He and *Life* went back twenty-five years, and there was nothing personal intended in the end of their relationship: *Life* had simply gone out of business. There was no longer a market for a weekly picture magazine that depended on static images—photography—and text set in type, not when you could have moving, real-time electronic images with sound. *Life*, too, was an artifact of the pre-1968 world that had to undergo demolition.

His talents, however, remained in demand. He still got assignments from other Time-Life publications as well as freelance work. He also had a new assistant, Lorenzo, one of his twin sons. In the manner of his own father, Gordon Craig, David was estranged from the other son, and for a long while he and Lorenzo hadn't been close either. They hadn't lived together for as long as Lorenzo could remember. Before he was born, before she married David, Lorenzo's mother had been a widow. As it turned out, Lorenzo might have thought, she'd become a widow twice over.

But when Lorenzo was sixteen, in glorious, ignominious 1968, his father persuaded him to come to a shoot. David was working in Rome at the church of San Andrea della Valle, at night, as was his wont, so that he and his setups wouldn't be disturbed. That evening Lorenzo discovered photography, and he seemed to have also discovered something about churches, and about faith.

He continued to work with his father, and David taught him photography, not just about the technical things, but about what went on in the photographer's mind and eye. "Every picture begins *here*," David would say, tapping his head. "And then you *wait* for it to happen, because it always *will* happen." It was like hunting, or like prayer. You held yourself still and waited for the thing—the thing as it truly was—to appear.

After *Life* ended David and Lorenzo worked together, mostly out of Milan, doing architectural and industrial photography. And then, in 1978, Lorenzo got his own chance to shoot for Time-Life: Pope Paul

VI had died and Lorenzo photographed the funeral for *Time*. David had covered Paul for so long that the Pope always recognized him instantly, calling out, "How is my English Florentine friend?" Now Lorenzo would take the final pictures of that assignment.

At some point he and David talked about David's absence while Lorenzo and his brother were growing up; the life—the greater part of the boys' entire life—he didn't share with them. But what would David have been able to do, having had the father *he'd* had, the genius Gordon Craig, himself the son of prima donna genius Ellen Terry? All David could tell Lorenzo was that, really, he loved Lorenzo more than his mistress, more than any of his women. He had always tried, if not quite enough: being so much under the influence of others— Craig, the art, and all the rest—he had done as he could.

As of 1972 Joe Nkrumah had been working among the damaged books of Florence for six years. He'd traveled elsewhere in his work as a now eminent conservationist, but he always came back here. Tony Cains had stayed until just last year. There was still a mountain of books to rescue—it was better not to think about how many—but they'd had some memorable experiences, heroic, moving, and absurd. In 1968, a year and a half after the flood, he, Tony, and Nick Kraczyna had gone up to Germany to buy a used Volkswagen, which they totaled on the way home. Joe finished up on crutches. But it was an adventure. It was fun. Why this should have been the case would escape any normal, sane person, anyone who hadn't spent the last eighteen months as a mucker and navvy of books and art in Florence. It was a story with an end, a punch line, unlike the flood.

Still, things were being wound up. CRIA was closing its office, and while it would remain in business a little longer, it was looking farther afield for projects; in Venice, for example, which was in its way flooded in perpetuity, sinking into the Adriatic. The *angeli*, of course, were long gone: they'd left by the end of 1967, perhaps to go to Paris or another zone where 1968 was being played out. There were still students coming to Florence from abroad, but they'd come to study art or art history, as they'd been coming for 150 years. Nick was teaching them in American overseas college programs.

He was still painting, drawing, and—more and more—etching Icarus. But the Pietàs were gone. Now he was preoccupied with Vietnam, another of those things that moldered without end. He'd traded one tragedy for another, but he imagined this one as a chess game, death and power hopping from one square to another in Machiavellian gambits. Icarus was still the central figure, though this time the victim of other people's heedless wishful thinking.

Then, in March 1978, the Red Brigades kidnapped and murdered Aldo Moro, leaving his corpse in the trunk of a Fiat in Via Fani in Rome, in what came to seem the final, shabby butt-end of the 1968 *événements*. For a long time afterward Nick worked on a series called *Labyrinth of Via Fani*. Everyone—Icarus, the Madonnas, the *angeli*—was trapped inside the labyrinth with everyone else, holding one another prisoner. There was no way out, no end, infinite leaves of infinite books.

In 1973 Joe finally had to go for good. The CRIA grant that had kept him, Tony Cains, and the others at the Biblioteca had run out. Perhaps it was time anyway, time to go back to Ghana and do something with art there. He'd miss Nick and Amy's daughter, Anna, who'd been born the spring after the flood. She'd miss him too. Now six, she liked to look at him, even to touch him, and he'd laugh. She'd say, "You're *so* black," as if this was the most marvelous thing she'd ever seen, as if his lovely color was the deepest image, the labyrinth she could lose herself in.

9

*H*ere is where we begin, Umberto Baldini might have thought. By the beginning of 1975 the cross was as dry as it had been before the flood, nine years before. In February it was sent to the Fortezza carpentry shop and when it emerged six months later in most respects it looked no different than when it arrived. That had been the intention. But inside, the cross was now very much the "machine" Baldini had alluded to in "Firenze Restaura": it had been taken apart and reduced to its smallest components, in places down to nails and slivers. Cracks and fissures were filled with new but well-seasoned poplar from the same Casentine Forests that had supplied Cimabue's timbers seven hundred years earlier.

Inside the flesh of the wood, there was now a matrix of Inox screws, resin plugs, and composite materials. To hold the crossbeam and the upright together, stainless-steel rods were threaded through the members and then every trace of their insertion removed. All these additions or alterations had been designed to disappear inside the original remnant of the cross but also to be removable. If another team of restorers needed to overhaul the *Crocifisso* in two hundred years, they could remove practically every trace of Baldini's restoration and start from scratch.

By the autumn the cross and its painted surface had been reunited. In most ways the *Crocifisso* looked the same as the day it had been brought to the Limonaia in December 1966 save that the cleaning of the canvas had made the gaps even more glaringly visible.

As an intervention, *tratteggio*—hatching applied with a fine brush—would be the obvious approach and the surest bet. But no one had ever dealt with gaps like those in the Cimabue, some of them in excess of four feet long. You couldn't fill them with one color or even several: what had originally been in the gaps was full of varying brushwork, shading, and built-up or compounded hues. Moreover, to the eye of a spectator any sizable gap not only interrupted the visual field of an artwork but dominated it, becoming what the eye most noticed, reducing the extant parts of the original to background. Filling the gap with one or another selected hue from elsewhere in the painting would only change the color of the gap.

Baldini's idea was to infill with something that would allow the eye to keep moving in its search to apprehend the object before it; filling the gaps with something neutral that it could scan right by and through without interruption. In small, monochromatic patches, *tratteggio* accomplished exactly that: unless the viewer examines the infilled gap closely—in effect, scans the gap at its own level—the eye passes right over it. But a *tratteggio* of, say, one by three feet done in one or another selected color could scarcely disappear into the remainder of the painting.

The solution was to rely on another habit of the human eye called "the contrast of succession." Shown one color, the eye demands its complementary color: red followed by green, yellow by violet, blue by orange. If the complementary color isn't present, the eye—or rather the brain of the viewer—will supply it. It's this ability that allows the eye to fabricate the "true" color from a printed image or television picture made of dots or pixels in only three primary colors.

It was not Baldini but Ornella Casazza, Edo Masini's prize student (and by now, it was said, Baldini's lover), who discovered how to put this principle to work on the Cimabue. Casazza realized that you could measure the relative quantities of colors in the *Crocifisso*, then fill the gaps with "pixels" in the same proportions, and the eye would average out the hues that ought to be in the gaps from the surviving image surrounding them. And it would create not just the color that should be in the gap but also—from the colors extant on either side of the gap—its correct gradations as it scanned by.

Instead of dots, however, Casazza would use overlapping *tratteggio* brushstrokes in three colors—yellow, red, and green—plus black. She'd also angle her brushstrokes to correspond with the flow of the adjacent surviving image—the curve of Christ's head or the angle of a limb—to give the eye's scan a boost in the right direction. Taken all together, this "chromatic abstraction" would fill the gaps with both color and a kind of guided movement.

Casazza and her regular partner Paola Bracco began work in the autumn of 1975. The aim was to finish by November 1976, the tenth anniversary of the flood. Now employed full-time by the combined Laboratorio and Opificio, the restorers were obligated to work only six hours a day, but often put in twelve. They had to cover nearly fifty square feet of gaps four times over (one application for each color plus black) with quarter-inch brushstrokes.

You could have called the gaps that needed to be filled injuries, insults, and wounds to the figure of Christ except for the fact that they were more akin to decapitation, dismemberment, or flaying. The forehead and right side of the face were destroyed. So too was the center of the torso, the breastbone and heart down to the navel; and so too the left-hand side of the rib cage, upward to the armpit. Below the waist there was still less: the left hip and the belly, the genitals, both of the upper thighs, the lower left thigh and knee, most of the right knee and upper calf, the left ankle and instep, and instep and toes of the right—all annihilated. The left arm was broken into three segments at the bicep and the upper forearm. The palms of both hands were destroyed precisely in the places where Christ's real wounds ought to have been.

All that would be covered in chromatic abstraction—in what from a distance would look like a loosely woven mat of green-gold flesh—and perhaps abstraction was precisely the right word. Because when on the tenth anniversary of the flood the *Crocifisso* was returned to Santa Croce, you could not say it had been restored in the sense that something that had once been part of it and lost had now been put back; nor could you say that the wounds had been closed or healed. Rather, they'd become like the phantom limbs of an amputee: they were, for all their self-evident absence, still there, still palpable to the eye even as the eye registered the space they'd once occupied and moved on. In sum, what was once concretely present and then concretely absent in the *Crocifisso* was now present again, but as an abstract presence. You couldn't put your finger or eye on it, but your mind grasped its reality, the specter of what had been lost.

*D*ecember 14, 1976, was a Wednesday night in Advent, all chill expectation, and it was the last time they would gather in this particular constellation, the living and the dead, the restorers and restored; at the foot of the Borgo Allegri, in the once-upon-a-time shadow of Cimabue's studio; Bargellini in his library a block away, worrying his books and his prayers; Ruskin's ghost sprawled in ecstasy on the paving stones of the Peruzzi Chapel; and Francis, Francis and his brothers, watching over them all, looking down with Christ from the tattered heaven of the *Crocifisso*.

The same truck piloted by the same driver who'd brought the *Croci-*

fisso from Santa Croce to the Limonaia ten years and a week ago drove it back today from the Fortezza. Then he and a work crew hung it in the sanctuary of the church for the first time since Vasari's day. Art, it often seemed, was the province of geniuses and scholars, but as had been true ten years ago, it was just as much about laboring men: haulers, hod carriers, and carpenters—all heavy lifters, good at plodding and grunt work, the people the Casa del Popolo was supposed to shelter. They carried that carpenter's cross this night, hefted it and bore it up.

The organist played Bach, and the restorers sat in the half-light of the cold church flanked by Michelangelo, Galileo, and Machiavelli. Then a film was shown, a documentary that recorded the work of the last decade: Procacci at the Limonaia, misting the cross with fungicide; Baldini pacing the Laboratorio, willing it back to life; Casazza in a lab coat and pearls, hand suspended over a gap with brush cradled in her long Maddalena fingers.

At the end the organist played more Bach, the Toccata and Fugue in D Minor, and perhaps it was the wrong choice. Virtuosic and darkly majestic, even bombastic, it was a magnificent end to an evening celebrating an accomplishment for which, however fine, magnificent was not quite the right word. The *Crocifisso*, after all, was ultimately meant to be an emblem of humility, of God brought low on account of his love for humans, lodged in the church of the humble Francis. It had been shunted into the refectory by Vasari and into art historical oblivion by Berenson and his ilk. Then it was drowned, muddied, stripped, and bloated by the Arno, humbled still more. Now it had been pieced back together, its skin grafted with hatching, and for a few days it would get to preside over its old home before returning to the refectory. It was not made for glory.

*B*aldini was proud of what they'd accomplished. Of the completed *Crocifisso* he wrote:

> *In spite of irretrievable losses, it is now once again recognizable in*
> *that indescribable beauty which—now, more than ever, owing to an*
> *interpretation deeper than any before—justifies its position as the*
> *absolute masterpiece of Italian painting.*

That judgment was one not even Ruskin would have rendered. Until 1966 art historians had not much mentioned the *Crocifisso* at all, except as a milepost on the way to greater things. Now Baldini seemed to be according it the status of, say, Duccio's Rucellai *Madonna*.

Perhaps he meant that it *now* was the masterpiece of Italian painting. In the same passage he'd said the restoration "produced a genuinely new painting." Maybe he meant this new painting was in some way a greater painting than the preflood *Crocifisso*. It was a short step to assuming that, on account of the "interpretation deeper than any before" they'd formulated, the authors of this new masterpiece were Baldini and Casazza.

The Cimabue was an important painting, its restoration one of the major projects in the history of *restauro*, and Baldini himself was a large target. He was, like Procacci, respected, but he was not revered. For all his insistence on his own work's rigor and even scientific basis, *restauro* remained a personal and therefore subjective business: the final and unanswerable criterion in evaluating someone's work was to ask how someone else—most probably yourself—would have done it.

By the end of 1976 and into 1977, there had been not a few comments from highly placed restorers and art historians suggesting that the job indeed could have been done differently, which was to say better; which was to say, more implicitly but no less clearly for that, that Baldini had botched it. Paolo and Laura Mora—Baldini and Casazza's

252

counterparts at the Istituto Centrale per il Restauro in Rome—felt that chromatic abstraction did rather the opposite of what it claimed; that in its desire to avoid falsification of the artwork it drew attention to itself, especially with the coarse hatching of its *tratteggio*, which a less decorous person might have described as chicken scratchings. The prominent Florentine restorer Dino Dini was blunt: "They can do it if they want to," he allowed. "I don't care for it."

Those amounted to disagreements, even quibbles, over technique. Others would raise the question of whether *restauro* of this kind should be carried out at all. Chief among them was Alessandro Conti, a young art historian at the University of Bologna who was building a considerable reputation as a historian of *restauro* itself. He intended, in the tradition of the Casa del Popolo, to foment civic discourse and published a screed in the Florence evening paper.

Contrary to the mood expressed in the public events held the previous November, Conti said the return of the *Crocifisso* to Santa Croce was not a triumph but a tragedy. A treasured piece of Florence's heritage had indeed been injured by nature in 1966, but the Laboratorio had destroyed and defiled it. An "inattentive" Superintendency (which, in fact, had no jurisdiction over the restoration) had allowed "a rash restorer to jeopardize the very physical essence of a work of art, indeed to make such a mess of it that there's scarcely anything left to see."

Baldini and Casazza had defenders, and powerful and influential ones at that. In the journal *Critica d'Arte* Procacci's eminent old colleague Carlo Ragghianti pointedly wrote, "I have to say . . . that the skepticism and nay-saying in this matter are entirely unfounded and prejudiced, based on ignorance or a deficiency of knowledge of the historical and cultural conditions of artistic endeavor."

Baldini himself didn't respond to his critics, indeed scarcely seemed to be conscious of their existence. Florentine *restauro* had never taken much interest in the world beyond the city walls, and wasn't going to begin now. And if the world wanted to know what Baldini thought, he obliged them the following year in his theoretical masterwork, *Teoria del Restauro e Unità di Metodologia* ("Theory of Restoration and Methodological Unity"). The first rule, Baldini's existential imperative, was "The intervention should happen!" without "alibi[s]" founded on theoretical dithering or cowardice in the face of practical obstacles.

And with that, he continued on his way, and so did Casazza. Her and Baldini's respective divorces came through, and to cap that year of 1978, they were at last married. Together, they continued to make interventions happen, and at a very high level. For a long time Baldini had had his eye on the Brancacci Chapel and its Masaccios at the Church of Santa Maria del Carmine in the Oltrarno. Vasari had called its frescoes *la scuola del mondo*, "the art school of the world," the essential foundation that every great Renaissance artist had studied and learned from.

For perhaps the first time in his career, Baldini met resistance, and from a formidable opponent: the Istituto Centrale per il Restauro in Rome. With both Cesare Brandi and Procacci retired, the long-standing mutual nonaggression pact between Florence and Rome was null. The Brancacci was, after the Sistine Chapel, the biggest prize in Italian *restauro*, and the Istituto wanted to claim it. It pressed its case with the national government, citing its putative jurisdiction over any and all churches in the country as well as its unrivaled expertise with fresco. But the Istituto hadn't reckoned with Umberto Baldini. Not satisfied with simply snatching back the Brancacci from the Roman carpetbaggers, he seized control of the Istituto and got himself appointed its director.

On leaving in 1982 for his new post in Rome, Baldini put Casazza in charge of the Brancacci. She and Paola Bracco had just completed another high-profile restoration, the *Primavera* of Botticelli, and her qualifications for another important project seemed unquestionable. But Casazza had never, in fact, worked on fresco. Alessandro Conti, who'd decried their restoration of the Cimabue *Crocifisso*, issued a public plea not to let them touch the Brancacci. But the project went forward as Baldini intended, with Casazza in charge.

The *Crocifisso*, meanwhile, had scarcely been forgotten. Baldini sent it on a world tour, underwritten by the Olivetti Corporation, first to the Metropolitan in New York and the Louvre in Paris in late 1982, and then to the Royal Academy in London and the Prado in Madrid the following spring. When the cross came back to Florence, he persuaded Olivetti to underwrite the restoration of the Brancacci too. In that year, 1984, you might have commissioned a vast mural to commemorate a great man at the height of his powers, *The Apotheosis of Umberto Baldini*, which lacked only a Giorgio Vasari to paint it.

Casazza, however, seemed to some observers a little weary. She was in fact doing an extremely credible job at the Brancacci. But when visitors or journalists came by, wanting a look at the most important restoration project in Italy, she was curiously dispassionate, flatly reciting the theory of chromatic abstraction by rote. Asked if she was excited, she'd say she didn't get emotionally involved in her restorations. There was always, she said, another one waiting.

Casazza was perhaps tired, but, at age forty-four, she was scarcely old. Baldini, on the other hand, being an employee of the state and age sixty-five, was compelled to retire in 1987. The Brancacci still wasn't finished, but he was no longer in charge. He didn't like it. Ugo Procacci seemed amused at how his protégé had ended up: "This is what happens to a historian when he retires. He loses all his influence. It happened to me. And now it has happened to Baldini."

The Brancacci *restauro* was completed at the end of February 1991. Ugo Procacci had died a week earlier. Baldini remembered the last time he'd seen him, perhaps a year before. They'd talked as two old men, retirees, about the past. Procacci was, as ever, "a limpid, transparent man"—there was nothing hidden, least of all his passion for art—and of course as they talked, as they untwined the past together, he cried.

A few months later Frederick Hartt passed away in America. He'd died an eminent man, his textbook on the Renaissance still the standard work in its field. In retirement he'd turned his expertise to connoisseurship and paid authentication, and had a final, unintended Berensonian moment: learning he'd taken a commission on the sale of a Michelangelo sculpture he'd also authenticated, a London newspaper branded him an unscrupulous art hustler in the mode of BB. Hartt sued and was awarded a token settlement. But the judge opined that Hartt had acted "dishonorably" if not illegally in a technical sense.

It was perhaps the only stain on a career that was in every other respect remarkable for its idealism and unselfishness. And perhaps this one blemish was only the acquisition late in life of a kind of birthmark, a baptism as a *vero fiorentino* in the waters of the Arno where art and money mingled so promiscuously. His memorial service was held in San Miniato, overlooking the city, and his body was brought from America and buried nearby.

Nearly seven hundred years after he'd painted his last panel, Cimabue, or at least his reputation, knew no rest. He'd had his *Maestà* reattributed to Duccio nearly a century ago, and now, in 1997, another art historian was saying that not only was Cimabue not Duccio's teacher but that he hadn't even influenced him. It was the other way around: Cimabue had seen Duccio's work and incorporated it into his own style, including, presumably, the *Crocifisso*. The following year another art historian, Luciano Bellosi, published a huge monograph designed to rehabilitate Cimabue's reputation and put his work back in its Vasarian position as the "first page of Italian art." But Bellosi felt the need to pause to regret the unfortunate tampering with the *Crocifisso* by means of "so-called chromatic abstraction": even those charged with saving Cimabue's masterpiece could not be trusted to treat him respectfully. Another standard text cited the *Crocifisso* as an egregious example of a *restauro* "dominating the original work of art" which "cannot be accepted."

Nor was nature done with Cimabue. Thirty-one years after the flood, on September 26, 1997, an earthquake struck Assisi. Inside St. Francis's basilica, plaster and the frescoes painted on it rained down. Among the works demolished was Cimabue's *Saint Matthew*, part of the cycle that had convinced Ruskin that "before Cimabue, no beautiful rendering of human form was possible"; that he was the master "even more intense, capable of higher things than Giotto . . ."

Cimabue's greatest gift, Ruskin had thought, was his compassion, and perhaps compassion, *conpassione*, must always be accompanied by *passione*, "submission to suffering." That was what Francis had meant all along; that love consists of coexisting with the pain borne by others. Maybe Cimabue had known exactly what to expect, exactly what he had bargained for.

One hundred and twenty thousand pieces of Cimabue's fresco were found in the wreckage of the basilica at Assisi. The job of sifting and sorting them was given to the Istituto Centrale per il Restauro. In 2006 the fresco was reinstalled on the ceiling of the basilica using 25 percent of the original painted fragments, with the lacunae infilled with a "neutral" hue based on the color range of the surrounding painting.

Baldini and Casazza might have shrugged, and perhaps that explained Casazza's apparent indifference or resignation when she was working at the Brancacci: there would always be another artwork that needed restoring, so it was foolish to get too excited about or attached to any one project. Beauty, like truth, was supposed to be timeless, but the fact was that beauty was always falling apart or decaying. It needed constant shoring up, and the labor could make you weary. Beauty was, *al fondo*, in the final analysis, very like human flesh and bone. In Florence, where they'd made so much of it, there was that much more of it to break or injure. Left alone, without *restauro*, it would all eventually disappear. Really, art was always dying, beauty forever decaying. "I had not known death had undone so many," Dante marveled.

Ugo Procacci and Frederick Hartt believed that saving art was worth crawling through rubble under sniper fire. Thousands of *angeli* fought the mud and the mold under the same conviction, and for a while it seemed that almost the entire world joined them, as though culture, true to its linguistic root, really was the soil of our humanity. But if Adolf Hitler had donned his sunglasses and spent his ten days incognito in Florence among the masterpieces, might anything really have been different? Is the world a different, better place because the Cimabue *Crocifisso* survived the flood of 1966, however altered?

But the art in an artwork might not be located precisely where you thought it was. Perhaps it was just as much in the damage and decay as it was in the intact original. Perhaps it was in the gaps—in contemplating and tending those insults and injuries—that we find ourselves, by compassion; by bandaging, however imperfectly, those wounds. Art may be a species of faith, the assurance of things hoped for. It contains nothing so much as our wish that we persist.

Six

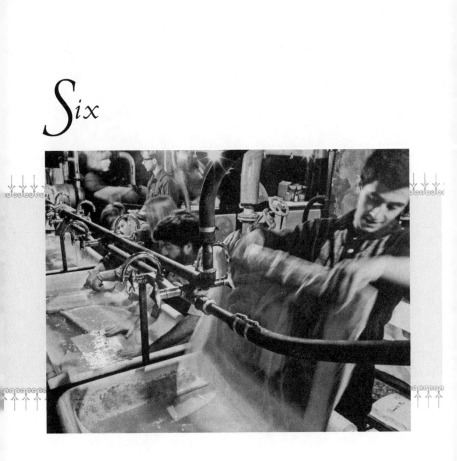

I forget the names of the towns without rivers.
A town needs a river to forgive the town.
Whatever river, whatever town—
It is much the same.
The cruel things I did, I took to the river.
I begged the current: make me better.

—RICHARD HUGO, THE TOWNS WE
KNOW AND LEAVE BEHIND, THE
RIVERS WE CARRY WITH US"

Angels washing books, November–December 1966 *(Photograph by David Lees)*

*T*he morning of the 1997 Assisi earthquake I was in Rome. I had come for the art; or rather, I was writing a book about how, for me at least, beauty and art seemed to imply faith, or something close to it. It was about two in the morning and the quake came as a single jolt, a momentary shudder. I'd been awake or sleeping fitfully: the night was hot and the street was noisy. I waited for the shaking to continue, as it would have done at home, on the Pacific coast. When it didn't I went back to sleep. It didn't seem to have been, by my definition, an earthquake after all.

In the morning I learned it had indeed been a quake, with its aftershocks a significant one, albeit far away in Assisi. It didn't preoccupy me. I'd been to Assisi, but my spirituality just then was more Baroque than Franciscan. I suppose the frescoes, hailing down on the stone floor of the basilica, must have made an enormous sound—like a landslide of glass and pebbles, a cascade of Scrabble tiles, a clatter of bones— but I didn't give it a thought. I was intent on other things: on art and the self I was busy discovering in art's reflection. Sometimes beauty can blind you to truth.

៛

*T*hirty years before, in December 1966, on the long cusp between Thanksgiving and Christmas, I'd been looking at David Lees's photographs: the restorer Dino Dini and his workers clambering up the scaffold of the Gaddi *Cenacolo*; the plaintive, empty-handed Virgin of Santa Croce in her field of *melma*; Baldini in his azure sweater at the moment they'd discovered the ruined Cimabue *Crocifisso*. I was fourteen years old.

I looked at them lying, belly down, on the blue sofa in our blue living room, the magazine laid on the floor, my chin on the welting of the cushion, one hand slung to the floor in order to turn the pages. It was an odd way to read—though perhaps it was the only way for me to accommodate the sprawling fourteen-year-old body I was not quite used to—but I looked more than I read. It's unlikely I took in any of the particulars of the flood or of Florence, never mind of Gaddi and Cimabue. Mostly, I was struck by the colors: gilded, molten, mounting upward into human yet magisterial figures, stern, compassionate, and pitiful; dolorous Mary, Christ suspended in death, Francis among the birds. I loved photography and I had also been religious—not prayerful and certainly not given to good works, but pulled irresistibly toward what seemed to me must be the numinous and infinite: colors, ceremonies, hierarchy; a kind of love and beauty limned with purposeful tragedy that went back two thousand years.

But just then I was giving those things up, my photography and my religion: my novitiate in beauty, in the tears of things as manifested in Jesus and his tender suffering. I'd gotten my first camera in December 1963 and joined the Episcopal Church the same month. I would not have connected the two, but the correspondence now seems unmistakable. Those next three years were happy. My mother and I might have been Dorothy and David Lees—my father was not an artist, never mind a genius, but he had absented himself years before—she practicing such bohemianism as could be mustered in St. Paul, Minnesota, I taking pictures. My heroes, beyond Jesus, Mary, and Francis, were the great *Life* photographers: Eisenstaedt, Mydans, Feininger, and Bourke-White. And during those three years, the photographs of David Lees—his shots of popes, the Holy Land, the Vatican, Assisi and its frescoes, the hills cowled and vested with olive trees—figured large. I didn't know his name but I would have envied his life: his Nikons and Linhofs, his spools and sheets of Tri-X and Ektachrome to take hold of the world's lineaments and shadows and to extract its colors.

But I put that away just then, in December 1966, God and the image, the craving for the luminous and profound. It had nothing to do with the flood, unless the flood in some uncanny way marked those things for me as spoiled, tarnished, and merely old rather than ancient. Soon I'd be remaking myself; driving around in my mother's car, listening to the top-forty songs on KDWB or WDGY, smoking Marlboros and, later, pot, aspiring to sex and, finally, idealism. But by then, after 1970, it was too late to join the *angeli*.

I doubt I made, that December, much of the flood itself, only of David Lees's photographs; and then as pictures, as things in themselves—artworks—rather than as a record or evidence of something else that might have corresponded to something I knew; say, our Mississippi to their Arno, our Mondrian print on the living room wall to their Cimabue, my father to their Azelide. Soon I would pass from seeing photographs to looking at not much more than television or the merest reflection of myself in a mirror. All the rest—the imperative, joyous hunger for created, creaturely beauty and its Creator's love and glory, my own original *vita nuova*—was swept away. It couldn't be recovered, still less restored.

I'd come back to Italy again in 2005, eight years after the Assisi earthquake. This time I was in Florence, trying—so it seems to me now—to write another book about those same things, the things I had lost, and I was flailing. When I noticed the flood marker above our mailbox, the thing that drew me to it, I think, was the concreteness of what it commemorated: it dealt with a fact, anchored in the past, that wove together Florence's art with its history and people. It seemed to contain and connect everything I was interested in but had not been able to grasp. And investigating it would give me a reason to stay longer in Italy.

The flood was by then thirty-nine years in the past, recent enough that memories were still relatively fresh but also sufficiently distant to have become no more than a historical event. It was over, the story complete, so I thought.

But the first week of November it began to rain. I should say that it had been raining a great deal even by Pacific Northwest standards ever since we'd arrived in September. There'd been thunderstorms and weekly downpours. The ceiling of our apartment began to leak. The landlord didn't seem very alarmed by this. When it rained a little more, we were told, everything would swell up and the leaks would stop. This proved to be correct. The central maxim of Tuscan home maintenance—maybe of Italian problem-solving in general—was "Ignore it and it will go away." And although it wouldn't work in America or perhaps anywhere else, more often than not, here it seemed to hold true.

There was no reason, therefore, to pay any attention to this latest onslaught of rain. But I crossed the Ponte alla Carraia several times a day and I couldn't help but notice that the river was rising. Trees, branches, and vegetation were piling up around the piers of the bridge. The river was murky and umber, a turbid orangish brown reminiscent of nothing so much as diarrhea. Pausing on the bridge to gaze at the water rushing under it was now both heady and slightly nauseating, like vertigo.

By the third day, November 5, the water was still rising, and when I crossed the bridge that day I was not so much intrigued as apprehensive. The speed at which the water was tearing downstream made me nervous, as though it were a roller coaster that was, if not out of control, moving faster and more precipitously than I'd bargained for. I wanted to get off.

Neither the river nor my anxiety abated. It was not only ironic but creepily ironic that no sooner had I begun to look into the flood of November 4, 1966, than it had risen from its crypt and was chasing me down. Stranger still was the sense that no one but me was remotely alarmed by this.

It seemed, I learned from reading the papers and talking to neighbors, that the river rose nearly every year in early November. This time the water was indeed a bit on the high side, but not excessively so. It didn't present any danger, but it did afford the opportunity—as in almost every year—for Florentines to rehash the 1966 flood, the matter of who was to blame for it, and the likelihood of it happening again. Inevitably, the supposedly unsolved mystery of the dams would be raised and inevitably ENEL, for the thirty-ninth time, would deny they'd played any role in the deluge. Inevitably too the likelihood of such a flood occurring again would arise—it was said that nothing had been done, or even that things were worse—and inevitably the responsible government agency, L'Autorità di Bacino del Fiume Arno, would respond that, no, a flood on the scale of 1966 almost certainly wouldn't occur again and that much had been done since then to ensure against it.

So regardless of the state of the river, the beginning of November marked Florence's annual *festa* of muttering, backbiting, obfuscation, rationalization, and paranoia that ran for perhaps ten days on either side of the fourth. Beyond the matter of the dams and the potential for future floods, the other perennial debate centered on the current status of the art and books damaged in 1966. And as with the dams and flood prevention, suspicion trumped probability: the operative principle was a corollary to "Ignore it and it will go away," one that stated that if there is something to hide, someone somewhere will be hiding it.

One ingredient in that latter discussion was Giorgio Vasari. Like most people I had heard of Vasari because of his *Lives of the Artists*. In fact I had just finished writing a novel that borrowed that very title for satiric purposes. I also knew, like most people, that he had been some sort of artist himself. On the other hand I couldn't by any stretch of the imagination have named one of his works, still less one that was considered important. Vasari, then, was well known, even famous, in a very modern way: he was a famous artist based on his being an artist who was otherwise famous.

As CRIA had discovered, there was a bottomless market for masterpieces to rescue. Thirty-nine years after the flood all the obvious ones had been saved, but surely, as with the dams and flood abatement, the authorities were hiding something, and a Vasari would suffice to prove it. That was how I encountered Vasari's *Last Supper*. It was mentioned in the Italian newspaper I read every morning and also in the national newsmagazines, and the nub of the story was this: bureaucratic ineptitude and cynicism had allowed the painting to molder, unseen, for the last thirty-nine years. It was the scandal of an abandoned masterpiece. That it was a masterpiece that no one knew the name of—that no art historian or connoisseur had ever claimed was a masterpiece—was either beside the point or in some way made its neglect that much more criminal.

Dark Water

Typically, *The Last Supper* was portrayed as having just been discovered—every November somebody seemed to be stumbling across it—in a pile of junk in a cellar or a barn, but the actual story was a little more complicated and a little less scandalous than that. It was merely pathetic in the quotidian mode, sad in that middling sense that characterized almost everything that touched upon Giorgio Vasari.

The Last Supper had not, in fact, ever really been lost, any more than hundreds of other panel paintings that had had to wait their turns for restoration at the Fortezza. In 1982 its "desperate condition" was publicly noted and an initial plan had been mooted, a *trasporto* that never went forward. The problem was twofold: on the one hand the painting was severely damaged and its restoration would therefore consume vast quantities of money and time; on the other it wasn't, by anyone's lights, a very important work of art. Decisions about which pieces got restored first were similar to choosing a patient for a rare, costly, and difficult operation: which one had the best prospects and would, recuperated, lead the fullest life and make the largest contribution to society? Subjected to that sort of cost-benefit analysis, the Vasari finished in limbo. It wasn't a write-off but neither did it make a compelling case for immediate action.

So *The Last Supper* remained in storage near the train station until 1991, when it was moved to another building near the Uffizi. Five years passed and in November 1996, the thirtieth anniversary of the flood, the central panel was put on display in an exhibition titled "Salvate dalle Acque," "Saved from the Waters." It had to be exhibited laid flat: the surface, though still secured with Marco Grassi's application of rice paper, was too fragile to risk dislodging by hanging it upright. Only the head of Peter was visible; the rest of the panel, including the figure of Jesus, was concealed beneath the murky, translucent mask of *velinatura*. In the catalog it was described as "moribund" and its injuries enumerated: "shrinkage, deformations, and fractures of the

267

wooden support (some several centimeters in size), loss of cohesion of the layers of the ground with consequent loosening and detachment of the painted surface." That diagnosis referred only to the central panel: the other four, back at the warehouse, were in considerably worse condition.

Three years later the Vasari was moved "temporarily" to another storage room at the Palazzo Serristori. In 2000 the restorer Giovanni Cabras prepared an estimate for the *restauro* in the amount of 500 million lire, about $400,000, as much as had been spent on any panel painting at the Fortezza thus far. As though in response, *The Last Supper* was moved back to another storeroom in the Palazzo Pitti, which a journalist would later describe as "squalid." Returned to the vicinity of the Limonaia, the Vasari had come full circle in thirty-five years, still in exactly the same devastated condition in which it had arrived there in December 1966. An official from the Superintendency explained that in "meritocratic" terms its *restauro* could not presently be justified.

For the succeeding three Novembers *The Last Supper* did not attract much attention or comment: the usual conspiracies surrounding the dams as well as forecasts of future cataclysms were rolled out and the customary official responses volleyed back, but conditions on the art front remained relatively calm. However, on November 1, 2003, a journalist named Marco Ferri, writing in Florence's *Giornale della Toscana*, published an article that was, compared to previous exposés on the flooded artworks, explosive.

Ferri was not only a professional journalist but an academically trained historian. In composing his story, he didn't simply marshal the usual statistics of unrestored objects and the neglect of supposed masterpieces, but put in months of legwork around Florence and the surrounding countryside with Superintendency inventories, a flashlight, and a photographer. What he found did indeed seem to be a scandal, extending from the "morgue" that contained the Vasari at the Palazzo Pitti to a hundred thousand unrestored books (36,000 of which were still mud-encrusted) at the Biblioteca Nazionale to the "Dantesque" conditions at a former Medici farmstead in the hills. The latter contained literal heaps, ton upon ton, of damaged furniture, artworks, and furnishings—a near landslide of candelabra, for example—from flooded churches. Amid those darkened rooms and cellars, Ferri also discovered the disassembled altar of Vasari whose *ciborio* had replaced the Cimabue *Crocifisso* in Santa Croce four centuries earlier.

Ferri's exposé produced outrage in Florence, but thanks to the media empire of sometime Italian prime minister Silvio Berlusconi, it acquired a national and international audience as well. The Berlusconi-owned newsweekly *Panorama* gave Ferri's story a second life (even if no credit to the reporter himself), dubbing the storage sites he'd uncovered "depots of shame." And with that, the relatively measured annual discourse about the flooded art took on an unpredictable, even frenzied character. The room where the Vasari *Last Supper* was housed was, *Panorama* reported, "cold and dusty, with broken windows and heaps of tools dangerously close to other artworks, which are piled here and there protected only by cellophane."

Suddenly, reporters and photographers were converging around the Fortezza on the track of heretofore meek and anonymous art historians and restorers. The press and the public it purported to represent insisted on statements, explanations and, still more, immediate action. Pumped for answers, one official allowed that it might take ten years just to remove the *velinatura* from the Vasari. This was not what people wanted to hear, not this November.

But within a short time the Fortezza summoned up the public relations skills it had possessed during the Baldini regime. Florentines wanted results and the press had already produced a poster child in the form of the Vasari. Suddenly, it made sense to revise what had previously seemed a well-reasoned restoration program for all the flooded artworks and make *The Last Supper* a top priority. If it hadn't been a masterpiece before, it had just become one.

The official put in charge, Marco Ciatti, the Fortezza's expert on panel paintings, hadn't seen the Vasari before. After examining it carefully, he said to his superiors, *Ma voi mi chiedete un miracolo*, "But you're asking me for a miracle."

The Fortezza could try refastening the paint to the warped panels or attempt a *trasporto*. But neither of these were likely to succeed: where the Allori *Deposition*, for example, had cracks, ridges, and valleys, the Vasari had chasms. Ciatti could only plead for time, the principal thing a scandalized public and a voracious media would deny him. He'd made his own discovery in a Palazzo Pitti storeroom thirteen years ago: a *Deposition* by Salviati, also from Santa Croce, in a dank stack of planks. They'd been working on it ever since then and it would need two more years. With *The Last Supper* he would have liked to take a couple of years just to do tests and consider his options: the most likely outcome of any hasty intervention would be to make things worse, to do irretrievable damage. Yet people seemed to expect to have the Vasari, restored, better than new, the day after tomorrow.

Still, the public had to be satisfied. A gesture toward at least the appearance of action had to be made. In January 2004, two months after Ferri's story appeared, the Vasari, now insured for €100,000, was moved to the Fortezza with film crews from the BBC in train. Inside, the panels were ceremoniously laid into a custom-built steel storage cradle, a sliding drawer for each of the five panels. And with that procession and display finished, Ciatti hoped, there would be time to think, to conjure up his *miracolo*.

Dark Water

*B*y the second week of November the river had returned to its normal level, but every day I saw the tangle of flotsam wrapped around the northernmost pier of the Ponte alla Carraia, a haystack-sized islet upon which birds and nutria—the possum-sized rodents who live along the banks—had begun to install themselves. I assumed their residence would be short-lived. I'd been in Florence two months and although I could manage in the Italian language, my grasp of how things were done here—how actions and reactions unfolded—was childlike. That it might sit there indefinitely, like the pile of rubble and debris in our cortile, was a notion beyond my imagination.

Similarly, when I read a feature story in one of Italy's most important national newspapers, *Corriere della Sera*, about the unrestored artworks in storage, I was scandalized, but scandalized in the American mode: why, I wondered of this state of affairs, didn't they *fix* it? It would take me some time to understand that Florentines would be scandalized in an almost radically different way: of course they wanted the art restored, but the essence of their preoccupation was the certainty that someone, corrupt and/or derelict, ought to be hung out to dry, but, just as certainly, that nothing would be done. You might imagine that given this combination of convictions, there was little point in becoming outraged in the first place. But being Continental Europeans, they were scandalized dialectically; they could maintain their hope and cynicism simultaneously, their faith in art and in the infinite, incorrigible variety of human misbehavior perfectly intact in parallel lines of thought.

As an American, I also didn't understand the Florentine dialectic of art and life: I assumed that the scandal of the dams was vastly more significant than that of the artworks. Human lives, after all, had been at stake, and I'd managed to collect quite a dossier of supposedly undisclosed truths around the neighborhood. For example, everyone knew they'd never released the real death toll: the official number, thirty-three, was *assurdo*; the true count must be ten times that. Who knew? And of course, there were the warnings that had obviously been given to well-connected people who happened to be rich, goldsmiths and dealers in gems—*che coincidenza!* Finally, it went without saying that everyone knew they'd panicked at the dams and dumped a tidal wave onto the city. Then they'd covered up the whole thing, the *capo* "they" on behalf of the minion "they." Within these other dialectics there was, I guessed, a third dialect of power and secrecy, just as eternal, consisting of "everyone" and "they."

With my American naiveté I imagined there was someone "in charge" and that if I could interview this person, I could get to the bottom of things. As it happened, there was: the director of L'Autorità di Bacino del Fiume Arno, who, more amazingly, was willing to speak to me. He was a wiry, visibly intense man about my own age. Inside the palazzo housing the Autorità we sat in his frescoed office—such offices in Florence have frescoes the way offices in America have framed posters exalting "teamwork" and "excellence"—and with his computer and maps he told me about the river. When he was done, I had to admit that to maintain that the dams had caused or even significantly exacerbated the flood was itself *assurdo*.

I hadn't been taken in or snowed. The director was a specimen of government official I'd never encountered, deeply versed in art, film, history, and poetry. He was just then in the midst of compiling a *Dizionario dell'Arno*, a gazetteer of everything there was to know about the river from hydrology to Leonardo to wildlife to Dante. He'd had a good education—as classical as it was scientific—at a school in Santa Croce called Pestalozzi, which had unfortunately been wiped out in 1966. He'd wanted to help with the flood then, but his mother hadn't let him, not initially. Now he was in charge of the whole river.

Giovanni Menduni knew art, literature, and politics—with his tapered goatee and fine hands, he looked very much the Florentine humanist savant—but he also knew his science and his facts: short of blowing up both dams simultaneously, there was no way anyone either accidentally or deliberately could have started or seriously augmented the flood of 1966. And it was extremely unlikely a flood on that scale would occur in the future: human interventions that had decreased the Arno's capacity or increased its velocity had been ameliorated, and a network of overflow basins had been built along the river into which future floodwaters could be diverted. And if there was a flood even bigger than 1966 that could overwhelm these new defenses, there would be effective warnings. A much more extensive and sophisticated system of meteorological and hydrological data collection tied together by computer modeling would assure that everyone and everything could be moved to safety in advance.

In all this Menduni hadn't quite carried out Leonardo's grand scheme—although it was five hundred years ahead of its time, it wasn't perfect—but da Vinci was his mentor, his patron saint. Leonardo the engineer had created a reclamation plan for the Arno that in its scale and invasiveness was, by modern standards, scarcely environmentally sensitive. But Leonardo the artist had drawn and, still more, dreamed a river that was both terrifying and sublime, not a channel for carrying water but an organism, an entity that embodied chaos, making and unmaking itself. The effects and images it produced—sculpted, tinted, and curved—were stunning and almost always beautiful where they were not terrible. The Arno was no work of art, but perhaps it was an artist.

Giovanni Menduni had the sensibility and vision of Leonardo, but he also required some of the skills of Machiavelli. When—and it was never a question of "if"—a major flood did come, he would be more involved than his mother forty years before could ever have dreamed. In the interim, and particularly each November, he was Tuscany's chief fielder of riverine speculation. Florence wanted to hear that everything could be made reliable, predictable, and safe, and they also wanted someone to blame when, inevitably, it didn't turn out that way. They wanted what they imagined was scientific certainty when the best Menduni could offer them—and he was honest and frank, a realist if not a cynic—were likelihoods. His science and, even more, Leonardo told him that the Arno was an organism, a machine, if you liked, whose nature was to flood. It was made to flood, even in some providential way intended to flood, and you really couldn't expect it to do otherwise. It did what it could do, not what it ought to do.

*A*dvent and Christmas came and went, and the weather grew bitter. It was hard to imagine this was paradisal Italy, land of Goethe's blooming lemon trees. The freeze held into January, and day after day I shuddered on a park bench while Andrew played soccer, oblivious to the viscously cold air through which he and his friends moved. I was busy learning about the Arno, not just in 1966 but all the deluges going back to Roman times. I wanted to catch up on everything there was to know about the subject before next November, the fortieth anniversary of the 1966 flood.

There would doubtless be the habitual recriminations, but I'd also been hearing that preparations were under way for exhibitions, memorials, and a grand reunion of mud angels. But on January 19 someone jumped the gun. Italy's minister of civil defense in Rome, Guido Bertolaso, announced that he had found €250,000 with which to restore Vasari's *Last Supper*. This might not have been surprising—in Italy's various state and local departmental treasuries money got "found" rather like old, apparently lost bags in a railroad station checkroom— but the source of the funds was incongruous, rather as if the U.S.

Army Corps of Engineers were gifting the National Gallery a piece of its budget to buy a Giorgione.

The Vasari had, of course, been damaged in a flood that, after a fashion, was within the Department of Civil Defense's portfolio. The following week Bertolaso announced, as though an afterthought, that €200,000 was needed to make the Arno "safe" (whatever "safe" meant), albeit without any mention of where or when the €200,000 might be "found." All this was news to Giovanni Menduni.

The officials of the Superintendency and the art historians and restorers of the Fortezza were even more puzzled. Bertolaso was a Berlusconi appointee, dubbed *l'uomo dalle mani d'oro*, "the man with the golden hands," by one newspaper, and a bit of a grandstander. No one knew anything about the money: where precisely it had come from, when it would be disbursed, or what restrictions might be attached to its use. The money ought to have represented good news, but if Bertolaso turned out to be a loose cannon and his money disappeared back into the lost-and-found depot where it had come from, the Vasari's prospects would be that much worse: the Fortezza had been trying to raise restoration funds from the national government through its own channels, and the appearance of Bertolaso's €250,000 might make that effort look redundant. Moreover, in parallel with the Fortezza an Anglo-American charity, "The Angels of Florence," had been pushing forward with its own appeal for a major grant to perform the tests and studies Marco Ciatti needed to start the *restauro*. Now that too was in jeopardy.

Nor was Rome quite finished with Florence. Later in the spring, the Istituto Centrale per il Restauro launched a new sortie against the Fortezza, appealing to the incoming government of the new prime minister, Romano Prodi, to "rationalize and unify" *restauro* in Italy by placing the Fortezza under its control. I had wanted to talk to Marco

Ciatti for some time, but through the spring he was obviously preoccupied, not to say harried, his Fortezza under an almost literal siege.

In May I finally got to see him. Ciatti was a slight man with a pendant walrus mustache and wore a tie with a collar that was just a little
too big for him. A pair of spectacles dangled from a chain around his
neck. In all, he looked long-faced and stooped. We talked about the Istituto's power grab. For him, it wasn't about Procacci versus Brandi or
Baldini and Casazza versus the Moras or a high art variant of Florence's ancient feuds with Siena or Pisa. It was now a matter of two different styles of doing *restauro,* both of which ought to be honored and
preserved. Florence had no problem with Rome's handling of Assisi
or its controversial role in the cleaning of Michelangelo's Sistine
Chapel frescoes during the 1980s and early 1990s. Why couldn't the Istituto extend the same regard to the Fortezza?

On Bertolaso's €250,000 (of which there had been no sign or news
after four months) and on funding in general, Ciatti seemed to be of
two or even three minds. On the one hand, of course, he needed
money, perhaps something on the order of €500,000 to begin with.
And he had 40 percent less money overall to work with at the Fortezza
than he'd had five years ago. But then he seemed to reverse himself:
"If I had Rockefeller's millions, it wouldn't change anything," he said
almost dolefully. "It just takes time." Given the duration of projects
like the Cimabue *Crocifisso* or the Salviati *Deposizione*—ten and fifteen
years respectively—that seemed self-evident, even if the public and
media would never grasp or accept the necessity. More than anything,
I felt, Ciatti wanted to be left alone.

But as he walked me back to the area of the Laboratorio where the
planks of the Vasari were kept, he brightened. We maneuvered past
dozens of artworks undergoing *restauro*, some of them as massive as
the Cimabue cross, others small as icons; some brilliantly colored and

gilded, others extraordinarily worn, shabby, and dull, junk from a Renaissance landfill.

The racks on which the panels of the Vasari lay were dark blue steel surmounted by a sign with their corporate sponsor's name. When Ciatti reached down to pull one of the five out on its rollers, I held my breath. I was about to see a work of art I had never seen except in pre-flood photographs (only black-and-white images had ever been made), a relic untouched since November 1966, panels that five centuries ago had been touched by Giorgio Vasari. It wasn't a Michelangelo, but it was by someone who'd *known* Michelangelo, who'd claimed to have been Michelangelo's pupil and friend.

But what Marco Ciatti revealed to me was nothing at all: a dirty gray board pasted over with what might have been toilet paper, breaks in the tissue patched with further scraps of toilet paper like stanched shaving cuts. The panel was cracked and fissured, incised and pocked with welts and blisters. It wasn't even a ruin. It wasn't picturesque. If you'd found it in your barn or cellar, you would have thrown it out. It wouldn't be worth the trouble to burn.

After some time, on the central panel, in the upper-left-hand corner, I was able to make out a little of what must have been Peter registering his shock at Jesus' prophecy from under the grime. But that was all there was to see.

Why, I wanted to know, had Vasari's painting fared so badly in the flood, worse in many ways than the Cimabue *Crocifisso*, which had been completely immersed? Cimabue, Ciatti explained, had been meticulous in his selection of materials and preparations. He had the best heartwood sawn from poplar logs for his panels, laid down his gesso in smooth, polished layers, and sheathed it in one continuous piece of canvas. Vasari, by contrast, used "tangential" cuts of lumber from the sides of the logs, put a thin layer of gesso on the wood, and painted directly upon it. Perhaps it was a matter of how the two painters had viewed themselves. Cimabue saw himself as a craftsman. His carpentry, his preparation of the ground, and the image he brushed and gilded onto it were all essential parts of the object he was making. Vasari, on the other hand, was an artist, a role he himself had helped invent. His eye was on the classical geniuses of the past and the posterity that he hoped the future might bestow on him, on Neoplatonic conceptions of beauty and the ideal rather than wood, glue, and gesso, on the art rather than the artwork. He wasn't unique in this: painted panels from the sixteenth century were among the most severely damaged victims of the flood.

"An American restorer told me it would be impossible to do anything with it," Ciatti said, his hand outstretched, palm up, in a gesture that might have signified either revelation or resignation. Maybe he thought I would come to understand the enormity of what he'd been asked to undertake if the assessment came from a fellow citizen. But I didn't need convincing. There was a tawdry coating of failure and loss all over Vasari's panels. I couldn't wait to get away from them.

Still, we stood there. Ciatti shook his head, and then he said, "There's something that might work." *Trasporto* was, of course, out of the question. You couldn't excavate the wood away from behind in the usual way, not when in some places the paint had erupted a half inch upward from the original panel. After *trasporto* you'd have a crumpled, brittle membrane of paint that would disintegrate if you so much as looked at it sideways.

And, after all, what, Ciatti asked, was a panel painting without a panel? *Trasporto* was as falsifying as it was risky: in sacrificing the wood panel, it destroyed an entire physical and visual dimension of the artwork in order to save the two-dimensional image. It was only defensible as a last resort, even assuming you could carry it off. Ciatti had something else in mind, something he'd tried on a less ambitious scale almost twenty years before. There'd been a flood-damaged panel *Cro-*

cifisso by Giotto's contemporary Lippo di Benivieni from Santa Croce, in similar condition. As Baldini had done with the Cimabue, they viewed its wooden support as an essential part of the work and therefore ruled out *trasporto*. Instead, they'd used a custom-made saw to slice the paint and its ground longitudinally from the panel in one piece. The paint—now two millimeters thick—was intact, as was the original panel. After the rucked and blistered ground of the paint was leveled and reconsolidated it was reunited with the panel. The only inauthentic ingredient in the entire work was the thin layer of bonding that held them together.

Ciatti's saw was analogous to a microtome, a device used to cut tissue samples for lab analysis. But with the Vasari, to maintain a consistent thickness the blade would have to move not just through the wood laterally but up or down relative to the uneven surface. Ciatti was thinking that by using new technology, the irregularities could be mapped with lasers and the blade guided by computer. It was all speculation at this point. They needed money and time—especially time— to see what was possible.

As we walked back Ciatti greeted several of his staff. One of them was Paola Bracco, who I knew had been Ornella Casazza's partner on the *Crocifisso*. She'd also worked on the di Benivieni that Ciatti had just been telling me about. She stood in her white lab coat next to a small panel painting, a late medieval saint from the look of it. Her hand rested on an adjacent table crowded with chemicals, paint, brushes, and tools. Bracco looked to be about sixty-five, keen, genial, but unassuming. Unlike Casazza, she was still, now, a quotidian practitioner of her craft, an artisan-physician to wounded artworks. I imagined she must be content, although I knew nothing of her life. As Ciatti and I departed I shook her hand. I'd spent a lot of time by now studying Cimabue, and this was the hand that for an entire year had tended his broken Christ.

*I*t was May and in a month I'd have to return to America. On the Ponte alla Carraia there was a truck with a hoist and a team of laborers with chain saws, some of them wearing scuba gear. They were standing on the tangle of debris wrapped around the north pier, cutting through the larger trunks, then attaching the hoist's cable to pull them loose. But beyond clipping back some of the longer trees and limbs, they didn't succeed much in reducing the bulk of the islet. Five months of the Arno bearing down on it had compacted and consolidated the snarl of flotsam into an impenetrably solid mesh. The workers might have been embarrassed to have accomplished so little with their engines, cables, and chain saws. Surely their ancestors seven hundred years ago hadn't been so easily stymied.

It was by then time for me to find Umberto Baldini. He was eighty-four years old, but by all accounts vigorous. After his retirement he'd founded a private college of *restauro* and museum curating, the Università Internazionale dell'Arte, where he was still teaching. I'd gotten his phone number and I'd been told he was approachable, that he even liked to give interviews.

I dialed the number and I was afraid he wouldn't answer. Or that he would answer. Baldini was by now a legendary figure in my mind, maybe mythic. He had become the central figure in my story—at least among the living—without my quite intending it, almost as large as the river. But he, or someone, answered. It was an old if not weary voice, cultured and modulated. It was Baldini. I told him who I was, and his tone rose, as though he knew who I was. Maybe he'd heard about the American asking questions about the flood, asking questions about him.

He told me to call back in a week. He was busy reading papers and exams. It was the end of the academic year. I shouldn't worry—we'd talk. I felt relieved.

Seven days later, to the day, to the hour, I telephoned again. He knew it was me before I'd said three words, and I was taken aback at this eerie prescience. (It didn't occur to me that my execrable Italian delivered in a Midwestern buzz-saw accent might distinguish me from his other habitual callers.) He told me to call back next week. He was still reading exams.

When I called back a week later a woman answered. I asked if Dottore Baldini was there. No, she said. I told her that he had told me to call him today, as though this would somehow have precluded him from going out. "He's in the hospital," she said. I asked, densely, when he'd be back. "I don't know. He's old. He's sick," she replied, and hung up. Months later I realized the woman must have been Ornella Casazza.

Two weeks afterward I was back in Seattle. I spent the summer reading about Cimabue, Vasari, Leonardo, and the first art tourists and expatriates who followed them to Florence. On August 17 I read Umberto Baldini's obituary in the Seattle *Post-Intelligencer*. He had, indeed, been a great man, great enough to have his passing noticed far away in a medium-sized city in America. "Savior of Florentine Art," the subheadline said.

I felt dread: I'd lost my chance to speak to my protagonist. There were things he knew that no one else knew. But I was also strangely re-lieved. I wouldn't have to undergo the trial of trying to appear com-petent before him, to ask intelligent questions, to extract the truth I wanted from him. Just a month earlier I'd had dinner with a prominent art historian. Hearing I was researching the *Crocifisso*, he said, "It's Baldini who should have been crucified for what he did to that Cimabue."

Perhaps I feared I wouldn't know what to make of him; that I'd be either taken in or too suspicious, that I wouldn't be able truly to see him or—perhaps just as likely—to see past him. But now he'd eluded me, slipped away into the great sea. That, people might have said, was just like him.

Whatever I wrote now would be, by necessity, a variety of *restauro*, with all its concomitant dilemmas of falsification; of infilling, abstrac-tion, and synthetic bonds. If I was fortunate, it might be as good as his Cimabue, or at least not worse: 20 percent of Baldini would still be ap-parent in it and the rest wouldn't be a gross distraction or distortion. But then I'd been to see the *Crocifisso* a dozen times and I couldn't make the least sense of it—of whether it was a masterpiece and whether Bal-dini's *restauro* added or detracted from it. It was tempting to use the word "enigmatic," surely one of the great clichés in discourse about art: there was the enigma of the *Mona Lisa*, of Piero della Francesca, of Caravaggio, and, later, of much of the entire modern movement. It might indicate mystery, the refusal of the work of art to resolve itself in an expected way, or pure incomprehension on the viewer's part—a failure of imagination, vision, or simple nerve.

But Cimabue's *Crocifisso* was no enigma at all. It was, I thought, what it was, and it remained so: Francis's fully human Christ. To claim that the chromatic abstraction somehow prevented one from seeing it was to be thick as a plank or maybe just God's fool, as Francis himself claimed to be. But, still, was it beautiful? Was it art?

When I returned to Florence in September I discovered there had been, beyond the death of Umberto Baldini, other developments. In July, Guido Bertolaso of the Department of Civil Defense had announced that he'd found another €200,000, which he was earmarking for the *restauro* of Donatello's *David* in the Bargello. As with *The Last Supper*, no one in Florence knew anything about it. Also, as before, none of €250,000 promised for the Vasari earlier had yet turned up at the Fortezza. Regardless, the Angels of Florence group announced they were withdrawing from the *Last Supper* restoration. There were other worthy projects, and the grandstanding and incoherence surrounding the Vasari made it an untenable situation.

Meanwhile Marco Ferri's investigations on behalf of *Il Giornale della Toscana* had turned up another eight abandoned paintings in a Palazzo Pitti storage room that was supposed to be empty. When interviewed, the official in charge of the *deposito* explained that *that* particular *deposito* was outside her jurisdiction. But apparently it wasn't under anyone else's either.

I'd gone back to work interviewing people and reading old records and newspapers. Late in September, the month of the lowest water on the Arno, the divers and chain saw cutters came back again to the north pier of Ponte alla Carraia. It was a reassuring sight. After a few days they disappeared, and, although I was quite convinced they hadn't made so much as a dent in the thicket, that too was reassuring. I was becoming, I imagined, acclimated in Florence.

Through the autumn my intention was to learn everything I could about *restauro* and, more particularly, about Umberto Baldini. I went to see Cristina Acidini, who was superintendent of both the Fortezza and the Uffizi. She'd been a mud angel at age fourteen and now she held Ugo Procacci's old position. When Baldini had died in the summer of 2006, she wrote the official tribute on behalf of the Superintendency.

Acidini's conversation seemed to me a curious mixture of official discretion and frankness. She didn't volunteer anything about Baldini that wasn't in the obituary she had already written, but was happy to discuss the parlous state of the Superintendency itself. She didn't, for example, have money in her budget to buy fuel for the motor fleet, but there was, on the other hand, several €100,000 earmarked and ready for projects there wasn't time or staff to launch. Her responsibilities overlapped with other directors of other agencies. Only Rome, apparently, had a copy of the organization chart. "We're all pieces on the ministry's chessboard," she sighed.

Acidini had, however, news regarding the Vasari *Last Supper*. Bertolaso had in fact finally issued a check for the €250,000, but had sent it to the wrong bank account. It should have gone to the Patrimonio Storico Artistico at the Palazzo Pitti. I should go talk to its director, an art historian named Bruno Santi.

Santi too had been a mud angel, an art history student in 1966, who nearly forfeited his last exam on account of the flood. Now he held one of the most important cultural posts in Tuscany. We sat in his office in the Palazzo Pitti, the rooms Ugo Procacci had occupied when the Germans blew up the bridges and Frederick Hartt rolled up in his Lucky 13. Like Acidini, Santi offered me only the customary boilerplate about Baldini, but he did tell me he'd first met him in the Limonaia just after the flood: he and another mud angel, an English kid named John Schofield, had been put in charge of keeping mold off the Cimabue *Crocifisso*. Baldini and his restorers hadn't even realized that the cross was being consumed from the rear by runaway mold. But he and Schofield had gotten it under control; or, really, John had. All the ideas, right down to buying a drugstore perfume atomizer, had been his. John Schofield was one of the people, as much as Procacci and Baldini, who'd saved the *Crocifisso*. I should call him—I promised Santi I would—and say hello from Bruno. Maybe they'd see each other again this November.

*T*he fortieth-anniversary commemorations of the flood were already in evidence by early October. A mud angel reunion had been scheduled, discussion panels organized, and exhibitions curated. Nick Kraczyna's photographs from the first few days of the flood were going to be published by the press of Syracuse University, on whose Florence faculty he now taught printmaking. Marco Ciatti had composed a massive catalog to accompany the unveilings of the Fortezza's *restauro* of the Salviati *Deposition* and other works from Santa Croce. Giovanni Menduni would do a reading from his *Dizionario*.

The habitual discussions and suspicions of every other anniversary of the flood were also surfacing, albeit more prominently and insistently than in other years. Giorgio Bocca, perhaps the most distinguished journalist in Italy, weighed in on the dams. Bocca had fought as a partisan against the Nazis, which lent him an authority, at least on the political left, few commentators could match. He lamented the "recklessness of those who had allowed the flood to take place" and cited the *Sunday Times* investigation of forty years earlier as his authority, the gospel in what had long ago become a matter of belief rather than fact.

Meanwhile Marco Ciatti launched an uncharacteristic preemptive counterattack against the accusations he correctly assumed would come with the anniversary. The legend of the Cimabue *Crocifisso* floating facedown in the refectory—everyone knew it; people had seen it, regardless of what *they* had said—was by now an old if unforgotten canard. But Ferri's exposé and Bertolaso's showy largesse from Rome had sharpened the media's taste for stories of the Fortezza's supposed ineptitude and procrastination. In his catalog for the Fortezza's exhibition Ciatti wrote, "Only the arrogant superficiality of a few journalists has allowed the responsible methodological attitude followed in projects [by the Fortezza] to be interpreted as an incapacity to act." Not since Baldini had appealed to the evidence of David Lees's photographs of the upright *Crocifisso* had the Fortezza been so assertive in its self-defense.

For whatever reasons, by the beginning of November it seemed to me that the predicted carping had been replaced by a sense of occasion, of a suddenly recognized need to remember and to think rather than speculate and blame; to recollect the losses and the deeds of those days in a serious and even self-critical manner. I was surprised, for example, to read an interview with Antonio Paolucci, one of Cristina Acidini's predecessors at the Superintendency, that seemed to suggest Florence's art was at the root of some of the city's problems rather than purely its crowning glory. The city was a "monoculture," "a kind of victim of art," that was driving out traditional artisans in favor of "shows" rather than genuine new artwork and *restauro* of the old. Florence was in real danger of becoming a museum of itself, not just in the highbrow Berensonian sense, but in embodying all the worst aspects of the contemporary world of blockbuster exhibitions: the museum as a brand, a theme park dislocated from place, time, or context; from what Ruskin would have simply called the real.

The Arno too was being seen in a different light. Florentines had never imagined it as simply the villain of 1966, but as a moody, obstreperous relation, half child and half paterfamilias. You couldn't really blame the river; if Florentines hadn't wanted to deal with it, they shouldn't have moved their settlement down from Fiesole two millennia ago.

That attitude was manifest at a reading and panel discussion of Giovanni Menduni's *Dizionario dell'Arno* a few days before the anniversary. There were questions about the Arno as a present danger to be controlled as well as the possibility of being able to predict its floods. Menduni responded to these a little impatiently. It was Leonardo's Arno, it seemed, that he wanted to talk about and to reflect upon, the Arno as metaphor, as the connecting thread that ran through Florence and Tuscany's heart and soul, the creative force that sculpted and washed it away, so as to begin again. The Arno was, for Menduni, the Hammond B-3 he'd never owned—the one that the river itself had drowned and smashed to splinters—upon which he could improvise and compose.

I'd imagined November 4, 2006, would be something like November 4, 2005, or perhaps even November 4, 1966. But it resembled neither of those. It was eerily clear, still, and cool, like a placid summer day with the temperature lowered by thirty degrees. I got up early. There were a half dozen events I wanted to attend, most of them overlapping.

The first was a mass in the Duomo presided over by the archbishop of Florence, Cardinal Antonelli, in memory of the dead and in honor of the city emergency workers who'd rescued the survivors. On an ordinary day, the Duomo was divided into two parts, the rear two-thirds swarming with tourists and the area around the altar reserved for prayer and services, nearly deserted but thrumming with the overspill of tourists' voices. But today the whole place was opened up, filled from one end to the other with neither tourists nor the devout, but ordinary Florentines, working Florentines who normally stayed in their own neighborhoods, in San Frediano or Santa Croce. A large number of them wore the uniforms of police, firefighters, and paramedics. These were the Florentines you never saw anywhere near the Duomo, reclaiming the heart of their city for a day.

The mass began with a procession, the same slightly disconcerting mix of the ecclesiastical and the civic, the Franciscan and Machiavellian, that had attended Pope Paul on Christmas 1966. Men in martial Renaissance dress carried the Gonfalone, Florence's republican flag, followed by a line of priests, deacons, acolytes, and the cardinal. The Duomo was crammed with people, and I pressed myself up against a column perhaps thirty feet from the altar. A portrait of Dante—Giotto's friend, the recorder of Cimabue's declining fame—was fixed on the wall opposite me, and above me was Vasari's painted cupola, the vast rendering of Heaven and Hell that covered the inscape of Brunelleschi's dome. It was Vasari's last public work and his most prestigious, the plum project he hadn't lived to see finished.

The mass began and I watched the demons and the damned they tormented hovering above me. Their heavenly counterparts seemed a little bland in comparison. That was the usual complaint about Vasari. He hadn't *painted* God and Christ in their majesty and mercy, but flattered them. But his monsters were monstrous.

Then came the readings. The first was the story of Noah. I'd wondered if anyone would allude to it today, and had imagined no, it would be obvious or corny and possibly in bad taste. It seemed neither apt nor kind to impose this fairy tale on people who'd lost real loved ones, homes, and livelihoods in the flood: their story was a fact while this was a "story." But although I thought I knew a fair amount about how to "read" a work of art like the Vasari looming overhead, I'd seemed to have lost the capacity to read a story like this one.

I couldn't see that Noah's story was the story of both *the* flood and every flood, as Mary was both *the* mother and every mother in all the *Maestàs* of Cimabue, Duccio, and Giotto. It's in this way that images and stories extend themselves outward to include and comprehend each and every particular; come to mean rather than merely stand apart as objects, to incorporate us and our experience within them.

That capability, before we started calling it art, was art. And that was why, in Cimabue's day, when every *crocifisso* was the *Crocifisso*—particular and universal, every example an exemplar—the maker took such pains over his timber, his ground, and his paints.

So, as they listened to the Noah story, there were three or four thousand Florentines—cops, nurses, firefighters, people who ran cafés and bars, bakers, clerks, and carpenters—who understood this, even if it was beyond me. And what happened at the end of the Noah story was a promise: that, when the waters withdrew, there would be a new *alleanza*—a compact or alliance—between God and man, between Creator and creature, between hope and this broken, drowned, sodden world. So Noah and the deluge, in fact, was precisely the story to read on this occasion. There was no irony in it. For Francis, Cimabue, and even Vasari, the promise was going to be fulfilled, and that was why you painted *Last Suppers* and *Crocifissi*. There'd been a flood and there was loss and now there would be consolation. And so we go on.

Maybe, huddled against my pillar, scratching in my notebook, I didn't really "read" anything as well as I thought I did, least of all art. Maybe I didn't even understand the Vasari looming overhead, at least not well enough to claim that my taste was of a higher order than Vasari's technique.

After the readings the cardinal rose to give his homily, and I expected truisms and uplifting hooey from him, or at best elegies. He mentioned, of course, the rescue workers, the *angeli*, and the patient, sometimes misunderstood Catholic humanism of Mayor Bargellini. But he also took up the notion of a new *alleanza* from the Noah story and asked what it might mean. What kind of city would Florence be after its flood? The cardinal was tough-minded. As matters stood, Florence hadn't done much on its side of the bargain. Today the *centro* was dominated by offices, high-end shops, tourists, and overseas students able to pay exorbitant rents while artisans and working families were abandoning their historic *quartieri*, leaving a lonely and sick population of the elderly behind. It was a harsh assessment, but, he said, a necessary one. The energies people had found in themselves forty years ago needed to be revived. Community, family, and faith would help, but so too would art, leading into and out of them. I couldn't make out the last few words of the cardinal's homily, but I know—I heard it clearly—that the final one was *bellezza*, "beauty."

*A*fter the mass, I went to the Palazzo Vecchio for a reunion of the *angeli* held in the building's grandest public room, the Salone dei Cinquecento. By my reckoning—no one knew exactly—there had been at most fifteen hundred *angeli*. If so, it seemed that almost all of them were here, a mass of late-middle-aged people who looked surprisingly youthful—the mud had preserved them, someone joked—talking ebulliently, almost desperately, in the manner of people who have shared an adventure and haven't seen each other in a very long time. They were surrounded by a younger generation of television crews, reporters, and organizers, men and women who might have been their children; not much older than they'd been in 1966.

The official program began with flags, more men in Renaissance costumes, and welcomes from civic officials. John Schofield's friend from art school in London, Susan Glasspool, spoke. In many ways she embodied the collective experience of the *angeli*. Bilingual, possessed by a love of art, she'd come from another country, but had stayed. She'd saved books and artworks, and best of all, she'd found love, a husband among her fellow *angeli*. Like everyone else's subsequent life, her story was not quite the one they'd all envisioned forty years before: the world had not been transformed, was arguably no better than it had been, and maybe a little worse. But they had saved a bit of the better parts of it, maybe even some of the best of it, a masterpiece here or there. They'd believed, against cynicism and despair, that there was something in it worth saving; things that meant more than themselves, things that could save you by your saving them.

The *angeli* were by no means congratulating themselves, but they seemed pleased and somehow surprised to be in Florence again, together. Had they really been here all those years ago, in all that cold, damp, and mud? They hadn't been heroes: they'd been having the time of their lives. The odd thing was not so much the memory of what had been, but that they'd ended up here, after all this time, as old people, having persisted all that while just like everything they'd saved in Florence. I'd been looking for John Schofield—we'd talked on the telephone several times—but he hadn't been able to come. He was busy renovating his family's old home in Cornwall, busy tending his mother, who was old and ailing. *Restauro, sempre.*

My eye wandered up the high walls and ceiling, tumescent with gilding and murals. Here, as in the Duomo, we were being overseen by another gargantuan Vasari, his *La Battaglia di Marciano*, whose clashing armies formed a kind of counterpart to the milling *angeli* below. It was said that Vasari overpainted his mural on an unfinished Leonardo masterpiece, *La Battaglia di Anghiari*; genius wallpapered over by competent mediocrity, as the connoisseurs would have it. In upper center was Vasari's cryptic legend *cerca trova*, "seek, find," which some believe is a coded reference to the painting underneath, which might even be intact, protected behind a hollow cavity. The word "enigma" again came uselessly to mind. Vasari was famously practical, not someone given to sly mysteries or hoaxes. So perhaps *cerca trova* meant no more or less than the tale of Noah did; perhaps it meant to simply get on with your work, mine, Vasari's, or anyone's.

Just before noon I went to the Arno, to the Ponte Vecchio. It was full of people but didn't feel crowded in the usual way. It was almost silent. The bells would begin to toll soon, all over the city, up and down the river. Drummers in Renaissance dress would pound out a dull funereal beat. Children in red jackets were standing by, waiting, holding lilies and marguerites. All this for the dead.

At noon the bells and drums began and the children gathered at the center of the downstream side of the bridge. They had perhaps three dozen flowers in all, one for each victim; one at least for the youngest, Marina Ripari, who would now be forty-three; one for the bravest, Carlo Maggiorelli, who stayed at his post on the aqueduct until the water siphoned him away; one for the one who suffered most of all, Azelide Benedetti, who drowned in the cage of her apartment, lashed to her window bars.

The children began to throw their flowers over the parapet into the river. The flowers would float on the Arno all the way to the sea. They'd drift in the Tyrrhenian like beautiful wreckage. But the river was slack today, dead still, so unlike itself. The flowers languished motionless, almost beneath the arch of the bridge. Then—perhaps an invisible puff of Shelley's west wind came up, or perhaps it was a trick of the eye—the river almost seemed for an instant to be flowing upstream, carrying the flowers with it, against itself, back toward Monte Falterona. *Cerca trova.* You might seek, and find—not an enigma but a small miracle, a fragment of *bellezza*, a leaf or a flower on the stream, ascending.

*T*he restorers and conservators who'd come from overseas and worked as or alongside the *angeli* had their own reunion a few days later at La Pietra, Harold Acton's villa, which was now owned by New York University. Nick Kraczyna had told me about it. He was excited. He was going to see people like Joe Nkrumah and Tony Cains for the first time in decades. I found a way to go along.

The Conservation Center of the Institute of Fine Arts at NYU was sponsoring the event, and scholarly papers—some of them quite technical—would be presented. Nick would settle down Nkrumah and Cains and they'd reprise the tale of the totaled Volkswagen and Joe's broken leg. But the formal point of the symposium was to examine the legacy of the flood as it applied to restorers and conservators. The book conservators formed the largest contingent, people from overseas who'd come to Florence's libraries and had invented their profession in the process. The presiding genius of the entire operation, Peter Waters, had died the previous year, a victim of the asbestos tools he'd used in his work. His wife, Sheila, spoke in his stead without sentimentality or conceit. They'd done a good job. They had learned a lot.

In another session Marco Grassi, who'd pasted *velinatura* on the

Vasari *Last Supper*, looked back with some amusement on what they'd all accomplished, given their age, inexperience, and naiveté, their capacity to slap together jerry-built solutions and recover from their own blunders. It had been an achievement merely to slog through the mud, the liquefied chaos that clung to your feet, hands, and entire body, that was always slowly, tirelessly laboring to pull you in and under.

Now they were all grown up: Grassi himself was a beautifully spoken, elegant gentleman who divided his time between Manhattan and Florence. These one-time *angeli* held positions of great responsibility, were *dottori, professori, gran' signori*. But together they'd had this grimy golden youth. Afterward, lunch was served and people made plans to meet in the city that night for drinks and dinner, to talk into the night, to laugh and reminisce.

Then Joe Nkrumah took the podium. He'd always cut a large figure, physically and in the gravitational force of his character. Now the director of the Foundation for Contemporary Art in Accra, he'd come all the way from Ghana. He'd aged magnificently. Vested in a blue and gray boubou, he looked like a prophet or a king. He began in his customary manner, sly, jocund, and self-deprecating. And then he said, "Joe Nkrumah is a very angry man." He repeated this twice more, and he laid into all of them, and especially into himself. "We can't finish even *one* thing," he continued. "Half our work is still awaiting completion. We couldn't create an institution to finish it." He shook his head. "If art is important, if culture is our soul, our identity . . . " His voiced ebbed into silence.

He began again. "So I'm angry. Forty years on, I can't see much of what I—what we—did." He shook his head again, as though he'd had a text he'd misplaced, or thrown away. "Why do we even care . . . to disturb the dead, to disturb the dead, if this is how we are—not finishing this work." And he stepped off the dais and went back to his seat near Nick Kraczyna.

Afterward there was a presentation about loose vellum bindings, and another about the solubility of acrylic resins. Or I think they were. I was preoccupied. I couldn't quite understand what Nkrumah had been so angry about, why he'd trailed dejection through the room amid all the fond nostalgia, the hard-earned ease of these people who'd saved so much. And statistically, he wasn't right: I'd checked, and there were at most 25 percent of the Biblioteca Nazionale's flooded books left to restore.

The next morning I went down to the river and crossed the Ponte Santa Trinità to a photographic exhibition at the Palazzo Vecchio. I'd seen Nick's photographs—grainy, angular, and precipitate—and Zeffirelli's film, with its gyres of water and floating cars and the bleak overcast of Burton's voice. But these were David Lees's photographs. They'd been enlarged to a massive scale and hung, illumined by pools of light, within a shadowy, vaulted room.

I'd seen them again and again over the last year, and I knew, of course, who David Lees was. So I must have known that his were the photographs by which I'd come to know about the flood when I was a boy: it went without saying. But I hadn't seen it. It was a face I hadn't recognized. And then, gazing at the Madonna poised on her delta of mud, I remembered.

In many ways the other photographs I'd seen were more immediate, and I suppose they gave a truer impression of what the flood had really been like: the disorder and filth, the unraveling of every normalcy and routine, the panic, misery, tears, and shrugs. But the profound impression I received from Lees's photographs was of an eerie motionless silence, peace as far as the eye could see; Leonardo's infinite water, now calm, and a bird settling upon a drifting tangle of bodies, an islet of stilled flesh.

It was terrible, or at least sad, and yet I might have just then been back in Minnesota forty years before, looking—languid and spread upon the sofa or the blue wool carpeting—at a magazine, seeing tragedy five thousand miles distant rendered into beauty, entering me, asking me to give it its due. It made me think of those forty years, and what I'd made of them, and I think then I knew a little of what Joe Nkrumah had been trying to say. In my life, in all the things I might have saved and remade, I hadn't done the half of it, either.

I wanted to know everything about David Lees. I was sure he was dead, but I looked in our two-year-old telephone directory, and he was listed as residing just down the street from us, opposite the Piazza Santo Spirito. There was no answer. He'd been dead two years. But the catalog for the exhibition listed a Lorenzo Lees among the acknowledgments. Surely this was a relative and surely, given the unusual name—half Italian, half English—he could be tracked down.

I typed the name into an Internet search engine, but the only result that made any sense was on a site belonging to the Archdiocese of Westminster, the Roman Catholic see of London. The "Lorenzo Lees" listed there had conducted a catechism class at some point. It didn't seem likely this was who I'd been seeking, someone off in England, teaching Sunday school. But I sent an e-mail, apologizing for the intrusion, but asking that in the remote event that this person was connected to David Lees to please get in touch.

I was still, all that while, also looking for Umberto Baldini. I knew, of course, a lot about his career as well as the odd shred of gossip but I wanted to get a feel for him; a sense of his motivations, this great man who'd saved—or destroyed—the Cimabue *Crocifisso*. There was nowhere left to go but to Ornella Casazza.

I'd avoided her until now; or, as I preferred to think, left her in peace. She might still be in mourning, and I'd been told repeatedly she was a difficult, opaque person. She'd talk shop a little, but she wouldn't let you in.

Still, I had to try. I had Cristina Acidini and Bruno Santi to refer me, and just after New Year's I had an appointment. Her office was in the Palazzo Pitti, across a cortile from Santi's. I was nervous. Apparently she spoke English but would prefer not to. That was her right. We were meeting on her turf, not mine.

An assistant led me down yards of corridors to her office. It was frescoed and overlooked another smaller, more isolated cortile. Casazza rose from her chair, walked over to me, shook my hand with both of her hands, and smiled a winsome, blazing smile. By my calculation she should be sixty-three or sixty-four years old. She was beautiful; in fact, she was sexy. I would have done whatever she asked.

She'd been talking with an American-born colleague, perfectly bilingual, and it was agreed he'd stay and sort out any linguistic confusion over technical matters. I had a list of questions that would slowly narrow down to the matter of the *Crocifisso*, and the critics of its *restauro*. I began, and Casazza continued to smile. She would spread her arms and turn her palms upward, as though the answers were floating down from overhead like feathers and all she had to do was catch them. She'd offer an answer, and for good measure refer it to her colleague for confirmation. I sat, hunched over my notebook, nodding with canine avidity.

She was still raining down warmth on me, but nothing intimate about Baldini had come across the two-foot gap between us, still less about her and Baldini. I played the Mora card: a historian of restoration at the La Pietra Symposium had told me that people often referred to Baldini and Casazza in tandem with Paolo and Laura Mora—Cesare Brandi's prize students and his successors at the Istituto Centrale per il Restauro in Rome—as rival husband-and-wife teams of *restauro*.

What did she think of their work? I asked. Casazza was kind and condescending: it was fine as far as it went, but ultimately it was subjective. It was distorted by the Moras' reliance on their taste, by the limitations of Brandi's theory. By contrast, she and Baldini had let Cimabue be their teacher, had followed his lead. They built a neutral bridge across the gaps from the artwork back to the viewer. It was like conducting a musical score: every conductor had an interpretation, but when the orchestra played Beethoven it was still Beethoven. But in Rome at the Istituto, with the Moras, it wasn't Beethoven anymore.

And what of the critics of the Cimabue *restauro*? Chromatic abstraction was as valid now as it was then, Casazza told me. Since then, tests and studies they'd done with computers had confirmed the choices they'd made in applying Baldini's theories. Today she would do the Cimabue, the *Primavera*, and the Brancacci—their three most important projects—exactly the same way they'd done them originally. There were no regrets, no second thoughts, no doubts.

We looked at some photographs I'd brought: in one, an unknown hand holding a brush was laying down *tratteggio* on the head of the *Crocifisso*. She'd never seen it before. I asked her to look closely and she bent down over the photograph. "Yes," she said, "that's my hand." It was a discovery that seemed to please her. Then, as now, she was beautiful. Her hand might have been cast of silver, or of bronze.

She was a kind woman too—at least to me—and maybe Baldini had, in fact, been a kind man. As for their affair, their age difference, the way he was supposed to have eased her passage through exams and job competitions—well, this was Italy; and now I couldn't say that I didn't understand exactly why such things might have happened. He did what anyone might do when seized by overwhelming *bellezza*.

Dark Water

A few days later, I got an e-mail from London: "I am David Lees' son," it said. I could write back or we could talk on the phone.

When I telephoned Lorenzo Lees, he told me that as it turned out he was coming to Florence in a few days to arrange for the sale of his father's old apartment. Lorenzo was a Catholic missionary in an inner-city part of London and had accustomed himself to a modest way of life, but his twin brother in Rome had insisted that they realize the considerable profit the apartment would yield on the Florentine real estate market.

Later that next week I sat with Lorenzo in the apartment, unchanged from his father's last occupation of it. It had the austere but expansive feel of an artist's home or studio from some moment in the fifties, the white walls, geometric splashes of primary colors, and nubby, rough textures woven in earth tones. It could have been our house when I was a boy had we dared to be more bohemian, had we, I suppose, loved art more.

Lorenzo was, it turned out, precisely my age: my St. Paul with my mother had paralleled his Rome with his mother. He was frank with me about his life—or, for a long time, the lack of it—with his father; the things he'd missed, the things he imagined David had missed with Gordon Craig. But he was proud of them too, Craig and his internationally famous mother, Ellen Terry, David's own fearless and tender aesthete mother, Dorothy, and David most of all. Lorenzo was a devout Catholic: he'd dedicated his life to the Church and to making a family of a kind neither he nor his father had ever known. The first time he mentioned he had ten children, I thought I misheard him. Yes, ten. I should come to London. I could meet them. That was where he had his father's things: the negatives, the papers, the notebooks. I said I would try, maybe in March. He really seemed to want me to come, as though it would do me good, as though I needed saving.

7

*T*he phrase "the religion of art" seems to have originated with Walter Pater, the Oxford don and aesthete who famously said that all art ought to aspire to the condition of music, and that life should aspire to the condition of art: "to burn always with this hard, gem-like flame." It was an imperative compelling enough to draw Dorothy Lees and thousands more to Florence. Perhaps it had moved me here too.

Nietzsche had taken the idea a little further: "Art raises its head where religions decline." It's a truth that can't be proven, but the decline of religion in the nineteenth century did indeed parallel the rise of connoisseurship, aestheticism, and art tourism rather neatly. For myself, I would have said I was beyond that. Certainly when I was growing up, what I craved in art and music and idealism was a life of the spirit, a meaning that felt to me lost or never acquired in the first place. But as an adult, I'd found a middle way. I decided I did believe in God—or at least in something spiritual, some great numinous intention—and I did believe in beauty: one, in fact, was a sign, a revelation, of the other.

But on a morning in Florence in February I woke up and I didn't believe in God anymore; or, rather, I had the belief but not the feeling of believing, which I suppose was to say that I had lost faith. I still had the idea of the divine, but couldn't quite touch it, not to say *see* it. It had become an abstraction at a very great remove. The loss didn't seem to make any great difference to me except when I thought of it. It was as though I'd been entertaining a great hope for a very long while—say, a windfall, an award, the perfect job—which had been in the end disappointed, but whose reality hadn't quite sunk in.

That I should have felt this was odd, because on the principle just enumerated, I should by rights have been up to my neck in God because I was up to my neck in beauty. Maybe I needed to try a little harder. I should put art to the test and see if it actually did what I thought it was supposed to do. I went back to see the Cimabue *Crocifisso*. Cimabue's purposes were strictly spiritual and in that regard even practical. That's not to say the labor did not give him pleasure or despair, or that he wasn't proud of it and pleased to think about what it would do for his reputation. But he'd made an object, a tool to effect Christian worship, prayer, fear, and consolation. As the Arno was a machine made to move water, the *Crocifisso* was a machine to move sinners to salvation. I had a feeling I would not be so easily converted. But maybe I would have a transcendent moment, or at least a powerful sense of "tactile values." The beauty would turn me back onto the path whose track I'd lost.

I went to Santa Croce first thing in the morning so I could have the *Crocifisso* to myself, and I was indeed the only person in the refectory. But on the way, I stopped for a moment to look at the cross by Lippo di Benivieni, whose wood support Marco Ciatti had been able to preserve using his microtome saw technique. It was more striking, more compelling, than I'd remembered. Its Christ was an obviously young, even handsome man and perhaps because of that, he projected an innocence that could only produce a concomitant sense, in me at least, of the outrage and cruelty that had been perpetrated on his body. Mary and John, on either end of the horizontal spar, look shattered, their faces wrenched by grief. In the Benivieni there's what Ruskin called the sweetness of Giotto in the rendering of Jesus; in the tender-limbed body, the way the toes of the right foot are curled around the left, as though to protect them, this one little thing, from harm. It moves you to pity, and perhaps to the thought that God might pity you.

After seeing the Benivieni, the Cimabue looked different to me. I couldn't now say how many times I'd visited it in the last two years, never mind how many times I'd seen it in photographs. But now it seemed darker, stiller, more silent and cold than I recalled. Viewing it wasn't an entirely pleasant experience. It wasn't consoling or uplifting. What it manifested more than any other quality was the absolute dead-ness of Jesus. It seemed to enclose and hold fast the minute just after his last breath, his final heartbeat. Mary and John are not so much grieving as stunned; they're still taking things in; the tears haven't come yet. And the resurrection doesn't even register as a possibility. It's as though he's swallowed death whole.

I was thinking that Cimabue's *Crocifisso* wasn't beautiful by any normal standard of beauty. Nor was it shocking or transgressive in the manner much contemporary art claims to be. Of course there were things in it that I might have called beautiful: the majestic arc of the body like a sickle moon, broad-hipped and rounded in the belly, femi-nine, almost fecund in its collapse. And there was his one surviving eye—God's eye, you could say—that was also curved in the manner of the body, shut tight, not asleep, but exhausted beyond measure. There was not an ounce of life in the entire painting. This is the vast-ness of the Crucifixion, the painting said; the extent of the annihilation necessary for Christ to kill death. Now there's nothing, no place to go. The next move belongs to God.

For me the overwhelming feeling was one of devastation, of loss and absence far beyond sadness or grief. The *Crocifisso* now simply stated, This is death; this is suffering pressed to and beyond its limit. No wonder the Arno, in its raging self-abnegation, came looking for this particular object and drowned it with such care. They were brothers under the skin.

Of course the meaning Francis and Cimabue intended only begins here: the rest of the story, life without end, followed from this absolute dying by Christ. You might as well embrace him, they would have said. That's the next step, if you're up for it. As if you had any alternative.

I didn't know if I could go that far. I felt that the *Crocifisso* had, instead of offering me transcendent beauty—one standard definition of art—asked me to transcend beauty itself, to press beyond it; not necessarily to religion, but toward something very insistent in its demands; something emphatically real rather than hollow. As matters stood, I saw only darkness in the Cimabue. Perhaps Baldini's *restauro* had made it darker still. I could see the chromatic abstraction at work. The two dominant colors in the painting—gold/yellow and blue— combined in the eye to make green in the gaps. Or that was what my eye did. The entire *Crocifisso* seemed to have a greenish cast, a hint of the sickly that perhaps suited its intention, that perhaps was there all the time.

The Cimabue was high up the wall, fastened from above by cables with which the whole cross could be raised to the ceiling should the Arno come again. Now, at worst, the flood could only nip at its heels. Consequently, you can't inspect most of the surface. At the very foot of the cross, however, I could get a fairly good look at an infilled gap. The color—or rather what my eye was making of the patch—seemed a kind of algal brown, the hue more or less of mud. It took me a few moments to make out the hatching—it was that subtle—and I wondered if the work had been Casazza's or Bracco's. It was, as Baldini's theory provided for, angled up to the left, northwestward, toward the sagging crescent of Christ's leg.

So had they wrecked the *Crocifisso*? I couldn't say. And had the *Crocifisso*, by way of its art or its example, exercised any kind of *restauro* on my faith? If it had—and I doubted that as I doubted everything— it meant to save me in a wholly confusing, unexpected way. It wanted me to go with it beyond art, which had already been as far as I thought I could go. But on either account, Baldini's or mine, yes, the Cimabue was ruined. It had been ruined, I now understood, from the beginning.

I came out of the refectory into the light of the second cloister, the lawn deep green, shot through with pink and yellow roses. I heard a crackle of birdsong and for a moment—perhaps I was still under the influence of the Cimabue—I thought I saw books afloat on water, the maelstrom of paper that Casamassima had seen forty years ago, that the Franciscan brothers had had to navigate to enter the refectory. It was over in an instant, this vision: the flood had receded, ancient as Noah. Outside, in the piazza, tourists were milling, waiting to see the art. Women, immigrants who'd come here all the way from southeast Asia, were selling silk-screened scarves.

Giorgio Vasari had been a realist. He knew the kind of things people could and would say about one's work, starting with his loathsome antagonist, Benvenuto Cellini. Or there was this, from an art historian four hundred years later referring to one of his paintings as "a *Last Supper* in a lifeless manneristic style. St. John is outrageously sprawled and the Judas is a poor borrowing from Sodoma . . . dull and undigested." And he knew what mere time and nature could do, not to say a flood: *l'acqua rintenerì di maniera il gesso . . . fece gonfiare il legname di sorte che tanto quanto se ne bagnò da piè si e scortecciato*, "the water is absorbed by the gesso and makes the panel swell so that it's soaked from the bottom and the surface peels off like bark." He and his art had been through it all.

But now a great deal of attention was being lavished on him. The press of the twenty-first century had made him a painter of masterpieces, or perhaps it was really the flood, the Arno. When I went back to the Fortezza in the spring, three of the five panels of *The Last Supper* were missing from their cradle. The tests Marco Ciatti had wanted were finally under way.

In the lab he showed me panels 1 and 2, now mounted on upright supports so their surfaces could be laser-scanned millimeter by millimeter. Panel 2 was in the worst condition of any section of the painting: besides being fissured and rucked, it was two centimeters smaller than the paint that was supposed to be covering it. It was Judas's panel. Somewhere under the *velinatura*, he was lurking, holding his body in that fey twisted pose Vasari had gotten from Sodoma. Before Ciatti could even think about separating the image and its mismatched support, they'd have to make a molded replica of the entire panel for the saw to track. And then there was the question of the saw itself, which would have to be custom-built at massive expense. It would be a formidable, even infernal machine: there was some question about whether Ciatti could obtain the necessary safety certifications that would allow his team to operate it.

But they were going forward regardless. On the central panel, number 3, they'd conducted tests to see if the *velinatura* could be removed and the paint underneath consolidated securely. They'd had to apply a solvent gel, let it sit for two weeks, and then gently work the paper free using only water and a fine brush. Once the *velinatura* was out of the way, loose and flaking paint had to be secured in place, using a syringe to inject threads of animal glue beneath the surface. All these procedures had worked as they'd hoped. They had a plan and three of the Fortezza's best restorers plus two student assistants to carry it out. They also had, it seemed, some of the money that had been promised from Rome.

Ciatti took me over to see the results: I knew from the old black-and-white photographs that panel 3 was the center section containing the figure of Christ. John would be collapsed against Jesus on the right and, on the opposite side, Peter. After forty years of being ignored and shunted between cellars and storerooms, veiled in rice paper, I was going to see part of the uncovered *Last Supper*.

It was Peter I could see, Peter who'd surfaced from under the dirt and the mud, not perhaps good as new but very close to it. He was stunned as though lightning-struck, nearly falling over backward at hearing Jesus' declaration that one of them would betray him. He was shocked, it seemed to me, but also simply affronted. He couldn't imagine that one of them was capable of this.

But of course one of them was, and for not much money. And so was another: Peter himself, who would deny knowing Jesus three times in the next twenty-four hours. Judas was, you could argue, simply bad, playing his assigned role in the drama of redemption. But Peter's betrayal was of another magnitude exactly because it was so ordinary, committed almost innocently by that most ordinary of the apostles. It was beyond his imagining that he might do such a thing, and then he did it twice more, willed and willfully, all the while mystified at himself.

Peter had done what anyone could have done and maybe would have done under the circumstances. As an evil it was inconsequential, but consciously shamefaced in execution, a mediocre, tawdry little thing. It was the kind of sin Vasari especially could understand: "I am as I can, not as I ought to be . . ."

I looked for a long while at Peter and the field of gray *velinatura* around him. The rest of the rice paper and Kleenex would soon be stripped away, although in *restauro* "soon" could mean five years. For now there was Peter, flabbergasted by an event we couldn't yet entirely see; or perhaps he's taken aback by where he finds himself, dirty but intact after forty years of sleep. As I moved away from the panel, I saw that some dirt had stuck to my sleeve. I was sure I'd never come in physical contact with the painting. Ciatti was under no obligation to let me see these things, and it went without saying he trusted that I would be careful around them. But there was the spot, the mark of my unwitting touching of what I was not supposed to touch. I was soiled by the same dried Arno mud as Judas and the rest of them who lived inside Vasari's painting.

Ciatti saw me to the door. He had to take a telephone call and while I was waiting I noticed a bust near the entrance. It was carved by Pellegrino Banella, who had restored Donatello's *Maddalena*. The subject was Ugo Procacci. Returning, Ciatti saw me looking at the statue, and we talked about Procacci and of Ciatti's admiration for him. If he could be just a little bit like Procacci, he said, he'd consider his life a great success. He didn't want to sound pretentious, but he was trying to run this *laboratorio* as Procacci would. Of course he was only human. We were all merely human, perhaps even the geniuses. One did what one could, and perhaps brushing up against all this beauty—devoting oneself to it—helped one to do a little better.

As we went toward the door, I mentioned the death of Umberto Baldini eight months before. Would there be a bust of him someday? Of course Banella was dead, but someone could doubtless attempt it. "Perhaps, perhaps," Ciatti said. In Florence, at the Fortezza, eight months scarcely counted as time at all.

8

*I*n March I went to London to see Lorenzo Lees. I telephoned him from the sidewalk outside my hotel. Where was I? he asked. Maybe he could pick me up. I looked behind me, hoping to see a street sign. But there was only a blue plaque. They're everywhere in London, marking the former homes of historic figures. This one recorded that at this address in Barkston Gardens, Earls Court, lived Ellen Terry, actress, from 1889 to 1902. Ellen Terry was Lorenzo's great-grandmother, the mother of Gordon Craig, the absentee father of Lorenzo's absentee father, David. She'd moved on just as Dorothy Lees was embarking for Florence, for art's sake and, later, love's.

We decided it would be easier if I simply met Lorenzo at the church in south London where his wife was working. I took the underground to Brixton and arrived at the church, Our Lady of the Rosary, in advance of Lorenzo. At the back, in the sanctuary, there was a woman standing on a scaffold with a brush in her hand. She was painting a mural that ran fifteen feet up the wall and wrapped around either side of the altar. It was in the Greek style, the style from which Cimabue had decisively freed Italian art. The artist here in Brixton was painting an *Anastasis*, one of the principal images in the Eastern tradition, in which

Christ was shown retrieving the dead from Hell, the event that follows what Cimabue had portrayed in the *Crocifisso*.

This painter was no Cimabue or even a Vasari. But there was a boldness to her lines, shapes, and colors that was compelling. You wanted to look, to go a little further with the image than you might first think. That was nothing negligible. In Florence, in the epochs I'd been studying, seeing an artist on a scaffold painting in a church would have been a nearly daily event. Today, he or she would likely be a restorer. But this little parish in a downtrodden part of London was an unlikely place for any kind of art at all. The painter, Lorenzo told me when he finally arrived, was his wife, Maurizia.

They'd lived in England for twenty years now, painting, catechizing, and doing good works, but they had remained thoroughly Italian. They wanted to speak Italian and when we got to their home in Peckham for lunch we would eat Italian, right down to debating the merits of long pasta versus short. The kitchen was presided over by an archetypal signora of immeasurable years who had also been caring for Maurizia and Lorenzo's youngest child. When we sat down, there was an *antipasto*, a *primo*, a *secondo*, wine, and a *dolce*, all modest but correct. We were a long way from south London.

But in fact that London was just outside the door. In the last month there'd been a chain of murders two blocks away. A fifteen-year-old boy had been shot in his bed, and three others stabbed or shot within a few days by rival gang members. A neighbor told the BBC that Peckham was "England's Bronx." I asked Lorenzo if they'd considered leaving. He said they had "no plans."

Lorenzo showed me what he wryly called the "archives," a dead space at the top of a stairway crammed with files and boxes. Most of his father's negatives were here as well as an extensive hoard of Gordon Craig memorabilia. Among the latter were wooden figures, beautifully carved and worn by handling, that Craig used to block his actors and build mock-ups of his stage designs. Maybe I would like to take one? But I declined, blind to what Lorenzo was offering. I was here to talk to him about his father and to look at his photographs. I'd hoped there might be unpublished shots of the flood and the subsequent restorations.

Lorenzo stood on the top step and handed boxes and sleeved transparencies back to me. We found a set of slides taken in 1972 that I'd never seen before, but other than that there were no other flood and *restauro* photographs. Then I noticed a book that looked familiar and I asked Lorenzo to hand it to me. It was a Time-Life book from the late fifties called *The World's Great Religions*, and we'd had a copy when I was a boy. I leafed through it and I stopped at a photograph from the interior of the Church of the Nativity in Bethlehem. A silver star was set into the stone floor and it was exactly here, the story went, that Jesus was born. I told Lorenzo that I remembered seeing that photograph. In fact, I'd been fascinated by it. It contained for me at age ten or eleven the notion that the son of God could be born in so particular a place; a spot that could be touched and photographed, an intersection of the transcendent and the concrete that for me seemed to constitute the marvelous, the beautiful, and the holy. It was probably this photograph as much as anything that had launched me into that brief bout of faith in 1966 that had lasted until a little while after the flood.

"My father took that," Lorenzo said, and although as David was *Life*'s specialist in such subjects I shouldn't have been surprised, this fact too seemed a marvel. It wasn't a coincidence or a happenstance, but another point on a matrix that was becoming an image or at least a frame. Inside it I was beginning to see not just the flood or Florence or its art but my own life. Lorenzo asked me if I wanted anything from the archive, a photograph or a print. I took a 35mm slide, shot on what David liked to call "*mia amica* Nikon," from the 1972 sleeve we'd found. It was the bare cross of the Cimabue, leaning against a wall in the Fortezza, stripped of its canvas and paint as it had been shown in Baldini's exhibition. It was a transitory, temporary phase in the *Crocifisso*'s life, its heart laid bare, halfway between its drowning in the Arno and its resurrection ten years after, still precisely itself. The photograph itself was beautiful, as beautiful as the cross, as beautiful now as the one of Bethlehem had been once upon a time. Maybe it would lead me somewhere, to art or faith or something more.

I went back downstairs with Lorenzo. Maurizia and the signora were tending the baby. The child, I realized, was wearing tiny plastic spectacles, or rather the women were attempting to make him wear them, since he pulled them off—seemingly with great delight—every time they were put on him. Lorenzo and Maurizia had named him John Paul after the recently deceased pope. The fervency of their Catholicism made me a little uncomfortable: the enormous family; the cheerfully accepted privation of living in a blighted, dangerous neighborhood; the setting aside of larger ambitions they might have had for her painting and his own photography; and this blind or half blind child. None of it belonged to what I believed to be my life, my world of art and books and beautiful things.

John Paul seemed happy enough, as happy in fact as any baby I'd seen. I asked Lorenzo how well he could see with his glasses. They didn't know: there was no way to test a child so small. He might see blurs and shapes, or just colors, or merely light and dark—chiaroscuro. Just then, he squealed, the avian shriek that babies produce for a few months before real words come. He'd seen something, and the feeling it gave him—the thing it pulled out of him—had brought him to ecstasy, to a vision, a depth, that only he could take the measure of.

&—

Dark Water

*B*ack in Florence I went to see Giovanni Menduni at L'Autorità di Bacino del Fiume Arno one last time. He'd agreed to take me around to some places in the city that had been important to him at the time of the flood. As a high government official, he possessed that most envied of Florentine treasures, a parking permit that allowed him to drive and leave his car almost anywhere. When the next flood came, he'd enjoy, of course, the most privileged level of access.

So we drove to Santa Croce. He could have gone straight into the piazza and left his car in front of the Basilica if he had a mind to, but instead he found an ordinary, legal parking place alongside the exterior of the second cloister and the Biblioteca Nazionale. I wondered if he ever became tired of coming here, of seeing the church, the piazza, and the statue of Dante, Dante's face fixed in a severe, perturbed expression as though he were angry at nothing so much as Florence itself.

We turned right at the northeast corner of the piazza into Via San Giuseppe. A few blocks down was the old Pestalozzi academy, which had finally been restored and put back in use as an ordinary public school. Menduni asked the woman in the vestibule if we could come in, gently, shyly, rather as I suppose he had offered his help to the despairing custodian forty years before, *rastrello* in hand. He wanted to show me the *giardino*—what I would call the playground—where so many of what now seemed to him to be the happiest moments of his life had transpired. It had once been the garden of Santa Croce's monastery, on the far edge of the city, almost rural. It still enjoyed a view of the back of the Basilica that few people had ever seen.

We came out and continued right down Via San Giuseppe. I think Menduni was trying to give me a better, longer view of his old school, but my eye was struck and held by a plaque on a wall just ahead of us. It had been installed very recently, only a few months ago, and it marked Azelide Benedetti's apartment. She had been powerless, the plaque said, *una che deve morire e che vede la morte avvincinarsi,* "one who must die and sees death approach." She had not been a hero, but only a witness, like the Cimabue *Crocifisso* that still—once more— hung seventy-five yards from her barred window.

We walked back down the street in the opposite direction, past the intersection with the Borgo Allegri, and Menduni showed me Mayor Bargellini's old palazzo. Members of his family still lived there, he told me. The front was as badly defaced with graffiti as any building I'd seen in Florence: supersaturated red, blue, green, orange, and purple on a buff wall; inanities—beautiful in a certain vivid way—frescoing the house of Florence's great contemporary Christian humanist. Up the street was the old site of the Casa del Popolo, now vacated. Politics in Florence were, as Machiavelli knew, eternal in form, but subject to changes in substance. Across the street from the former Casa, a cortile now housed a mosque and on its door there was a poster expressing solidarity with the Palestinian people.

On our way back to his car we stopped again in the Piazza Santa Croce, the epicenter of the flood, the bottom of the spiral of the inferno of 1966. "You have to ask yourself," said Menduni, "why, knowing what they know, people keep rebuilding here, knowing that every hundred and fifty years there will be a deluge." He paused, as though the people walking by or sitting in the piazza might be the very ones who'd made this decision. "It seems irrational, but perhaps it's not. Maybe people weighed the benefits of being here against the cost of losing half or a third of it every century, and they decided it's worth it—to be here, on the Arno. There's tradition and pride, but Florentines are practical people."

Maybe, I thought, far from destroying their community, the floods were part of what makes Florentines who they are. I remembered what the politician Enrico Mattei had once said: "The most divided, most discordant, most quarrelsome people in the world found themselves united, brothers, in the immense pity of Florence."

Back at his office Menduni showed me some photographs. He loved computers and had become extraordinarily adept at scanning images and magnifying and analyzing them. "Look at this," he said. It was a map from Leonardo's *Book of Water*. Menduni zoomed in until we could see the finest lines, the threads of the smallest cross-hatching. He pointed. "Here's Florence. Now look at this. I don't think anyone's ever noticed it before." I could see what seemed to be the Arno entering and leaving the spot he'd indicated. But to either side of it the line of the river divided, forked into two branches, and reunited at the other edge.

"He wanted to put a *moat* around Florence," Menduni said. "Bisect the river and have flood control and defense in one stroke." He shook his head in amazement. "That's a pretty extraordinary idea."

In the excitement of hearing about this discovery, I realized I'd forgotten to ask if he ever got a Hammond B-3. No, he never had, he replied. And now they were out of production, collectors' items, hair-raisingly expensive. Seeing the wreck of the B-3 he'd coveted dragged out into the mud of the street had been his initiation into loss and disappointment—Virgil and Dante's *lacrimae rerum*, "the tears of things"—back in 1966. But look at everything he'd learned from the Arno by not having it.

I had not given up looking for Umberto Baldini. The memories of the people who'd known him had gone fuzzy or, I suspected, consciously protective of his reputation. But what of the end of his life? What had he done in those last few years of his life besides read examinations and essays? Something would have been possessing him, even in his senescence, an object for his outsized ambition, energy, and intelligence, probably right up to the moment he'd gone to the hospital. It would be, of course, a *restauro*.

And I found there was indeed a final Baldini restoration: the frescoes Giorgio Vasari had painted for himself in his house in Santa Croce, frescoes that told the allegorical stories of the arts he'd practiced and depicted the faces of the artists he worshipped. The *sala* of Casa Vasari was, even more than his *Last Supper*, his lost masterwork.

When the last of Vasari's heirs died 113 years after his death, the house was deeded in accordance with his will to a lay religious order based on Arezzo. The brothers sold off the furnishings and art and the house itself passed into the hands of several owners, most recently the Marrocchi family in 1842. Casa Vasari had undergone considerable alteration over four hundred years, but the *sala* had remained untouched. No one except the Marrocchis had seen the frescoes for 150 years but any restorer would have correctly surmised that they had deteriorated, perhaps badly. Baldini knew of the frescoes' existence, but it was during his retirement—when he became president of the Fondazione Horne, just down the street from the Casa—that he was in a position to act. In 2002 preliminary tests and evaluations were begun in conjunction with the Istituto in Rome. Beyond the expected grime, in places the frescoes had cracked or detached from the wall. The Arno had never reached the height of the *sala*, but there was extensive damage from water and damp.

Baldini's wherewithal was still intact: the latest technology—computer scanning and spectography as well as acoustic and nuclear magnetic resonance imaging—from the best-equipped laboratories was lugged up the deep stairwell of the Casa. Cleaning and restoration were begun later—*stacco*, the equivalent for fresco of *trasporto*, would be necessary in places—and was continuing the summer Baldini died.

Someday, although no one can yet say when, the *sala* will be open to viewing by small groups.

So it was Vasari—Vasari painted by Vasari; Vasari flanked by Cimabue and Leonardo, watched over by Michelangelo; Vasari's private, even secret gallery of Vasaris—that was Umberto Baldini's final *restauro*. I stood outside the Casa on a searing afternoon at the beginning of the summer after the fortieth anniversary of the flood, 435 years after Vasari painted the frescoes, the last works he completed with his own hand. I was frustrated. I'd been trying for six weeks to get permission to go inside, to see them, but the day before I'd been formally refused. Until the *restauro* was definitively completed, there could be no visitors. The shutters would stay fastened against the blaze of light streaming down the Borgo from the Piazza Santa Croce. "We cannot confer eternal life on paintings and statues and frescoes," Baldini had told an interviewer once. But for the indefinite future, the *sala* and its frescoes would belong only to Vasari, to Baldini, and the great men they had loved and devoted themselves to, their immortal intimates and brothers in art.

Nick Kraczyna and I were having coffee in the Caffè Ricci in the Piazza Santo Spirito. If we'd gone outside, I would have been in sight or at least easy reach of almost everything that had mattered to me for the last two years in Florence, to say nothing of Nick's forty-five: the piazza, of course, and Brunelleschi's church, and, beyond it, the great river; the river in which Brunelleschi's freighter of stone for the Duomo had foundered, whose hulk had so possessed Leonardo's imagination when he was a boy, as David Lees's photographs had possessed mine. And then, just beyond, its cities, Florence and Firenze.

That last pair did not make a distinction that Nick would much recognize, although it was still very real to me. He'd been in and out of this neighborhood since he was twenty, eating *ribollita*, drinking its tight-knit wine, and buying charcoal alongside people whose children had long since moved away. But he'd stayed. Unlike me and the line of English and American expatriates I felt descended from, Nick was an artist—not an aesthete, a scholar, a connoisseur, or a tourist—and for him there was no other place but this Florence, city of makers.

Here, he was midway between the Brancacci and the Pontormos in Santa Felicità. And here, for me, were Bernard Berenson's first lodgings in Florence looking down on the piazza, the Brownings' apartment a block away, Claire Clairmont's a little farther down the Via Romana, Dorothy Lees's tower by the Ponte Vecchio, and, on the Bellosguardo hill beyond, the villa where Henry James had lived. And over the river, always the river, were the homes of the Shelleys, the hotels of Ruskin and Forster, and the cellars that vibrated beneath Frederick Hartt's room during his first flood.

We'd both be leaving Florence soon, Nick for a year's teaching in America, a place that was now as "abroad" for him as any other. But then he had always been a refugee, except for here. And I was going home, even if after all this time here I was a little less sure of what constituted "home," just as I was about faith.

We talked, of course, about the flood. Did he still think it was, as he liked to say, the "monumental" moment in his life? He was now sixty-seven years old and he'd seen a lot of things. But yes, it still was. He'd felt, in those minutes on the crumbling parapet of the Lungarno, both entirely present and entirely unrooted, like Icarus first launching himself. Perhaps that roaring surge of time contained, ecstatically, the moment before the moment Cimabue had fixed in perpetuity on his *Crocifisso*; the instant Peter is about to enter emerging from the *velinatura* of *The Last Supper*.

I asked Nick what he'd been working on lately. He was very excited about the multiplate color etching process he'd invented and been teaching to students from around the world. But what about Icarus? He said he hadn't done much with Icarus in the last few years. He'd painted a huge outdoor mural in the Czech Republic in 2002, but nothing since. You had to wait for Icarus to come to you like you had to wait for these once-in-a-century deluges. The Pietà motif had come back for a while a few years ago—insisted on being worked on *right now*—and some other variation would doubtless present itself soon. Icarus was, after all, always and everywhere trapped in the labyrinth, trying to escape through his devices and fabrications. Weren't we all? We all wanted so much and would do so much, so strangely and unpredictably, to gain it.

So we'd talked about the flood and we'd talked about art. There was a pause and then Nick said, "Here's a puzzle, a labyrinth. The river's flooding. And there's a baby and there's a Leonardo painting floating down it. Which do I save?"

I spread my arms apart, palms up, in the Italian gesture that can mean "Who knows?" or "Suit yourself," or indicate several varieties of resignation. It's not, I realized, much different than Mary's posture in David Lees's mudflat photograph of Santa Croce.

Nick looked at me. "But you think you know what I'd answer, don't you?" And I thought, yes, I do. Because there's ordinary life and it's good and ought to be respected, but then there is also more, much more than we can imagine, beauty that runs on forever. There's Firenze and then there is Florence.

"But you'd be wrong," I heard Nick saying. "And you know why? Because, all right, there's a Leonardo floating away. But suppose the baby is the *next* Leonardo and there's all this work he's going to do? Suppose he's even better than Leonardo? You weigh all *that*, and you save the baby."

Nick seemed pleased to have confounded me. Still, I thought, suppose the baby is John Paul Lees, who can't even see, or scarcely at all? But who knew what he might be or do? It was beyond imagining. So any of us, really, was worth a Leonardo. Ruskin—who knew almost nothing of ordinary people or the real world, who lived from beauty to beauty—said, "You will never love art well till you love what she mirrors better." You should look, but you should also see. You should pay attention, render creation its due.

So there is the city and the river, what people make and lose and what survives; and then there is the beauty of it. Here is where we begin.

ACKNOWLEDGMENTS

This book owes itself entirely to the stories and, still more, the kindness of dozens of people in Florence and elsewhere who were generous in sharing their recollections and thoughts with me. In particular Nick Kraczyna, Lorenzo Lees, Giovanni Menduni, and John Schofield opened their life stories to me with an unstinting patience. Marco Ciatti, Susan Glasspool, Sandro Pintus, and Ilaria Sborgi were also extraordinarily helpful.

I am also indebted to the following individuals who gave me the benefit of their expertise and experience: Cristina Acidini, Kirsten Aschengreen Piacenti, Massimo Becattini, Carla Guiducci Bonnani, Paola Bracco, Anthony Cains, Ornella Casazza, Cosimo Chiarelli, Marco Grassi, Richard Haslam, Bruno Santi, Ken Shulman, Allesandro Sidoti, John Spike, Michelle Spike, and Joyce Hill Stoner.

I also owe a great debt to the librarians and staff of the following institutions: Archivio Contemporaneo, Biblioteca Vissieux, Florence; Biblioteca Berenson, I Tatti, Florence; Biblioteca Comunale, Florence; Biblioteca Marucelliana, Florence; Biblioteca Nazionale Centrale, Florence; Biblioteca Uffizi, Florence; the Conservation Center of the Institute of Fine Arts, New York University; Houghton Library,

Harvard University, Cambridge; and the Sterling Memorial Library, Yale University, New Haven.

Much of my stay in Italy was made possible through the vital support of the John Simon Guggenheim Foundation.

As ever, my reader and writer friends Patricia Hampl, David Shields, Jeff Smith, and Gregory Wolfe sustained and supported me in myriad ways as I wrote this book. I especially want to thank David, who selflessly brought his acute and generous intelligence to bear on several drafts of the manuscript.

My agent, Marly Rusoff, has been a constant and enthusiastic advocate of all my work and of this project in particular. Her energy and wisdom have been essential in inspiring, shaping, and completing the manuscript as well as in bringing the book to Charles Conrad, whose editorial acumen is equaled by his love of Italy. It has been a privilege to work with him and his assistant, Jenna Thompson.

Finally, my love and infinite gratitude to my children, Andrew and Tessa, and to my wife, Caroline, who have been *i migliori compagni di viaggio* on the Arno.

Florence and Seattle
2005–2007

1226	Death of St. Francis of Assisi
1246	Founding of Santa Maria Novella by the Dominicans
1265	Birth of Dante (Durante degli' Alighieri)
c. 1288	Cimabue begins painting the *Crocifisso* for Santa Croce
1294	Dedication of the Franciscan Basilica of Santa Croce
1299	Construction of the Palazzo Vecchio
1300	Arnolfo di Cambio begins work on the Duomo
1302	Exile of Dante
1304	Ponte alla Carraia collapses during a pageant depicting the Inferno
1321	Death of Dante in Ravenna
1333	Flood with three thousand dead
1334	Flood
1345	Flood Present Ponte Vecchio built by Taddeo Gaddi

1348	Plague. Sixty thousand—two-thirds of Florence's population—dead
1401	Lorenzo Ghiberti wins competition for bronze Baptistry doors against Brunelleschi
1452	Donatello carves the Baptistry *Maddalena* Birth of Leonardo da Vinci
1463	Duomo completed
1469	Birth of Niccolò Machiavelli
1475	Birth of Michelangelo
1478	Assassination of Giuliano de' Medici in the Pazzi conspiracy
1494	Deposition of the Medicis and founding of the Florentine republic
1500	Flood
1503	Leonardo and Machiavelli plan diversion of the Arno with excavation beginning in 1505, subsequently abandoned
1504	Michelangelo's *David* installed in Piazza Signoria
1505	Leonardo's *Battle of Anghiari* painted in the Palazzo Vecchio
1510	Machiavelli denounced for sodomy; subsequently begins *The Prince*
1511	Birth of Giorgio Vasari
1512	Restoration of the Medicis
1519	Death of Leonardo
1527	Death of Machiavelli Expulsion of the Medicis and restoration of Florentine republic
1531	Medicis restored
1546	Vasari's *Last Supper* commissioned by Pope Paul III

1547	Flood
1550	Publication of the first edition of *The Lives of the Artists*
1557	Flood
1560	Vasari designs and builds the Uffizi
1561	Vasari overpaints Leonardo's *Battle of Anghiari* in the Palazzo Vecchio
1564	Death of Michelangelo
1568	Publication of the second edition of *The Lives of the Artists*
1569	Vasari rebuilds the interior of Santa Croce; Cimabue's *Crocifisso* replaced by Vasari's *ciborio*
1574	Death of Vasari
1589	Flood
1646	Flood
1676	Flood
1688	Flood
1740	Flood
1758	Flood
1799	Napoleon Bonaparte takes Florence
1808	Dissolution of convents and monasteries; Vasari's *Last Supper* moved to Santa Croce
1815	Napoleon defeated at Waterloo
1819	Percy Shelley, Mary Shelley, and Claire Clairmont settle in Florence
1822	Death of Shelley

1830–35   George Fairholme studies the geology of the Arno

1843   John Ruskin begins writing *Modern Painters* (completed 1860)

1844   Flood
           City engineer Giuseppe Poggi proposes construction of flood works

1845   Giuseppe Aiazzi chronicles the history of floods in Florence
           John Ruskin arrives in Florence

1847   Elizabeth Barrett and Robert Browning settle in Florence

1848–49   Grand Duke Leopoldo II temporarily expelled from Florence by popular
           uprising

1851   John Ruskin's *The Stones of Venice*

1859–60   Final expulsion of Leopoldo II; Florence joins newly founded kingdom of
           Italy

1865–70   Florence capital of Italy

1869   Henry James arrives in Florence; on return to America he writes "The
           Madonna of the Future"

1873–74   Henry James returns to Florence and writes *Roderick Hudson*

1877   John Ruskin's *Mornings in Florence*

1879   Death of Claire Clairmont

1881   Henry James's *The Portrait of a Lady*

1888   Henry James's *The Aspern Papers*

1889   Bernard Berenson arrives in Florence

1896   Bernard Berenson's *The Florentine Painters of the Renaissance*

1900   Berenson buys Villa I Tatti

CHRONOLOGY

1901	E. M. Forster visits Florence
1903	Dorothy Lees arrives in Florence
1907	E. M. Forster's *A Room with a View* Dorothy Lees's *Scenes and Shrines in Tuscany* and *Tuscan Feasts and Friends*
1926	Vasari's *Last Supper* moved from chapel to refectory at Santa Croce
1934	Ugo Procacci founds the Gabinetto dei Restauri at the Ufizzi
1938	Adolf Hitler visits Florence and tours the Uffizi
1940	Mussolini declares war against the Allies; Hitler revisits Florence
1943	Mussolini deposed; Florence under German rule
1944	*August 3–4:* Germans dynamite Florentine bridges, excepting the Ponte Vecchio *August 13:* Frederick Hartt reaches Florence and meets up with Ugo Procacci *November 2:* Flood
1950	David Lees becomes *Life*'s chief photographer in Italy
1951	Nick Kraczyna and family granted asylum after eight years as refugees
1956	Construction begins on the Levane and La Penna dams
1958	Restored Ponte Santa Trinità opened
1959	Death of Bernard Berenson
1961	Head of Ponte Santa Trinità *Spring* recovered from the Arno
1963	Vajont Dam breached; two thousand killed
1964	Nick Kraczyna and Amy Luckenbach settle in Florence

1966   *February:* Death of Dorothy Lees

September: Stationary moist weather system stalls over Italy

November 2: Seventeen inches of rainfall in twenty-four hours at Monte Falterona

November 3, 7 P.M.: Sirens sound at the La Penna and Levane dams, followed by flash flood

9 P.M.: One inch of rain per hour falling on Monte Falterona

November 4, 1 A.M.: Romildo Cesaroni, night watchman on the Ponte Vecchio, feels vibrating of bridge and alerts shop owners

3 A.M.: Flood gauge at Ponte Vecchio records 28.5 feet before being ripped away and carried downstream

4 A.M.: First fatality: aqueduct worker Carlo Maggiorelli swept away and buried in a water tunnel

6:30 A.M.: Final edition of *La Nazione* goes to press

7:29 A.M.: Electricity fails citywide; clocks stop

10 A.M.: BBC broadcasts the first worldwide news bulletin on the flood; Franco Zeffirelli begins filming

11 A.M.: Ugo Procacci and Umberto Baldini rescue artworks from Corrodoio Vasariano at the Ufizzi

12 P.M.: Arno crests at a speed of 145,000 cubic feet per second

2 P.M.: Water in Santa Croce reaches 15 to 20 feet above street level; drowning of Azelide Benedetti

6 P.M.: Water receding; the Arno in equilibrium by 12 A.M.

November 5: 9 A.M.: Emmanuele Casamassima reaches Biblioteca Nazionale; monks of Santa Croce enter refectory by inflatable boat

10 A.M.: David Lees arrives in Florence by helicopter

11 A.M. EST (USA): Frederick Hartt prepares to leave Philadelphia for Florence

November 6: Ugo Procacci reaches Santa Croce refectory followed by Umberto Baldini
Marco Grassi and other students begin arriving in Florence

November 7: President Giuseppe Saragat tours the city and is heckled in Santa Croce; Edward Kennedy visits mud angels at the Uffizi and Biblioteca Nazionale

November 8: Casa del Popolo opens Santa Croce relief center and food bank, and organizes a march to the Palazzo Vecchio to confront Mayor Bargellini

November 10: Auschwitz survivor Luciano Camerini dead of heart attack while rescuing scrolls and manuscripts in the Via Farina synagogue

November 11: Art restorers from the United States, coordinated by Frederick Hartt, begin arriving in Florence; with Fred Licht, Millard Meiss, and Bates Lowry, Hartt begins foundation of the Committee to Rescue Italian Art (CRIA) in New York

November 13: London *Sunday Times* exposé blames dams for the flood

November 20: Zeffirelli's *Per Firenze* premieres in London

November 26: Book restorers Peter Waters and Anthony Cains arrive from Britain and establish a library rescue program with Emanuele Casamassima

November 28: CRIA officially launched with the presentation of a $70,000 check to Ugo Procacci

December 2: Cimabue's *Crocifisso* moved to the Limonaia

December 24: Pope Paul VI celebrates midnight mass at the Duomo and prays before Cimabue's *Crocifisso*

1967   *January:* Mud angel John Schofield begins treating Cimabue's *Crocifisso* for
        mold; Joe Nkrumah joins the book team, which receives £115,000 of
        funding from Britain

        February: ENEL issues a report denying La Penna and Levane dams' role in
        the flood

        May: CRIA reports having raised $1.75 million to date; Umberto Baldini
        moves restoration headquarters from the Limonaia to the Fortezza

1968   Cimabue *Crocifisso* dries to 25 percent humidity; emergency *trasporto*
        performed in September

1969   Ornella Casazza and Paola Bracco restore Allori's *Deposition* with chief
        restorer Edo Masini

1972   "Firenze Restaura" exhibition at the Fortezza, with bare *Crocifisso* on display
        Life magazine ceases publication

1973   Joe Nkrumah leaves Florence

1975   Support and planking of Cimabue's *Crocifisso* rebuilt; Casazza and Bracco
        begin chromatic abstraction restoration of gaps

1976   Restored *Crocifisso* returned to Santa Croce on the tenth anniversary of the
        1966 flood

1978   Assassination of Aldo Moro

1982   Umberto Baldini becomes director of the Istituto Centrale per il Restauro in
        Rome
        Ornella Casazza leads restoration of Brancacci Chapel frescoes
        Cimabue's *Crocifisso* exhibited in New York, Paris, London, and Madrid
        Survey of flooded artworks in storage notes "desperate condition" of Vasari
        Last Supper

1986   Twentieth anniversary of the 1966 flood

1991   Death of Ugo Procacci
        Completion of Brancacci Chapel restoration

Death of Frederick Hartt
Vasari's *Last Supper* moved from the Fortezza to a warehouse

1996   Thirtieth anniversary of the 1966 flood

1997   Assisi earthquake on September 26

1999   Vasari's *Last Supper* moved to a new warehouse

2003   Journalist Marco Ferri publishes an exposé of unrestored art in *Il Giornale della Toscana*, including the status of Vasari's *Last Supper*; national and international newspapers and magazines pick up the story

2004   Vasari's *Last Supper* moved to the Fortezza for restoration
Death of David Lees

2005   Initial assessment of Vasari's *Last Supper*

2006   Minister of civil defense allocates €250,000 for the restoration of Vasari's *Last Supper*, with a further €200,000 announced in July; test removal of *velinatura*
Death of Umberto Baldini
Fortieth anniversary of the 1966 flood

2007   Further tests and planning for restoration of Vasari's *Last Supper*

Unless indicated, all translations are by the author.

Part Two

14   *Or rather, Dante tells you:* Dante Alighieri 2000, XIV.10–54

17   *Two years later Francis was dead:* Sabatier and Sweeney 2003, pp. 124*ff*; Hudleston 1965

18   *They were going to make a man:* Baldini and Casazza 1982, pp. 7–16

22   *Their names and careers were always entwined:* Ghiberti 1998, II.2; Vasari 1991, pp. 33*ff*

23   . . . quando Icaro misero: Dante Alighieri 2000, *Inferno* XVII.109–11

23   *Dante was acquainted with Cimabue:* Dante Alighieri 2003, XI.94–96

25   *In subsequent years, fire:* Machiavelli 1960, II.31

26   *As in other floods:* Aiazzi 1845, pp. 2–10

27   Io fei giubetto: Dante Alighieri 2000, *Inferno* XIII.143–51

27   *It would take 150,000 gold florins:* Villani 1537, III.12.ii

28   *There were also individual witnesses:* ibid.

29   *However, as Niccolò Machiavelli:* Machiavelli 1960, II.32

30   *There was a decline of religious faith:* Filippo Villani quoted in Baxandall 1971, p. 73; Salutati and Ullman 1957, III

30   *Mars, deposed from his place:* Shulman 1991, p. 134

35   *For example, Brunelleschi:* Machiavelli 1960, IV.5

35   *A boy like Leonardo:* Starnazzi 2002, p. 132

35   Così, giù d'una ripa discoscesa: Dante Alighieri 2000, XVI.103–5

35   *Someone would have to write all this down:* Machiavelli 1960, VIII.20, VIII.9

36   *It was the time that would later be called:* Sieni 2002, pp. 53–54

36   *Leonardo escaped the charges:* Da Vinci, Codex Arundel, fol. 236v

37   *When the Medicis were deposed:* Da Vinci, Codex Leicester, fol. 15v

37   *The contents were to include:* Da Vinci, Codex Trivulzanius, fol. 35v

37   *Amid all the causes:* Da Vinci 1970, pp. 26–27

38   *In* The Book of Water: Da Vinci, Paris I, fols. 72r, 87r

38   *The mind of Leonardo:* Da Vinci, Codex Leicester, fol. 34r

38   *The next four years:* Nicholl 2004, p. 352; Menduni *Dizionario* 2006, p. 242; Nicholl 2004, p. 345

39   *Work began the following year:* Da Vinci 1970, pp. 428*ff*; Nicholl 2004, pp. 357–60; for a full and fascinating account see also Masters 1998

40   *Nicolo di messer Bernardo Macchiaveli:* Sieni 2002, p. 71

40   *Machiavelli lived on in his country house:* De Grazia 1989, pp. 320–21; Masters 1998, p. 4

41   *I liken her to one of those ruinous rivers:* De Grazia 1989, p. 211

42   *Divisions:* Da Vinci, Windsor Folios, fol. 12665v

43   *He did, however, find his way into the* botteghe: Rubin 1995, pp. 70, 80, 88

45   Quivi il silentio: Boase 1979, p. 28

45   *with Giotto's name:* Vasari 1991, p. 30

45   *Except for the month each year:* Rubin 1995, pp. 35–36

46   *Vasari seized on the idea:* ibid., p. 147

46   *In October 1546 the Farnese Pope:* Colti 1989, p. 68; Ciatti et al. 1999

47   *for the inscription above Christ's head:* Harpath 1981, pp. 63–64

48   *Vasari meanwhile flourished:* Boase 1979, p. 41

49   *Vasari was in the midst of these labors:* Aiazzi 1845, pp. 15–21; Baldini et al. 2006, p. 13; Boase 1979, pp. 183, 339

49   *the cellars flood every winter:* Buonarroti Archives, MIL clix, Rome, December 31, 1546

50   *But Vasari would always think of himself:* Nicholl 2004, pp. 391–94

50   *By way of thanks for this:* Baldini et al. 2006, pp. 33–36; Rubin 1995, pp. 35–40; Boase 1979, p. 183

51   *For his second edition Vasari:* Boase 1979, pp. 183, 149

51   *Vasari's tendency was to praise:* ibid., p. 142; Rubin 1995, p. 53; Boase 1979, p. 298

51   *On February 11, 1564, Michelangelo died:* Hall 2005, p. 224

52   *It would also be, insofar as Vasari could manage it:* Boase 1979, p. 385

53   *Over the next four years:* ibid., pp. 172, 218–20; Vasari 1991, p. 104

53   *Vasari went to Milan:* Boase 1979, p. 65

54   *to replace Cimabue's cross over the altar with a* ciborio: Leoncini 2004, pp. 67–71

54   *in his old age Michelangelo:* Hall 2005, p. 95

54   *Vasari understood this:* Boase 1979, p. 118; Frey 1923, I.133

55   *In Florence, more than anywhere else:* Vasari 1991, pp. 257–58

55   *varnished with* beverone*:* Shulman 1991, pp. 116–19

56   *Galileo Galilei, dead in 1642:* Menduni *Dizionario* 2006, pp. 134–35, 194–95

57   *Medici-era laws were rescinded:* Caporali 2005, pp. 180–81

57   *They were all here together now:* Leoncini 2004, pp. 97–101

57   *In 1854, like so much else, Vasari's ciborio:* Ferri 2006, p. 109

Part Three

62   *Percy took yet another river walk:* Holmes 1974, p. 547

63   *the Arno seemed a yawning gulph:* Shelley 1823, chapter 1

63   *a fond, foolish Icarus:* Shelley 1826, chapter 4

64   *Twentieth-century demographers:* Thatcher 1996

65   *At the bridges of Florence:* Menduni *Dizionario* 2006, p. 107

65   *The following year Giuseppe Aiazzi:* Aiazzi 1845

68   *You shall see things:* Ruskin 1887

69   *like a room in a novel:* quoted in "Elizabeth Barrett Browning's Florence," www.florin.ms/ebbflor1.html

69   *golden Arno as it shoots away:* Browning 1848–52, III

70   *The picture, not the king:* ibid., X

70   *I heard last night:* ibid., I

71   *There was another flood:* "Una città e il suo fiume," 2006.

72   *When the twenty-six-year-old Henry James:* Edel 1953, pp. 301–2

73   *In 1873–74 both Henry James and John Ruskin:* Edel *Conquest of London* 1962, p. 149

74   *The world as it stands:* James 1984, p. 998

74   *He was a man of personal genius:* Bradley and Ousby 1987, p. 318

76   *Goodness!—that I can't draw it:* ibid., p. 330

76   *Henry James heard about them in 1887:* Edel *Middle Years* 1962, pp. 217–19, 219–20

77   *Certainly there is a little subject:* ibid., p. 217

79   *But in 1889:* Samuels 1979, p. 89

81   *to scientific criticism Cimabue:* Bellosi 1998

81   *Bernard Berenson decided he must stay:* Samuels 1979, pp. 128–32

82   *Mary secured her separation:* ibid., pp. 193, 240–42

83   *giving tactile values to retinal impressions:* Berenson 1952

84   *To illustrate his point:* ibid.

85   *Lily was pleased by her view:* Furbank 1978, pp. 83–84

86   *Of course, it must be a wonderful building:* Forster 1907

86   *The art historian R. H. Cust:* Samuels 1979, pp. 390*ff*

87 *But after a few afternoons at Cust's:* Furbank 1978, pp. 84–85

88 *Evening approached while they chatted:* Forster 1907

88 *It looked little like what my imagination had pictured:* Lees *Scenes and Shrines in Tuscany* 1907, p. 2

89 *Towards four o'clock:* ibid., p. 4

89 *what it is which brings the Americans:* ibid., p. 39

90 *For my part, I love the story:* ibid., p. 296

90 *Ah, Madonna, how much:* ibid.

90 *That evening in May:* ibid., pp. 298, 278

92 *Laws of Art:* Sborgi 2001, p. 16

92 *Dine first—dine well:* Craig, Edward Gordon Craig Papers, March 1917

93 Incipit Vita Nuova: Lees, Fondo Dorothy Nevile Lees, Agenda 1917

93 *by-and-bye you may go:* Lees, Fondo Dorothy Nevile Lees, Corrispondenza DNL a David Lees, September 3, 1933

95 *In 1926* The Last Supper: Ciatti et al. 1999.

95 *But regardless of the condition:* Samuels 1987, pp. 342, 364–65

96 *Five years later Duveen:* ibid., pp. 432–35

98 *Kriegbaum was also an authority:* Menduni *Dizionario* 2006, pp. 231–32

98 *Afterward, atop a hill:* Huss 1942, p. 2

99 *Only a year after he'd joined the Uffizi:* Ciatti and Frosinini 2006, p. 249; Shulman 1991, pp. 57*ff*

99 *But Ugo Procacci was not simply an earnest young art historian:* Ciatti and Frosinini 2006, pp. 25–26, 42–43

99 *Despite that, when Mussolini declared war:* Carniani and Paoletti 1991, pp. 8–35; Ciatti and Frosinini 2006, p. 249

100 *Every day, another piece of good news:* Ciatti and Frosinini 2006, p. 140

101 *He was one of the most thoroughly humanized:* Samuels 1987, pp. 481–82

101 Chi potrebbe distruggere una tale bellezza?: Pieraccini 2003, p. 357

103 *Hartt would have found Procacci:* Hartt 1949, pp. 39, 41

104 *A little before nine:* ibid., pp. 42–43

105 *In the morning Ugo Procacci leaned out:* Ciatti and Frosinini 2006, p. 41

106 *The view that met the Allies:* Carniani and Paoletti 1991, p. 5

107 *Hartt made sure guards:* Hartt 1949, pp. 18–21

107 *The Wehrmacht continued to shell:* ibid., pp. 18–19, 34–35

108 *When Hartt reached the Pitti:* ibid., pp. 46–47; Ciatti and Frosinini 2006, p. 20

109 *Hartt made inquiries:* Hartt 1949, pp. 65–66

110 *Through luck and persistence:* ibid., p. 51

113 *The design for this masterpiece:* ibid., p. 36

113 *David Lees had been gone seven years:* "Da Agnelli al Papa, Una Vita Dietro L'Obiettivo di David Lees," in *Firenze Mostre* David Lees, L'Italia nelle Fotografie di Life (2003)

114   *Your time is too necessary:* Lees, Fondo Dorothy Nevile Lees, Corrispondenza DNL-ECG-David Lees, November 5, 1948

116   *Three years after the end of the war:* Procacci 1947, Mostra di Opere d'Arte Trasportate a Firenze Durante La Guerra (1947)

116   *Just then, it seemed that "Cimabue":* Maginnis 1997, p. 76

117   *Taking on Baldini:* Ciatti and Frosinini 2006, p. 250

118   *There would be no more floods:* Caporali 2005, p. 181

118   *Vasari's* Last Supper *remained in the refectory:* Ciatti 1999

Part Four

125   *"The Fatal Gift of Beauty":* Life International, February 11, 1963; *Life,* July 13, 1964

126   *David—now living in Rome:* Lees, Fondo Dorothy Nevile Lees, Agenda 1965

129   *From Dante's celestial vantage point:* Caporali 2005, p. 184

129   *This did not seem remarkable:* Pintus and Messeri 2006, pp. 18–19

130   *Upstream thirty miles from the city:* Gerosa 1967, pp. 12–13

131   *In the Palazzo Vecchio the mayor of Florence:* D'Angelis 2006, p. 74

132   *Nonetheless, by eleven o'clock:* La Nazione, November 4, 2006

132   *Romildo Cesaroni worked as a night watchman:* Nencini 1966, p. 33

133   *Later, around three .⅞.:* ibid., p. 11

135   *The first dead inside Florence:* D'Angelis 2006, pp. 76–77

135   *In most of Florence information:* Caporali 2005, p. 185

136   *Around five o'clock:* D'Angelis 2006, p. 80; Gerosa 1967, p. 54

137   *All at once, at seven in the morning:* D'Angelis 2006, p. 82

143   *The water has arrived in the Piazza del Duomo:* ibid., p. 94

144   *Still farther up the hill:* www.barbaraminitti.it

148   *Inside the Uffizi, Procacci:* Gerosa 1967, p. 70

148   *By now other parts of Florence's:* ibid., p. 57

148   *Closer to the Uffizi:* Carniani and Paoletti 1991, p. 168

148   *Another artist and writer:* Coccioli 1967, pp. 15, 23

149   *In the* salone *of a residential hotel:* Taylor 1967, pp. 34–35

149   *Some things could not be explained:* Pintus and Messeri 2006, p. 18

150   *For example, Delia Quercioli:* Coccioli 1967, p. 52

150   *Azelide Benedetti lived:* La Nazione, November 6, 1966

151   *By six o'clock that evening:* Menduni Dizionario 2006, pp. 31, 328

152   *More than once, Don Stefani wrote:* Stefani 1967, pp. 4ff; Batini 1967, p. 43

152   Per mezza Toscana si spazia: Dante Alighieri 2003, XIV.16–18

153   *No one could yet say:* D'Angelis 2006, pp. 104, 108

156   *Everyone was standing by the Baptistry:* Gerosa 1967, pp. 52, 80

157   *People had said the foundations:* Taylor 1967, p. 69

159   *It's said that Father Cocci:* Sebregondi 2006, pp. 26–27; *La Repubblica*, September 26, 2006; Gerosa 1967, p. 55

161   *It was almost as if the farther away:* Hughes 2006, pp. 331*ff*

163   *That is one kind of knowledge:* Taylor 1967, pp. 75, 58

Part Five

169   *As they waited, Procacci and Baldini:* Ciatti and Frosinini 2006, pp. 71–72, 253, 21; Gerosa 1967, pp. 84–85; Baldini and Casazza 1982, p. 24; *La Repubblica*, September 26, 2006

172   *The Casa del Popolo had managed:* Principe 1966, pp. 1362–65

175   *Luciano Camerino undertook:* Gerosa 1967, pp. 124–25; Batini 1967, pp. 63–64

177   *Nearby a group of neighbors:* Principe 1966, pp. 1367–68

180   *Simultaneously Procacci, Casamassima, and their colleagues:* D'Angelis 2006, pp. 128–29

181   *That was what began to happen to Cimabue's* Crocifisso*:* Carniani and Paoletti 1991, p. 198

182   *Talking of his first sight of Ugo Procacci:* ibid., p. 191; *Time*, November 25, 1966

182   *You might say all this:* Carniani and Paoletti 1991, p. 187

183   *No one in Florence thought that art:* Coccioli 1967, p. 25

183   *Don Luigi Stefani had other misgivings:* Stefani 1967

183   *There was a brother working in the Chapel:* Gerosa 1967, photo insert

184   *At eight o'clock on the morning:* Principe 1966, p. 1371

185   *When they got to the Piazza Santa Croce:* ibid., pp. 1368–70

189   *There were even rumors about art:* Baldini and Casazza 1982, p. 23; Hughes 2006, p. 340

190   *Later, in his study:* Baldini and Casazza 1982, p. 107

191   *A week after the flood:* Principe 1966, p. 1377

195   *there were two cities:* Gerosa 1967, p. 116

198   *But it was also dangerous:* The *Sunday Times* (London), November 13, 1966 (translated from Nencini 1966, p. 41)

199   *Lorenzo, Ida, and the rest:* Nencini 1966, pp. 39–42

201   *Even then, much of Florence was literally:* Bietti 1996, p. 4

209   *The* angeli *had their own rumors:* Taylor 1967, pp. 140–41, 149

227   *On February 24:* ibid., p. 177

227   *The* Crocifisso *of Cimabue was continuing:* Baldini and Casazza 1982, p. 31

228   *In some paintings:* Hoeniger 1999, pp. 151, 158

231   *CRIA's adoption list:* CRIA Archive (1966–), box iv

234   *The report laid the blame:* ibid., fascicle 7

235   *a fanciful, corny reimagining in pastel: National Geographic,* July 1967

238   *Although the painted surface of the Cimabue:* Baldini and Casazza 1982, pp. 31–32; Giusti 1981, pp. 72–74

239   *Unlike some of their predecessors:* CRIA Archive (1966–), correspondence, November 23, November 29, 1968; December 23, 1969

242   *Firenze Restaura also revealed:* Baldini 1972, pp. 56–57

242   *Nothing, absolutely nothing:* ibid., p. 57

247   *Inside the flesh of the wood:* Baldini and Casazza 1982, pp. 36–41; Giusti 1981, pp. 75–86

250   *December 14, 1976, was a Wednesday night: La Nazione,* December 15, 1976

252   *In spite of irretrievable losses:* Baldini and Casazza 1982, p. 29

253   *They can do it if they want to:* Shulman 1991, p. 209

253   *Contrary to the mood expressed: Paese Sera,* "Cronoca Firenze," August 29, 1977

253   *Baldini and Casazza had defenders:* Ragghianti 1977, p. 217

253   *Baldini himself didn't respond:* Baldini 1978, translated in Price et al. 1996, p. 356

254   *And with that, he continued on his way:* Giusti 1981, pp. 92ff

254   *On leaving in 1982 for his new post:* Shulman 1991, pp. 123, 139; Conti 1985, pp. 3–9; see also Beck 1993, pp. 33–62

255   *This is what happens to a historian:* Shulman 1991, pp. 212, 221

255   *The Brancacci restauro was completed:* Ciatti and Frosinini 2006, p. 255

256   *In retirement he'd turned his expertise:* The *Independent* (London), December 7, 1989

256   *Nearly seven hundred years:* Maginnis 1997, p. 71; Bellosi 1998, p. 273; Price et al. 1996, p. 7

257   *Cimabue's greatest gift:* Bradley and Ousby 1987, p. 318

Part Six

267   The Last Supper *had not, in fact:* Ferri 2006, p. 93; Menduni *Dizionario* 2006, p. 408

267   *So* The Last Supper *remained in storage:* Bietti 1996, p. 32; Ferri 2006, p. 93

268   *Three years later the Vasari was moved:* Ferri 2006, pp. 92–94

268   *Ferri was not only a professional journalist:* ibid., pp. 103, 107–9

269   *depots of shame: Panorama,* November 21, 2003

269   *Suddenly, reporters and photographers:* ibid.

270   *The Fortezza could try refastening the paint:* Ferri 2006, p. 95

276   *The Vasari had, of course, been damaged:* ibid., pp. 87, 96; *La Repubblica,* January 20, 2006

279   *And, after all, what, Ciatti asked:* Greco 1986, pp. 455–68; see also Ciatti et al. 1999

285   *Meanwhile Marco Ferri's investigations:* Ferri 2006, p. 39

287   *the recklessness of those who had allowed:* La Repubblica, October 8, 2006

288   *Only the arrogant superficiality of a few journalists:* Ciatti and Frosinini 2006, p. 21

288   *The city was a "monoculture":* Ferri 2006, p. 24

309   *Giorgio Vasari had been a realist:* Vertova 1965, p. 80; Conti 1973, p. 54

318   *The most divided, most discordant, most quarrelsome:* Pintus 2006, p. 21

320   *And I found there was indeed a final Baldini:* Baldini and Vigato 2006, pp. 35–37, 192–93

321   *We cannot confer eternal life:* Shulman 1991, p. 23

CRISTINA ACIDINI: High school student and mud angel in 1966. Now superintendent of museums in Florence and chief of the Opificio delle Pietre Dure

UMBERTO BALDINI (1921–2006): art historian and theorist of art restoration. From 1949 director of the Gabinetto dei Restauri and from 1970 of the Opificio delle Pietre Dure, which merged with the Gabinetto in 1975

PIERO BARGELLINI (1897–1980): belletrist and mayor of Florence

BERNARD BERENSON (1865–1959): art historian and connoisseur

BRANCACCI CHAPEL: Frescoed c. 1425 by Masaccio and Masolino, in Santa Maria del Carmine

CESARE BRANDI (1906–88): art restoration theorist and founder of the Istituto Centrale per il Restauro in Rome

FILIPPO BRUNELLESCHI (1377–1446): architect of the Ospedale degli Innocenti, Santo Spirito, the dome of the Duomo, and the Pazzi Chapel at Santa Croce

CAMALDOLI: monastery of the Camaldolese Benedictine order in the Casentine Forests

ARNOLFO DI CAMBIO (C. 1240–C. 1310): sculptor and architect of the Basilica of Santa Croce and the Duomo

CAPO D'ARNO: source of the Arno on Monte Falterona

CASA DEL POPOLO: Community center and Communist Party headquarters in the Santa Croce quarter

ORNELLA CASAZZA: restoration theorist/scientist and restorer, with Paola Bracco, of the Cimabue *Crocifisso* and the Brancacci Chapel

CASENTINE FORESTS: mountainous wilderness southeast of Florence that includes Monte Falterona

CENACOLO: a painting of the Last Supper (also referred to as *L'Ultima Cena*)

CHROMATIC ABSTRACTION: four-color infilling technique devised by Ornella Casazza for large gaps in the Cimabue *Crocifisso*

MARCO CIATTI: director of the restoration laboratory of Opificio delle Pietre Dure at the Fortezza

CIMABUE (C. 1240–1303): nickname ("bull head") of the Florentine painter Bencivieni di Pepo

EDWARD GORDON CRAIG (1872–1966): actor, producer, director, scenic designer, and author

CROCIFISSO: "crucifix," here one painted on large planks by Cimabue c. 1288, about fourteen feet in height, and hung over the high altar of the Basilica of Santa Croce

DONATELLO (C. 1386–1466): Donato di Niccolò di Betto Bardi, sculptor of the Baptistry *Maddalena*

DUCCIO DI BUONINSEGNA (C. 1255–C. 1318): Sienese painter and probable creator of the Rucellai *Madonna*

TADDEO GADDI (C. 1300–1366): architect of the Ponte Vecchio and painter of *The Last Supper* and *The Tree of Life* in the Santa Croce refectory

GIOTTO DI BONDONE (C. 1267–1337): apprentice to Cimabue and painter of the Peruzzi and Bardi chapels at Santa Croce as well as the Scrovegni Chapel, Padua, and frescoes at the Basilica of Saint Francis in Assisi

SUSAN GLASSPOOL: art student and mud angel in 1966. Now a translator and painter in Florence

GORGA NERA: "black throat," a lake near the Capo d'Arno, in legend connected underground to the Tyrrhenian Sea

MARCO GRASSI: restorer/mud angel in 1966. Later curator of the Thyssen art collections and now a private restorer based in Florence and New York

FREDERICK HARTT (1914–91): art historian and lieutenant in the Commission for Monuments, Fine Arts, and Archives of the U.S. Army. Author of *Italian Renaissance Art* and cofounder of the Committee to Rescue Italian Art in 1966

NICK KRACZYNA: artist, married to Amy Luckenbach

LA VERNA: rugged wilderness in the Casentine Forests where Saint Francis received the stigmata

DAVID LEES (1917–2004): photographer

DOROTHY LEES (1880–1966): author and journalist

LUNGARNO (PLURAL, *LUNGARNI*): streets fronting the Arno

AMY LUCKENBACH: artist, married to Nick Kraczyna

MAESTÀ: a panel painting of Madonna and infant Jesus with angels and saints

GIOVANNI MENDUNI: middle-school student in 1966. Now director of L'Autorità di Bacino del Fiume Arno (Arno River Basin Authority)

JOE NKRUMAH: chemist and book restorer. Now retired director of the National Museum of Ghana and conservator of the National Museums and Monuments Board in Accra, Ghana

GIUSEPPE POGGI (1811–1901): Florence city engineer and urban planner

UGO PROCACCI (1905–91): art historian and theorist of art restoration. Founder of the Gabinetto dei Restauri and later superintendent of monuments and fine arts for Florence

BRUNO SANTI: art history postgraduate student in 1966. Now superintendent for the historic, artistic, and anthropological heritage of the province of Florence

JOHN SCHOFIELD: art and art history student and mud angel in 1966. Now an architect and building conservator in Cornwall, England

TRASPORTO: separation of a work's painted surface (and sometimes ground) from its supporting panel or canvas; or, in the case of the Cimabue *Crocifisso*, the removal of painted canvas from wood panels.

TRATTEGGIO: fine hatching used to infill gaps in damaged painting. Applied with four colors in chromatic abstraction

GIORGIO VASARI (1511–74): painter, architect, courtier, and art historian

VELINATURA: securing and consolidating the painted surface of an artwork with rice paper (or, in emergencies, Kleenex) applied with Paraloid acrylic resin

Acidini, Christina. *Addio a Umberto Baldini*. Florence: 2006.

Aiazzi, Giuseppe. *Narrazioni Istoriche delle Più Considerevoli Inondazioni dell'Arno*. Florence: Piatti, 1845.

Alessandri, Silvia. *Contro al Cieco Fiume: Quarant'anni Dopo*. Florence: BNCF/Protagon, 2006.

Baldini, Umberto. *Firenze Restaura*. Florence: Sansoni, 1972.

———. *Teoria del Restauro e Unità di Metodologia*. Florence: Nardini, 1978.

Baldini, Umberto, and Ornella Casazza. *Il Crocifisso di Cimabue*. Bologna: Olivetti, 1982.

Baldini, Umberto, and P. A. Vigato. *The Frescoes of Casa Vasari in Florence*. Florence: Polistampa, 2006.

Barkan, Leonard. *Unearthing the Past: Archeology and Aesthetics in the Making of Renaissance Culture*. New Haven, Connecticut: Yale, 1999.

Batini, Giorgio. *Numero Speciale di Italia Artistica*. Florence: Bonechi, 1967.

Baxandall, Michael. *Giotto and the Orators: Humanist Observers of Painting in Italy and the Discovery of Pictorial Composition, 1350–1450*. Oxford, England: Clarendon Press, 1971.

Beck, James, with Michael Daley. *Art Restoration: The Culture, the Business and the Scandal*. London: Murray, 1993.

Bellosi, Luciano. *Cimabue*. New York: Abbeville, 1998.

Belting, Hans. *The Invisible Masterpiece*. Chicago: University of Chicago Press, 2001.

Berenson, Bernard. *Rumor and Reflection*. New York: Simon and Schuster, 1952.

Bietti, Monica. *Salvate dalle Acque: Opere D'arte e da Restaure a Trent'anni dall'Alluvione*. Florence: Centro Di, 1996.

Boase, T.S.R. *Giorgio Vasari: The Man and the Book*. Princeton, New Jersey: Princeton University Press, 1979.

Borsook, Eve. Eve Borsook Archive. I Tatti, Florence: Biblioteca Berenson, 2007.

Borsook, Eve. *The Mural Painters of Tuscany: From Cimabue to Andrea del Sarto.* Oxford Studies in the History of Art & Architecture. Oxford: Oxford University Press, 1981.

Bradley, John, and Ian Ousby, eds. *The Correspondence of John Ruskin and Charles Eliot Norton.* Cambridge: Cambridge University Press, 1987.

Brink, J. "Carpentry and Symmetry in Cimabue's Santa Croce Crucifix." *Burlington Magazine* 120 (1978): 645–52.

Browning, Elizabeth Barrett. *Casa Guidi Windows.* Florence: 1848–52.

Brugnara, Rita. *The National Park of the Casentine Forests.* Florence: Giunti, 2003.

Buonarroti Archives. Florence: 1546.

Burrows, Russell, ed. *David Lees for Life: Triumph from Tragedy.* Florence: Polistampa, 2006.

Caporali, Enrica. "The Arno River Floods." *Giornale di Geologia Applicata* 1 (2005): 177–92.

Carniani, Mario, and Paolo Paoletti. *Firenze: Guerra e Alluvione.* Florence: Becocci Editore, 1991.

Casazza, Ornella, and Paolo Franchi. "Trattamento Digitale delle Imagini e Conservazione e Restauro di Opere d'Arte." *Critica d'Arte* 50 (1985): 71–78.

Chesterton, G. K. *St. Thomas Aquinas.* San Francisco, California: Ignatius Press, 2002.

Chiesa, Mario. *Episodi della Tragedia di Firenze.* Florence: Chiesa, 1967.

Ciatti, Marco. *Angeli, Santi e Demoni: Otto Capolavori Restaurati per Santa Croce.* Florence: Edifir, 2006.

———. *Giorgio Vasari, L'Ultima Cena.* Firenze: Opificio delle Pietre Dure, 1999.

Ciatti, Marco, Ciro Castelli, and Andrea Santacesaria. *Dipinti Su Tavola: La Technica e la Conservazione dei Suporti.* Florence: Edifir, 1999.

Ciatti, Marco, and Cecilia Frosinini, eds. *Ugo Procacci a Cento Anni dalla Nascità. Florence: Edifir, 2006.*

Clarkson, Christopher. *The Florence Flood of November 1966 and Its Aftermath,* 2003.

Coccioli, Carlo. *Firenze Novembre 1966: Non e Successo Niente.* Florence: Club degli Autori, 1967.

Colti, Laura. *Vasari: Catalogo Completo dei Dipinti.* Florence: Cantini Editore, 1989.

Conti, Alessandro. "Attenzione ai Restauri." *Prospettiva* 40 (1985): 3–9.

———. *Storia del Restauro e della Conservazione delle Opere D'arte.* Milan: 1973.

Craig, Edward Gordon. Edward Gordon Craig Papers. Houghton Library, Harvard University, Cambridge, Massachusetts.

CRIA Archive. Biblioteca Berenson, I Tatti, Florence.

Dal Poggetto, Paolo. "Trasferimento delle Opere d'Arte." *Antichità Viva* 5 (1967): 56–64.

D'Angelis, Erasmo. *Angeli del Fango.* Florence: Giunti, 2006.

Dante Alighieri. *Inferno.* Translated by Robert Hollander and Jean Hollander. New York: Doubleday, 2000.

————. *Purgatorio.* Translated by Jean Hollander and Robert Hollander. New York: Doubleday, 2003.

Da Vinci, Leonardo. Codex Arundel. British Library, London.

————. Codex Leicester. Bill Gates Collection, Seattle.

————. Codex Trivulzanius. Biblioteca Trivulziana, Milan.

————. *The Notebooks.* Edited by I. Richter. New York: Dover, 1970.

————. Paris I. MS 2180, Institut de France, Paris.

————. Windsor Folios. Royal Library, Windsor, England.

De Grazia, Sebastian. *Machiavelli in Hell.* Princeton, New Jersey: Princeton University Press, 1989.

DiLeva, Giuseppe. *Firenze: Cronaca del Diluvio.* Florence: Le Lettere, 1996.

Edel, Leon. *Henry James: The Conquest of London.* New York: Avon, 1962.

————. *Henry James: The Middle Years.* New York: Avon, 1962.

————. *Henry James: The Untried Years.* New York: Avon, 1953.

"Fango e Ideali." *Doc Toscana 5* no. 20 (2006).

Ferri, Marco. *L'Eredità di Fango: Cosa Rimane da Restaurare a Firenze 40 Anni Dopo l'Alluvione.* Florence: Società di Toscana Edizione, 2006.

Firenze Mostre: David Lees, L'Italia Nelle Fotografie di Life. Florence: 2003.

Frescobaldi, Dino, and Francesco Solinas. *I Frescobaldi: Una Famiglia Fiorentina.* Florence: Le Lettere, 2004

Frey, K., ed. *Der Literarische Nachlass Giorgio Vasaris.* Munich: Georg Müller, 1923.

Furbank, P. N. *E. M. Forster: A Life.* San Diego and New York: Harcourt, 1978.

Gerosa, Guido. *L'Arno Non Gonfia d'Acqua Chiara.* Milan: Mondadori, 1967.

Ghiberti, Lorenzo. *Lorenzo Ghiberti: I Commentarii: Biblioteca Nazionale Centrale di Firenze,* II, I, 333. Edited by Lornezo Bartoli. Firenze: Giunti, 1998.

Giusti, Anna Maria, ed. *Atti del Convegno Sul Restauro delle Opere D'Arte.* Florence: Polistampa, 1981.

Greco, Gabriella, ed. *Capolavori & Restauri.* Florence: Cantini, 1986.

Greenfield, Howard. *The Waters of November.* New York: Follett, 1969.

Gregori, Mina. "Stralci di Diario." *Antichità Viva* 5 (1967): 40–47.

Hall, James. *Michelangelo and the Reinvention of the Human Body.* New York: Farrar, Straus and Giroux, 2005.

Harpath, R. *Giorgio Vasari: Principi, Letterati e Artisti nella Carte Giorgio Vasari.* Florence: EDAM, 1981.

Hartt, Frederick. *Florentine Art Under Fire.* Princeton, New Jersey: Princeton University Press, 1949.

Hoeniger, Cathleen. "The Restoration of Early Italian 'Primitives' During the 20th Century: Valuing Art and Its Consequences." *Journal of the American Institute for Conservation* 38 (1999): 144–61.

Holmes, Richard. *Shelley: The Pursuit.* New York: New York Review, 1974.

Hudleston, Roger. *The Little Flowers of Saint Francis of Assisi*. New York: Heritage Press, 1965.

Hughes, Robert. *Things I Didn't Know*. London: Harvill Secker, 2006.

Huss, Pierre. *Office of Strategic Services: Hitler Source Book*. Washington, D.C.: United States Office of Strategic Services, 1942.

James, Henry. "Ivan Turgenev (April 1874)." In *Henry James: Literary Criticism*. Vol 2, *European Writers and Prefaces to the New York Edition*. New York: Library of America, 1984.

Kraczyna, Swietlan Nicholas. *The Great Flood of Florence, 1966: A Photographic Essay*. Florence: Syracuse University, 2006.

———. *Icarus in Flight for Forty Years: 1962–2002*. Florence: Labyrinth, 2003.

L'Arno in Bottega: Imaginni Inedite dell'Alluvione del 1966. Florence: Cassa di Risparmio di Firenze, 1986.

La Valle, R., and P. Bargellini. *Paolo VI Viandante nel Dolore*. Florence: Monnier, 1967.

Lees, David. *Fotografiamo con David Lees*. Milan: Fabbri, 1978.

Lees, Dorothy Nevile. Fondo Dorothy Nevile Lees. Archivio Contemporaneo, Biblioteca Vissieux, Florence.

———. *Scenes and Shrines in Tuscany*. London: Dent, 1907.

———. *Tuscan Feasts and Friends*. London: Chatto & Windus, 1907.

Leoncini, Giovanni. "Santa Croce nel Cinquecento." In *Alla Riscoperta delle Chiese di Firenze: Santa Croce,* edited by Timothy Verdon. Florence: Centro Di, 2004.

Listri, Pier. *Dizionario di Firenze*. 2 vols. Florence: Le Lettere, 2005.

Macadam, Alta. *Americans in Florence*. Florence: Giunti, 2003.

Machiavelli, Niccolò. *History of Florence and of the Affairs of Italy: From the Earliest Times to the Death of Lorenzo the Magnificent*. New York: Harper & Row, 1960.

Maginnis, Hayden. *Painting in the Age of Giotto*. University Park, Pennsylvania: Pennsylvania State University, 1997.

Masters, Roger. *Fortune Is a River: Leonardo Da Vinci and Niccolò Machiavelli's Magnificent Dream to Change the Course of Florentine History*. New York: The Free Press, 1998.

Menduni, Giovanni. *Dizionario dell'Arno*. Florence: Aida, 2006.

———. "Per Borgo Pinti Camminando sul Fondo del Mare." *La Repubblica*, November 2, 2006.

Montanelli, Indro. *La "Mia" Firenze*. San Miniato, Italy: FM Edizioni, 2005.

Nardi, Bernardina Bargellini. *L'Alluvione di Piero Bargellini*. Florence: Polistampa, 2006.

Nencini, Franco. *Firenze: I Giorni del Diluvio*. Florence: Sansoni, 1966.

Nicholl, Charles. *Leonardo Da Vinci: The Flights of the Mind*. London: Allen Lane, 2004.

Perl, Jed. *New Art City*. New York: Knopf, 2005.

Pescioli, Idana. *Com'era l'Acqua: I Bambini di Firenze Raccontano*. Florence: La Nuova Italia, 1967.

Pieraccini, Monica. *Firenze e la Repubblica Sociale Italiana (1943–1944)*. Florence: Edizioni Medicea, 2003.

Pintus, Sandro, and Silvia Messeri. *4 Novembre 1966: L'Alluvione a Firenze*. Empoli, Italy: Ibiskos Editrice Risolo, 2006.

Price, Nicholas, M. Kirby Talley, and Alessandra Melucco. *Historical and Philosophical Issues in the Conservation of Cultural Heritage*. Los Angeles: Getty Conservation Institute, 1996.

Principe, Ilario. "I Ciompi." *Il Ponte: Firenze Perche?* 22 (1966): 1361–85.

Procacci, Ugo. *Mostra di Opere D'Arte Trasportate a Firenze Durante la Guerra*. Florence: Guintina, 1947.

Ragghianti, C. L., ed. *David Lees*. Florence: La Strozzina, 1971.

Ragghianti, C. L., Ornella Casazza, and Umberto Baldini. "Dialogo e Corrispondenza." *Critica d'Arte* 42 (1977): 217–19, 222–26.

Rubin, Patricia Lee. *Giorgio Vasari: Art and History*. New Haven: Yale, 1995.

Ruskin, John. *Mornings in Florence* (1877). Available at http://www.gutenberg.org /dirs/etext05/8fmrn10.txt.

Sabatier, Paul, and Jon M. Sweeney. *The Road to Assisi: The Essential Biography of St. Francis*. Orleans, Massachusetts: Paraclete Press, 2003.

Salutati, Coluccio, and B. L. Ullman. *Colucii Salutati De Seculo Et Religione*. Florence: 1957.

Samuels, Ernest. *Bernard Berenson: The Making of a Connoisseur*. Cambridge, Massachusetts: Harvard, 1979.

———. *Bernard Berenson: The Making of a Legend*. Cambridge, Massachusetts: Harvard, 1987.

Sborgi, Ilaria. "Behind the Mask: Dorothy Nevile Lees' Florentine Contribution to Edward Gordon Craig's 'New Theatre.' " In *Otherness: Anglo-American Women in 19th and 20th Century Florence*. Florence: Edizioni Cadmo, 2001.

Scudieri, Magnolia. *Piccoli Grandi Tesori Alluvionati*. Florence: Sillabe, 2006.

Sebregondi, Ludovica. *L'Arno in Santa Croce*. Florence: Polistampa, 2006.

Shelley, Mary Wollstonecraft. *The Last Man*. London: 1826.

———. *Valperga* (1823). Available at http://www.bibliomania.com/0/0/43/2398 /frameset.html.

Shulman, Ken. *Anatomy of a Restoration: The Brancacci Chapel*. New York: Walker & Company, 1991.

Sieni, Stefano. *La Sporca Storia di Firenze*. Florence: Le Lettere, 2002.

Starnazzi, Carlo. *Leonardo Acque e Terre*. Florence: Gran'Tour, 2002.

Stefani, Don Luigi. *Il "Bel S. Giovanni" in Arno*. Florence: Centro Lo Sprone, 1967.

Tartfieri, Angelo, and Mario Scalini. *L'Arte a Firenze nell'eta di Dante*. Florence: Giunti/Firenze Musei, 2004.

———. *Giotto: Guida alla Mostra e Itinerario Fiorentino*. Florence: Giunti/Firenze Musei, 2000.

Taylor, Katherine Kressman. *Diary of Florence in Flood*. New York: Simon and Schuster, 1967.

Thatcher, Roger. "The Living Dead." *New Scientist* (1996): 69.

"Una città e il suo fiume: la vita lungo l'Arno; la ricostruzione e la prevenzione." *Archivo Storico del Comune di Firenze*, 2000.

Vasari, Giorgio. *The Lives of the Artists*. Translated by Julia Conaway and Peter Bondanella. Oxford, England: Oxford University Press, 1991.

Vertova, Luisa. *I Cenacoli Fiorentini*. Turin: Edizioni RAI, 1965.

Villani, Giovanni. *Croniche*. Venice: 1537.

Villani, Matteo, Filippo Villani, and Giovanni Villani. *Istorie*. Florence, 1581.